People, Places and Piazzas

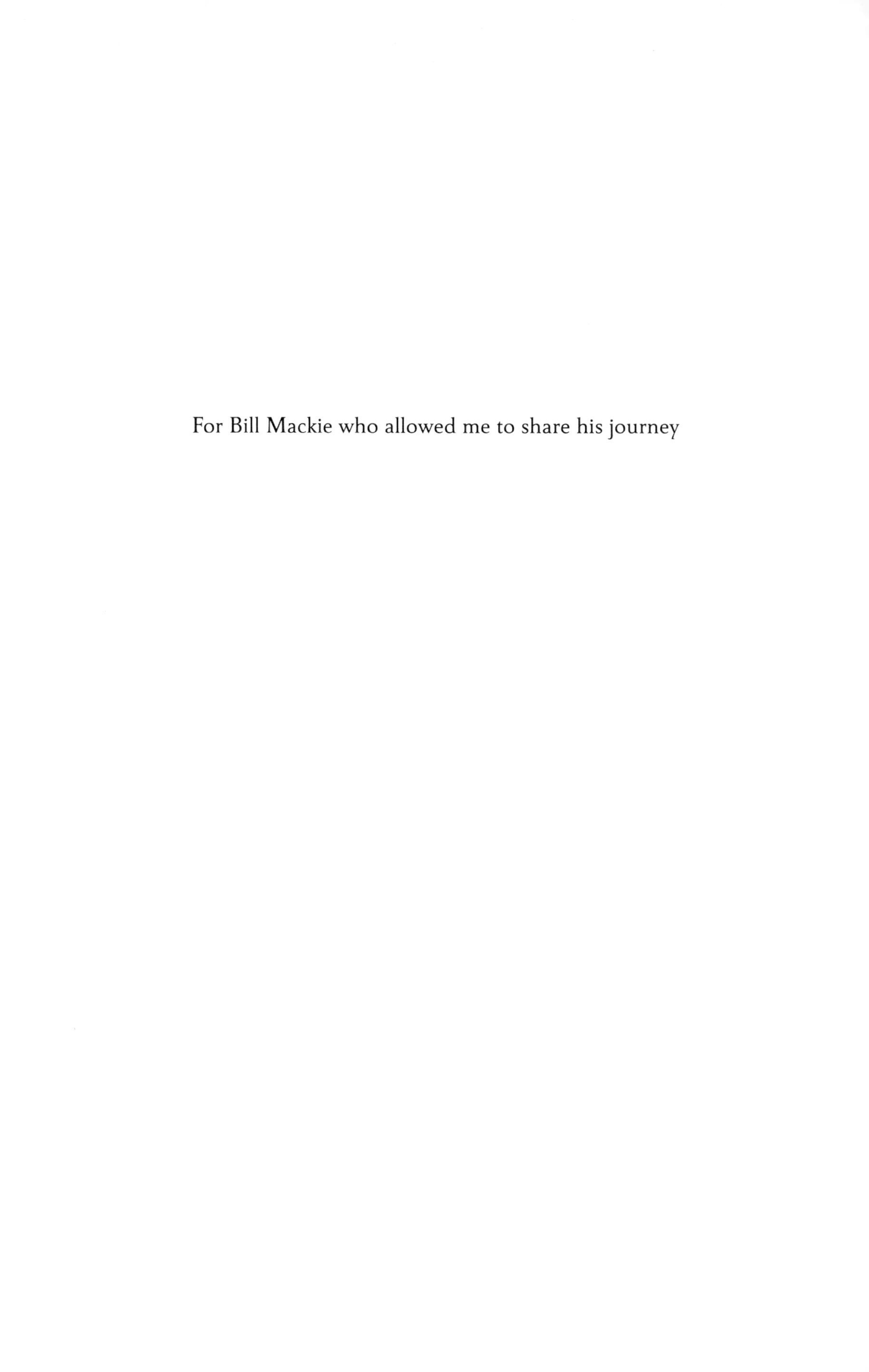

For Bill Mackie who allowed me to share his journey

People, Places and Piazzas

The Life and Art of Charles Hodge Mackie

Pat Clark

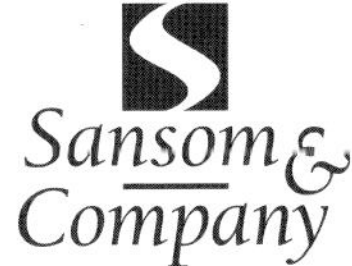

Sansom & Company

First published in 2016 by Sansom & Co
a publishing imprint of Redcliffe Press Ltd.,
81g Pembroke Road, Bristol BS8 3EA

info@sansomandcompany.co.uk
www.sansomandcompany.co.uk

© Pat Clark

ISBN 978-1-908326-91-1

British Library Cataloguing-in-Publication Data
A catalogue record for this book is available from the British Library

Text design and typesetting by Stephen Morris, www.stephen-morris.com
Set in Carre Noir
Cover and plate section design by Ian Parfitt
Printed and bound by Cambrian Printers Ltd

Contents

Author's Note 6

Chronology 7

Abbreviations 8

Introduction 9

Chapter 1   A nice paintable place 12

Chapter 2   Not a single rowan berry 28

Chapter 3   It is bad from cover to cover 37

Chapter 4   Very clever people, the French ... very clever artists 47

Chapter 5   Cabbages and sunsets 57

Chapter 6   Cherchez le gris 67

Chapter 7   A letter to the Queen 74

Chapter 8   A windmill of the imagination 87

Chapter 9   Water, wood and Walter 97

Chapter 10   La Serenissima 107

Chapter 11   An Immoral Display 118

Chapter 12   Vistas of enjoyment? 128

Epilogue 146

Index 152

Bibliography 157

Acknowledgements 162

Author's note

Conventional biography covers the period from birth to death, with due deference to chronological order. Since my approach has been thematic, I have provided a summary of the main events in Charles Mackie's life, for reference and to assist the reader.

A number of organisations are referred to in the text. On first usage, I have supplied the full title but thereafter used the more easily assimilated abbreviation e.g. Royal Scottish Academy becomes RSA. A brief list is included for ease of use. Specific page references for art journals are only footnoted when the quotations are of particular importance, otherwise they are cited by date in the bibliography.

Since the book has been written with a general readership in mind, I have provided a detailed bibliography to allow the curious to follow up any areas of particular interest. The illustrations have been chosen to complement the text, tracing Mackie's artistic career and its development. Further examples are available to view at www.artuk.org. In 2020 the City Art Centre in Edinburgh will be mounting a memorial exhibition for Charles Mackie, where a wider representation of his work will be on display. If readers know of any works in private hands which could add to our knowledge of the artist, please do contact the author.

I have been grateful for the cooperation, support and guidance given by all those mentioned in the acknowledgements. The opinions expressed and any inadvertent errors are my responsibility.

Chronology

1862   Born Aldershot, son of Captain Mackie

1871   Enrolled at George Watson's College in Edinburgh

1878   Left School; studied at the Trustees' Academy

1882   Visited London

1882-84   Royal Scottish Academy Life School

1891   Married Anne MacDonald Walls

            Helped found Society of Scottish Artists

1892   Visit to Brittany and Normandy; met Sérusier

1893   Paris and the Nabis

1894   Paris and Gauguin

1893-94   Murals for Patrick Geddes

1895-96   Established Coltbridge Studio in Murrayfield

1895-97   Designs for *The Evergreen*

1897   Birth of son Donald

1899-1905   Whitby, Runswick and the Staithes Art Club

1900   Elected Chairman of Society of Scottish Artists

1902   Elected Associate Royal Scottish Academy

1902   Elected to Royal Scottish Society of Painters in Watercolour

1903-4   Spain: Toledo and Madrid

1905-14   France, Venice and Italy

1912   Gold Medal Award in Amsterdam

1914   Fountain Sculpture

1917   Elected member of the Royal Scottish Academy

1920   Died at Coltbridge Studio

Abbreviations

ARSA	Associate of the Royal Scottish Academy
NGS	National Galleries of Scotland
NLS	National Library of Scotland
NMS	National Museums of Scotland
RA	Royal Academy
RCAHMS	Royal Commission for Ancient and Historic Monuments in Scotland
RGI	Royal Glasgow Institute
RSA	Royal Scottish Academy
RSW	Royal Scottish Society of Painters in Watercolour
SAC	Scottish Arts Club
SGPIC	Society of Graver-Printers in Colour
SMAA	Scottish Modern Artists' Association
SSA	Society of Scottish Artists
SSAH	Society for Scottish Art History
YUA	Yorkshire Union of Artists

Introduction

'Siberia' was accessed from a small landing and there hung a scene of Venice. Sunlight would occasionally fall across this painting and give it the warmth that was notoriously lacking in the bedroom that lay beyond, hence its name. In the composition, trees framed a subtly coloured canal scene and it was signed Charles Mackie 1910. The house itself was testimony to a family which had known more prosperous times in Glasgow before the Depression, when art had been collected and displayed in an even finer setting. The wealth of the Glasgow merchant class had allowed Andrew Clark, the family patriarch, to indulge his love of art and to build his own collection. The grand house 'The Cairns' later burned to the ground, after bankruptcy had already required the family to sell the bulk of their possessions. The Mackie was one of the few paintings that survived the fall from good fortune and it was the one which drew my eye, affording delight on every viewing. Aunt Evelyn (Andrew Clark's daughter) had insisted on bequeathing me the more valuable Dutch desk and I had to bid for my Mackie by telephone from the south of England. When I finally returned to Edinburgh, his painting took pride of place in my small flat in Wester Coates – as I was to discover, located only five minutes from the site of his former studio. It was there that curiosity led me to begin my journey of enquiry and discovery. Who was Charles Hodge Mackie?

On the other side of the world, a small boy could already answer that question, decades before I was born. Bill Mackie recalled that an impressive picture used to hang in the family dining room – as it turned out, also a Venetian scene, a print of children at play in the Palace Gardens (Pl. 25). He had been brought up on an occasionally drought-affected Australian farm and the other Scottish landscapes showed a country awash with water, a contrast which still holds true. His other discovery was a tin trunk in the chaff room beside the stables. This had been stored for fifteen years in a Melbourne garage when Bill's grandfather Copland Mackie and his family were in Ceylon. It had then re-joined them to travel to the farm one hundred and forty miles north of Melbourne. The contents had been protected from termites, mice and other antipodean rodents by its robust, tight closure. Inside, there were even more oil paintings, executed by the same artist. These now hang in Bill's home in Vermont, in the green Melbourne suburbs. The tin trunk resides in his daughter's garage.

For Bill, my original question was superfluous, since he was the grandson of Copland, Charles's elder brother. The latter had settled in Melbourne, following a spell as a tea-planter in Ceylon. The family had prospered, married well and put down deep roots in the state of Victoria. 'Uncle Charlie' had never visited Australia but had sent out a whole batch of paintings for sale in the Melbourne of the 1890s. Up to that point, gold had made the city flush with prosperity but Charles's timing proved tardy, since the art market had collapsed in a general economic downturn. The paintings were largely consigned to that tin trunk and almost forgotten.Bill's curiosity led him to unearth them and he started on his quest to uncover more about this Scottish ancestor. His research revealed a fascinating family, including a plethora of Annes, Annies and Nans, which still gives rise to confusion among those who write about Mackie. The most egregious example was one writer who said it was his sister Annie who was with him in Paris. It was, in fact, his wife Anne, an upstanding member of the Free Church of Scotland, who would not have welcomed the implications of this error. The path to unravelling the mystery of his life is strewn with such mistakes, repeated and handed on, as was the way in medieval manuscripts. Some questions might never be answered, such as his precise date of birth. Even the Aldershot garrison records in Kew would not yield it up, so the year 1862 will have to suffice. Captain Mackie never registered the birth officially and I have found no reference to birthday celebrations in any of the primary sources. Mackie's son confirmed that his father had been born to the sound of bugles, but baptism must have taken place at home, as was the practice for many soldiers on the move.

Sources can sometimes mislead, as is the case with a journal held in the National Library of Scotland. It was written by Mrs Mackie in her widowhood and is testimony to her loss and continued deep love of Charles — but thirty years had elapsed since the events she described. Understandably there are inaccuracies, since she conflated different events from his time span as well as sending off hares that could never be caught. The famous 'touch of gypsy blood'[1] has not been tracked down by any historical bloodhound, either in Australia or Scotland! It is his art that has stood the test of time and the evidence of a life which had an intriguing tale to tell. His story deserves to be told. Mackie produced works of sublime beauty and influenced others, whose names are better known and remembered. He was held in high regard by his fellow artists, made lifelong friends among their number and worked hard to promote modern art in an often critical and hostile environment. Gauguin, Vuillard and the Nabis were all known to him personally and Edward Hornel was a lifelong friend and associate. He found time to give lessons to the young Laura Johnson and to further his own personal experimentation in a range of media. Equally skilled in watercolours and oils, a colourist and an impressionist, he could capture the magic of a moment in time in a Venetian piazza as well as the challenges of a Scottish landscape, painted *en plein air*. His humanity and moral concern for others was noted in his obituaries but he was also known for his quick wit, sense of humour and sociability. He played an impressive game of golf, in the company of good friends from the Scottish Arts Club, and even took to a motorbike in pursuit of his art.

Chronologically, he fell between the Glasgow Boys and the Scottish Colourists, though he knew and was known by both sets of painters. The Great War stopped his travels on the Continent and cancer ended his life prematurely in 1920. As his impecunious widow noted, fashions change, and his art went out of vogue. The man and his work are now worthy of reappraisal, in terms of the people he influenced and helped, as well the places he visited and recorded in his art. When he painted the piazzas of Venice, he was nearing the end of his own artistic pilgrimage. Mine began with that painting outside 'Siberia'. It has led me to gallery basements, storage centres, dusty archives, Georgian mansions, Edinburgh flats and to Australia. Our travels together have thus spanned countries and continents, in a quest to uncover this artist whose long overlooked contribution to art stretched beyond his own canvas. Just as he found, the people and places proved integral to that journey.

NOTES

1 Unless indicated, all Anne Mackie's observations are taken from the journal in the NLS ACC 9177, quoted by kind permission of the National Library of Scotland.

One
A nice paintable place

Kirkcudbright and the Galloway countryside which surrounds it have afforded ample inspiration for artists, including Robert Burns, the painter, not the poet. He knew Charles Mackie well, having served together with him on the Council of the Society of Scottish Artists in Edinburgh. He had also contributed to *The Evergreen* for Patrick Geddes and was elected an Associate of the Royal Scottish Academy in 1902, the same year as Mackie. Burns's move to Galloway occasioned the epithet above – as depicted in the intense colours of Mackie's Kirkcudbright paintings. The hills, glorious woodland, Solway estuary and the buildings, whether cottage or castle, provided an ever-changing backdrop for the palette. It is not difficult to find fine landscapes and townscapes executed by names better known than Mackie.

The Faeds (John, James, Thomas and Susan) and William Mouncey, who married Margaret, Edward Hornel's oldest sister, were noted artists in Mackie's day. Both families opened their hearts to the young painter. Mouncey is recorded as the owner of Mackie's *Preparing for Dinner*, exhibited at the First Open Exhibition of the Kirkcudbrightshire Fine Art Association in 1887. At their Second Open Exhibition, in 1888, MacKie [sic] had three works for sale: *At Sundown on Peat Moss*, *A Field Worker* and *A Sower*. The rich abundance of such rural subject matter was linked to a strong artistic community spirit. It is for this reason that the town was sometimes dubbed an artists' colony, then and now. The local tourist board markets Kirkcudbright itself as 'The Artists' Town' and though less unspoilt these days, it is still possible to find a scene unchanged since the 1880s, when Mackie first visited and stayed to paint.

March 2013 saw snow and treacherous ice on the one-track, winding country roads overlooking the town. I was on my way to find *The Pool of Ness*, on the River Fleet, painted by Mackie c.1894, a living landscape of rocks, trees and tumbling waterfalls (Pl. 2). Executed *en plein air*, I admired his fortitude and determination as I struggled over muddy tussocks in a typically waterlogged Scottish field. The reward was to view it, virtually unchanged and certainly recognizable, as well as to feel the thrill of following, literally, in the artist's footsteps.

This work is now back home in Kirkcudbright, safely housed in the private collection of another Mackie devotee.

The Stewartry Museum in Kirkcudbright owns a Peploe (*Tolbooth*) and a Mackie, a head study entitled *John Copland*. An early work, possibly painted in 1883, it was given by the artist to his sitter in July 1884. Mackie is also known to have painted Mrs Copland and her son Sam at this time. Both artists, the better established Copland and the still to be recognized Mackie were based at nearby Dundrennan. The Mackies of Edinburgh were linked to the Coplands of Galloway. Helen Copland, who married William Mackie in Duddingston in 1815 was Charles's paternal grandmother. Her brother was John Copland. That John Copland had a son called James who named his son, in turn, John! So, Charles Mackie and the artist John Copland shared a common great-grandfather, Samuel Copland (1763-1825), the father of Helen and John (see family tree below). Charles's elder brother, it can be surmised, could have acquired the unusual forename Copland as a result of this common ancestry.

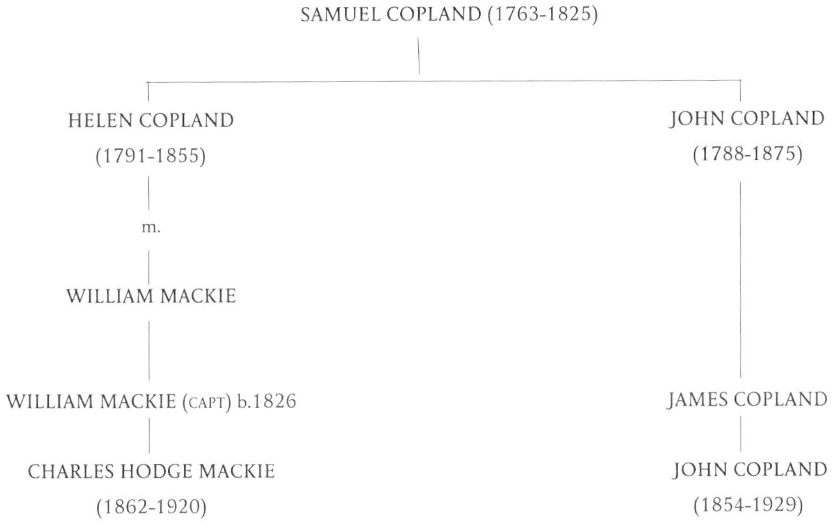

However, it was not this family link which was to prove the strongest pull for Charles Mackie. He had formed a close bond with 'Dear Eddie', better known as Edward Hornel, who would later become one of the well-known Glasgow Boys. The evidence for the depth and warmth of their friendship is to be found in the materials in the archives held at Broughton House, Hornel's grand residence in the town of Kirkcudbright. The letters are testimony to a strong and intimate relationship, founded on shared artistic values and ambitions for the future. The language can be somewhat verbose and flowery to the modern reader but Mackie's humour and honest expressiveness shine through the flimsy pages. Fellow artists, friends and acquaintances were not forgotten as gossip was exchanged between Antwerp and Galloway. He pours out his heart and allows us to glimpse the struggles, amorous and artistic, that beset him in those early years.[1]

Hornel had returned to the town in 1866, since his parents were Kirkcudbright folk, coming back home after a spell in Australia. He himself finally settled there in 1885 after completing his art training. Financial success rewarded his painting and he bought the eighteenth-century building on the High Street in 1901. At the time of his comradeship with Mackie, all that lay in the future. They were two young, struggling artists, trying to find the right training as well as their own distinctive style. The first note of friendship was a poem and drawing which Hornel kept (Fig. 1). It is dated August 1883 and the location was Dundrennan Abbey, very close to Kirkcudbright. This simple pen and ink drawing shows fine draftsmanship if limited poetic skill — a gift for an absent friend. It was possibly this palette which had served Mackie well as he executed the Copland family portraits.

> There rest ye now my trusty friend
> Too old for use too maimed to mend
> With nail where thumb
> Was wont to come
> Bent, battered, broke from end to end
>
> All projects, thoughts, ideas mine
> To thee in hope I did consign
> Thy beaming face
> Gave colour, grace
> And substance to my every line
>
> True sometimes I perverse would choose
> To mix to mud thy tender hues
> With well meant sweep
> Of knife I'd keep
> Thy purity I erst would lose
>
> Reader a Moral here you'll want
> Add it yourself. I've tried and can't.

The friendship between Mackie and Hornel perhaps began during the period when they both attended the Trustees' Academy, at the outset of their training. Their choices were limited at that time by what was publicly available in Edinburgh. Art training in Scotland had developed along a tortuous route, partly

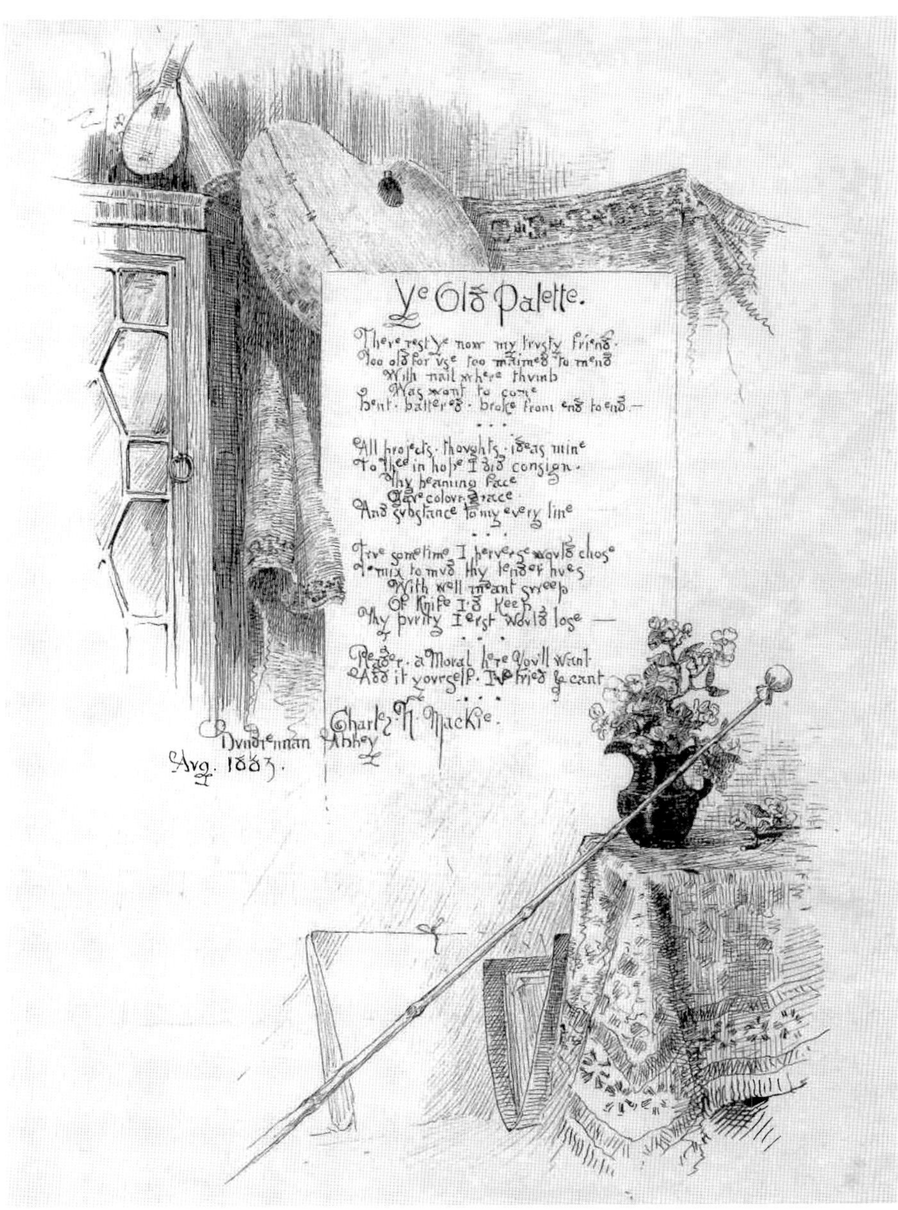

1 Signed Charles H. Mackie *Ye Olde Palette*, August 1883, pen and ink on paper, 9 x 7 cm.
Courtesy of the National Trust for Scotland, Broughton House archives. Author's photograph

dictated by the economic circumstances post-1707, after the Union with England. Since the reader will encounter these institutions again, the unusual structure of art education should be clarified at this point. It was not straightforward in its evolution and all these worthy bodies adopted elaborate titles, designed to confuse the unwary.

The Board of Trustees for Fisheries, Manufactures and Improvements in Scotland had been set up in 1727 to promote Scottish industrial development, to better integrate these interests within the new British economy. It was seen as complementary rather than competitive, encouraging the native Scottish industries of linen-weaving, wool and carpet manufacture. The long-winded title was usually abbreviated to the Board of Manufactures. It had set up its own Drawing Academy with the aim of improving industrial design, partly focused on patterns for textiles, and only shifted its emphasis to fine and decorative arts education in 1823. The Board of Manufactures had commissioned and owned the fine Playfair building at the foot of the Mound and it served as the Board's headquarters until all its remaining functions were subsumed within the National Galleries of Scotland in 1906. Since it also housed the Royal Institution for the Encouragement of the Fine Arts in Scotland (founded 1819) it became known as the Royal Institution building. Hornel and Mackie, like many students after them, would have attended their classes here. Hornel registered in October 1880 and Mackie is known have preceded him in 1878. Both would later apply for admission to the Life Class at the Royal Scottish Academy. Thankfully, their records have survived and show that Mackie was finally admitted to the Life Class of the RSA in November 1882. It is possible to view his actual signature in the attendance records. That signature was often first in the register, later flanked by life-long friends such as Robert Noble, Robert Nisbet and Tom Scott. Mackie's dedication was evident in the number of sessions attended in his first two years: November 1882-July 1883; November 1883-June 1884. It was only in the third and final year, November 1884-June 1885 that his attendance slumped visibly and he stopped coming after March. During this time, he would also have made the acquaintance of Tom Blacklock, Duddingston Herdman and William Robson, all of whose signatures figure in the register alongside C.H. Mackie. These early associations and friendships would count for more in the years ahead. He had also benefited from the tuition offered by the Visitors, Robert Gibb and William McTaggart and he had entered the august portals of the RSA.

The RSA had itself evolved independently of government direction and finance. Following in the steps of the afore-mentioned Royal Institution, it shared its aim of acquiring paintings to build a national collection. The RSA was set up in 1826 and granted its royal charter in 1838, always emphasizing its separateness from the Royal Academy in London and jealously guarding its Scottish identity. It became the awarding body for the distinctions of ARSA and RSA, with elevation to the rank of Associate or Academician being voted on by the artist and architect members. The emphasis of the RSA from the outset was on the promotion of the visual arts, their display, enjoyment and exhibition. Initially, it occupied space within the Royal Institution building which fronted Princes Street. When the second Playfair Parthenon was built in the 1850's, the RSA rented part of the new building designed to house the nascent national collection of the new National Gallery of Scotland.

Thus, the RSA had not viewed its function as primarily educational in the narrowest sense, given the existence of the Trustees' Academy. It was understood that the curriculum offered by the latter would focus on and conclude at the point where the 'Antique' was thought to finish, leaving the more advanced study of 'Life' to the care of the RSA. Naturally, the Life Class offered by the RSA played a vital part in the education of any Scottish artist and offered additional access to fellow journeymen whose mutual support could compensate for any deficiencies in the teaching.[2] The Annual Dinner held by its members paralleled the Banquet of the more distinguished Academicians and the speeches could touch on subjects dear to the hearts of the younger artists. In 1889 Alexander Roche, good friend of Mackie, spoke of the 'Art of the West', a topic close to him, as he hailed from Glasgow. For many of the younger men, Glasgow offered more in the way of inspiration compared to the academic strictures of the RSA. The Royal Glasgow Institute was also a more attractive proposition as it regularly sold three times the number of paintings managed by its Edinburgh rival. The healthy Glasgow art market outshone the east in every respect.

Both Hornel and Mackie were to become disillusioned and frustrated by what was on offer at that time to the aspirant artist in Edinburgh. They did not feel that they were learning how to paint, since they were set tasks such as copying from prints or drawing from casts. From 1858, the Trustees' Academy had been affiliated to the Science and Art Department in London and the consequent rigidity of the curriculum imposed from South Kensington, with its emphasis on payment by results, had done much to stultify the course of study. To those with means, there was an alternative path to follow — study abroad. This did not appear to be an option that Mackie could afford and he reminded his friend of the difference in their circumstances:

> I wish I had your advantages which I trust you fully appreciate and make good use of...

A number of Mackie's friends (including his future brother-in-law William Walls) accompanied Hornel when he went to study under Charles Verlat at the Academie Royale des Beaux-Arts in Antwerp. This was not an unusual path for Scots to follow, since connections with the Netherlands were of long standing. Indeed, Scottish artists often looked first to the Continent, rather than heading south to England. Hornel had chosen Antwerp because he considered Verlat to be in the first rank of teachers, inspiring him to be more adventurous with his brush and more forceful with his application of colour. Verlat encouraged freehand drawing, without models, believing the artist to be a craftsman who employed his eye, hands and materials in the service of art. All of this Hornel must have conveyed in his letters home to Mackie, who shared his delight that all had worked out well:

> I am very glad that your anticipations regarding Antwerp are not blasted. Two years of the training which your letter described should work wonders on you and your confrères.

(Hornel arrived in Antwerp in October 1883 and returned to Kirkcudbright in late summer 1885.)

Unfortunately, only one side of the correspondence is extant – the letters that Mackie wrote to Hornel still survive, despite their flimsy condition, in the Broughton House archive. They show that a home from home was provided by Hornel's mother and sisters, as he would visit them in the evenings: 'it was my wont to go over there'.

Mackie's two months stay in Dundrennan in 1883 had been productive, resulting in five 'Kirkcudbree' paintings sent in to the RSA Exhibition in 1884. He tells 'dear Hornell' (sic) that:

> The largest 18 x 24 is Mrs Copland of the Newlaw Dundrennan peeling potatoes à la Rembrandt... no.2 Master Sam Copland (as) scythe at rest he saunters home, as sunset gilds the eastern hills.

Beech trees, a turnip field and a small watercolour of Kirkcudbright Academy completed the submissions and he was hopeful of 'getting one hung'. In fact, three made the grade: *A homely old body* (cat. 624), *Sauntering home at sundown* (cat. 649) and *Kirkcudbright town* (cat. 871). The latter was bought by the Royal Association for the princely sum of six guineas.[3] This might well be the painting shown in Plate 1. In addition, he exhibited *Peeling Potatoes* at the RGI. Not one merited a mention in any of the reviews for that year in *The Scotsman*. There is no word of his 'Rembrandt' being bought in either Edinburgh or Glasgow.

He missed his friend Hornel:

> I could not help feeling the want of that cutty pipe and burglarian slouch hat of yours.

Having updated him on the latest artistic gossip, some personal matters are touched on. His heart had been warmed by an ambiguous amorous dalliance or two, hinted at but not pursued. With Tom Blacklock's sister there had been mere innocent recreation:

> We had a little walk in the grand old woods together occasionally which I have
> no doubt profited us both in a way.

The other maid remains unidentified, despite being 'lovelier than ever', with 'angelic form'. He had taken Blacklock to see her at one point. However, this came to naught as he reflects:

> Methinks her heart was heavy and beat in sympathy with mine which fairly jamp
> as I bid adieu to what might have been, had not Heaven guided me in better
> paths...

Temptation had been avoided. Tom Blacklock had proved a good companion and they had got on well together, though Hornel and his family appeared not to like him. Mackie judged him 'a nice, quiet, ill-used, inoffensive fellow very diffident of his own powers ... poor chap he needs every assistance'.

Mackie would have been aware of the crippling nature of the spinal condition which afflicted the young man he had first met in the RSA Life Class. Despite the support and friendship of artist brothers like Mackie, Blacklock met a tragic end, committing suicide in 1903.

However, as well as displaying compassion, the letters show that Mackie could be scathing when occasion demanded. He commented on Hornel's report of 'Brown's conduct at Antwerp' by saying that this 'tallies with his character as a thorough cad'. The confrères were not forgotten, since he asked to be remembered particularly to MacGeorge, Walls and Murdoch.[4] These three contemporaries would remain his loyal friends even after their bonds to Hornel were later severed.

At the end of this letter, dated 26 January 1884, he refers to his 'little blot', which might be the sketch described earlier: *Ye Olde Palette* (Fig. 1). It is of the right vintage and Hornel kept it till the end of his life. Mackie's honest feelings evidence how he felt about his art:

> I am glad I gave you it. There is nothing you know more pleasing to an artist than
> to know that the possession of something of his gives someone else even a small
> amount of pleasure.

Returning to the letter, he ends it with a final friendly admonition to his 'Red Republican' to 'See and behave yourself.'

The next missive was dated 2 March 1885 and there was a reason for the delay. His straitened circumstances meant he had 'lack of postage'. (Mackie still uses the correct spelling Hornell, since it was the latter who dropped the final letter, for no apparent reason.) Hornel was urged to enclose a few stamps, to expedite further correspondence. Mackie's self-effacement is to the fore in his report that he had just won the Stuart Prize, sharing this RSA award with Tom

Scott. The award had been endowed twenty years earlier by Lady Stuart of Allanbank with 'the idea that latent talent might often be brought to light by a timely call'. The monetary value was approximately £15 in total but it was surely the public recognition that would have mattered more to the two recipients. The Visitor's comment in the RSA records notes that the work submitted in that year had been 'much superior to those submitted in recent years'. Both young painters would surely have been encouraged by this compliment. Mackie's painting represented the busking of Culross Cross on the 1 July, St Serf's day. The children of this Fife town carried out the ceremony of decorating the town cross with flowers at daybreak, in honour of its patron saint whose bones were reputedly interred there. It was a lively and joyful scene, filled with the colour and animation that would have attracted a young painter's eye:

> On St Serf's Day, the populace paraded with branches of birches and other trees, in foliage, accompanied with drums and other musical instruments, adorning the cross and another public place called the Tron, with a great profusion and variety of flowers formed into different devices, and spending the evening in festivity and mirth.[5]

However, there is no record of any sale in the RSA records and no mention of the painting in any of the reviews. Mackie referred to it as his 'four feet abortion', not helped, in his opinion, by poor hanging in the RSA Galleries. Downplaying his achievement, he still felt sufficiently pleased to send Hornel a photograph. All things considered, there had been some small measure of recognition from the Edinburgh artistic establishment.

Despite this apparent upturn in his fortunes, all was not well, since he alludes to virtually all his Kirkcudbright work still being on his hands. There is a real artistic *cri de coeur*. Looking back, he thinks it 'a lost year' since he claims to have been learning nothing. There is a touching appeal to his friend to cost out and appraise the possibility of his coming to Antwerp.

> What would, say two months in Antwerp cost me? And would it do me any good?
> I could not spare more, as I have not made a cent lately.

Mackie never made it to Antwerp and, for the immediate future, had to content himself with Scottish landscapes and continuing disillusionment with artistic life in Edinburgh. He laments:

> I believe I have fewer than ever artist chums ... one looks askance at new faces and seeks to find more in the old ones ... it will give me unbounded pleasure to again behold that red republican visage of yours ... cutty-piped as of yore.

More 'lovelorn wailings' had been evoked by an unidentified fair maid from Perth, but he concedes the details would be wasted on Hornel, as someone 'born celibate, woman-hating and sentiment-scorning'. That verdict would be borne out by future events. Mackie was to make a happy marriage and Hornel stayed single all his life, setting up his bachelor home with his sister Tizzie. The warmth at the outset and end of the letter testify to the strength of their friendship at this embryonic point in their careers; he says 'I enjoyed your letter immensely' before signing off 'Your affectionate friend, Charles H. Mackie'. Despite challenging changes in circumstances and Hornel's increasing isolation from his fellow-artists, that affection endured.

There is a gap in the surviving correspondence, though its content confirms that the friendship had stayed strong. When Mackie next picks up his pen, he has been married for over three years and has returned to Gatehouse of Fleet with Mrs Mackie. She was the sister of William Walls, one of the old confrères from Antwerp. Mackie had married Anne MacDonald Walls on 30 April 1891, at Harriebrae in Dunfermline. The daughter of a Lord Provost of that fine burgh, she had travelled on the continent, was well-educated and had high moral standards. It was said that she would not allow the name of Goethe to be uttered in her presence, since he had mistresses. In the opinion of other family members she 'adulated'[6] Mackie and went with him on painting trips, as well as giving him a steady emotional foundation.

Hornell is invited not only to miss church, but to come over for tea at about six. The letter is merely headed Friday and is thought to have been written in 1894. Hornel is also asked to stay over and enjoy the comfort of the Mackie lodgings in the High Street at Gatehouse of Fleet, where they had moved after leaving Castle Cottage, Cardoness Castle.

The following three short letters of the same period were penned to 'Dear Eddie', definite proof of their continued amity and artistic interchange. They had much to discuss, since their careers had taken off, albeit on different trajectories. The letters are scant on detail but Mackie must have told him about his French travels and encounters with artists such as Gauguin, Vuillard and the group known as the Nabis (see Chapter 4). He had also made the acquaintance of Patrick Geddes, resulting in the commission of the Ramsay Garden murals, the inspiration for which was firmly rooted in the Galloway landscape.By contrast, Hornel and his friend George Henry had returned in July from their journey to Japan, which had been sponsored by the Glasgow art dealer Alexander Reid. Hornel's work had survived (unlike Henry's) to form the basis of the show in Reid's Gallery in Glasgow in the April of 1895. The Mackies' travels had only taken them as far as France and their life had centered on Paris, where a similarly strong interest in 'japonisme' had led them to amass many Japanese prints. The two friends must have shared this enthusiasm for all things Japanese. Hornel intimated to Mackie that he needed to prepare for a lecture, following the trip.

However, ignoring an earlier agreed understanding, the content of the lecture was drafted without any consultation with George Henry. While Hornel had headed straight back to Kirkcudbright on their return, Henry stayed in Glasgow. The press reported his 'daily levées in the Art Club', describing their time in Japan. News of this travel talk reached Kirkcudbright, including an unfortunate observation about Hornel. It was quoted in the *Kirkcudbrightshire Advertiser*: 'Hornel hadn't even to tie his own bootlace. That accounts for him being so stout now.' Perhaps Hornel felt his friend's behaviour and unflattering comments gave him carte blanche to write the lecture independently. However, for Henry, it must have rubbed more salt in an already bitter wound, since the latter had discovered that most of his canvases and materials had been damaged on the return sea journey. Their friendship did not survive either.

By contrast, there seems to have been considerable friendly help given by Mackie, despite his suffering from toothache: 'I have opened a fearful cavity in one of my grinders'. Mrs Mackie, with unidentified ailment, was being sent off to see a doctor in Castle Douglas while Charles went to the dentist. Their health must have improved sufficiently for the two of them to mount a tricycle for the expedition (there was no bus link until 1910). Mackie said he would bring some notes 'anent lecture matter', along the lines of 'what one would like to hear from an artist who had visited Japan'. Ever considerate, he hoped that they would talk it over together once the light had faded and Hornel had stopped painting for the day, since he did not want him to lose another day's work. Mackie's time at Gatehouse was to be cut short, as he had to head back to Edinburgh, albeit reluctantly, 'a nuisance as I have both my landscapes unfinished'. Despite this, he offered yet more assistance on the impending lecture. 'Whenever I get back to Edinburgh I shall gather together all the literary pabulum[7] to furnish your lecture', adding as a kind admonishment: 'I would advise you to read thoroughly and then note down in your own words any idea that seems useful, never allowing any other's phraseology to marr [sic] your essay'.

An active researcher on his friend's behalf, he promised notes and opinions to follow. Brimming with enthusiasm after the visit to Kirkcudbright, calling it 'exhilarating', Mackie felt that it had inspired him to work 'like a Trojan'. Ending the letter with good wishes to the whole Hornel family, he invited his friend to visit him in Edinburgh.

The mood of the final letter from this period is more downcast. Lamenting the contrast between Edinburgh and Galloway, his comments confirm how vital an inspiration Kirkcudbright had been:

> As far as art is concerned this is a city of the dead. You have much more art life down in your St Cuthbert's than we have here. Even in Gatehouse I think there was a consciousness of being a force and having a *raison d'etre* for being an artist that seems wanting here.

Despite a recurrence of toothache, his friend's impending lecture was not forgotten. He had done a lot of research on his behalf:

> I have hunted all through the Century magazines for material about Japan and I find there is much to send. But here is a list of the numbers useful for you. From Jan. to Dec. 1890 and these three I send you ... don't miss the 1890 volume. If I meet with anything on Jap. I shall send it to you.

Editorial assistance was also on offer: 'I shall wait till I see your first draft and interpolate', provided Hornel buckled down to work without delay. Mackie had detected some reluctance on the part of his friend, who had no burning desire to deliver the lecture. There is no further correspondence surviving on the Japanese lecture but it was duly given at 7pm on 9 February 1895 in Glasgow Corporation Art Galleries in Sauchiehall Street. *The Glasgow Evening News* had originally intimated that it would be given by Hornel in person and would be accompanied by illustrative lantern slides. In the event, it was delivered on Hornel's behalf by John Keppie, the architect, painter and art collector.[8] The excuse given was the illness of a near relative, which meant that Hornel had found it 'IMPOSSIBLE TO BE PRESENT IN PERSON'. The lecture was also repeated at the Walker Art Gallery in Liverpool, which had earlier courted controversy by buying Hornel's *Summer* in 1892. The *Liverpool Echo* had been critical of the Council's purchase of the painting, comparing its radical use of colour to 'an old woman's patchwork quilt'. However, the press furore had given the artist publicity, an aid to the sale of future works.

The author only lectured in person in his native Kirkcudbright in mid-March. The lecture gave a detailed account of contemporary Japan, describing its buildings, dancing, music and art. The only review that could be found was in *The Glasgow Evening News*, dated Monday, 11 February. Apparently, the main themes had been the society, customs and values of Japan, as well as some of the experiences of Hornel and Henry. At the end there was 'some small reference to Japanese art', which might have benefited from Mackie's input. However, no credit was accorded his friend, despite the time and care he had taken on his behalf.

By now both men were busy developing their careers and Mackie certainly spent further time down in Kirkcudbright and its environs, since he used it as inspiration for the Geddes murals, described in Chapter 2. 'Dunragit, Wigtownshire' was the postal address in 1896 for his copy of *The Evergreen*, despatched by Geddes himself. Above his name is listed 'E.A. Hornel, artist, Kirkcudbright'. Mackie might well have been instrumental in securing the Hornel drawing, *Madame Chrysanthème* for that publication in August 1895. It is one of the very few known drawings attributed to Hornel. Unfortunately, no correspondence has survived and there is no further evidence of direct contact between them until 1901.

In that year Hornel was to scandalize the Edinburgh art establishment of the RSA. The March 1901 election for Associateship resulted in three successful candidates: Gemmell Hutchison, William Walls and Edward Hornel; Charles Mackie was the next, unsuccessful, candidate with twenty votes. It must have been particularly galling for Mackie to lose out and then see his friend reject the nomination. It was the first time that this had ever happened and led to much critical comment in the press of the day. *The Scots Pictorial* was not sparing in its criticism of his behaviour: '[He] cannot be too strongly condemned ... a 2 days wonder ... lowering himself in the estimation of his brother artists in Glasgow and Edinburgh.' It continued to fulminate in the following December, 'Mr Hornel showed further contempt of the RSA by becoming at a later date an associate of the London International Society.'

Hornel had already alienated W. S. MacGeorge (one of the Antwerp confrères) after a fiery argument. A number of sources cite the latter's criticism of Hornel's heavy drinking as the underlying cause of the breach. Now, other artist friends who had argued his case for recognition as an Associate felt let down by his cavalier behaviour, since he had allowed his name to be put forward. A mutual colleague of Mackie and Hornel, Alexander Roche, remonstrated that he should have thought about his friends 'a wee bit' before taking such peremptory action. Hornel wrote to the RSA that he had declined on principle, reputedly telling his friend, Thomas Fraser, the publisher, 'I have been very happy as plain Hornel and I mean to remain such as far as these trumpery affairs are concerned.' It was felt at the time that he thought they had waited too long before making the offer, but the damage was done. His curmudgeonly response to all that transpired did not endear him to his supporters or the artistic establishment. Estrangement from these circles grew more marked in the years to come.

It is to Mackie's credit that their friendship survived, and the proof lies on Hornel's bookshelves in Broughton House. It was with some excitement that I opened a pristine copy of *Greeks and Persians*, a rather strange tome of doggerel verse by Elizabeth Pagan. Charles H. Mackie is on the front cover as 'Inventor and Printer', as he had 'aided by diversions in the manner of Greek Vases designedly discovered'. I could decipher a faint but clear handwritten inscription inside the front cover:

To my friend E.A.Hornell
C.H.Mackie
July 1902

This is sure testimony to his wish to keep the friendship intact, despite all the adverse criticism.

The final surviving letter in the Broughton House archive can be dated only

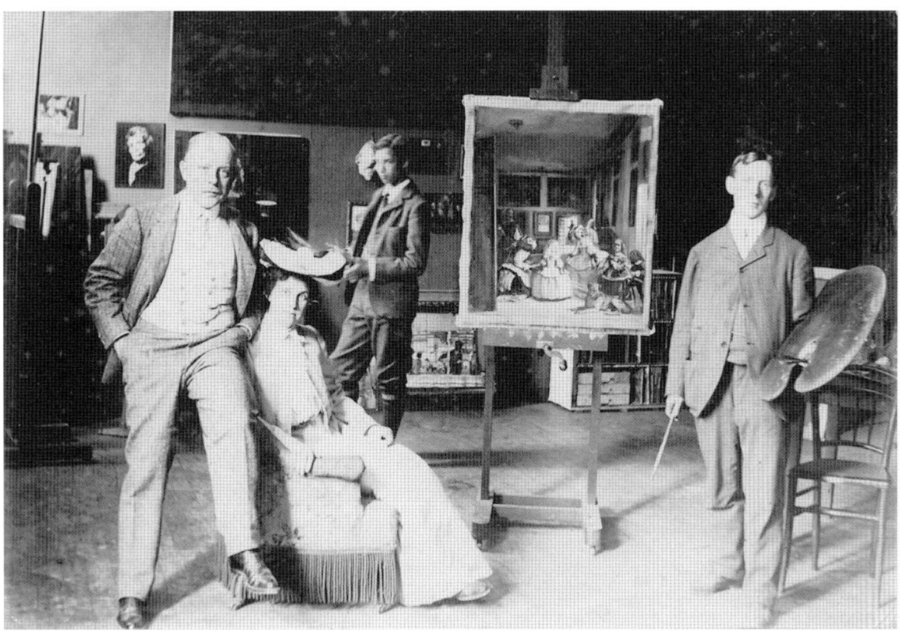

2 Family photograph taken in William (Willie) Mackie's Paris apartment 1904.
Charles Mackie is on the right, with palette and paintbrush in hand. Willie, his wife Fanny and son Torbet are to the left. On the easel is Charles Mackie's copy of *Las Meninas* from the Prado, Madrid. This was the result of a commission from a friend in Edinburgh, William Burn Murdoch, which had allowed Charles to travel and paint in Spain 1903-4. Courtesy of Bill Mackie

approximately since it has no month or year, but had been sent from Mackie's Coltbridge Studio, where he had moved in 1895. There are two references which help place it to 1903/4 – the RSA show containing Whistlers (held in 1903, the year Whistler died) and his planned April departure to Spain. Delighted at receiving a commission from 'our old friend Burn Murdoch' (one of the erstwhile confrères) to copy Velasquez's *The Spinners*, he was looking forward to visiting the Prado. He did head off to Spain in 1903 and 1904, producing some oils, including *La Senorita* and *The Little Dancers, Madrid*, as well as the commissioned work. There is also photographic evidence of his delight in seeing the Prado paintings (Fig. 2). Palette and paintbrush in hand, the artist stands in front of his copy of a Velasquez. The location was his brother Willie's Paris apartment and Willie is on the left, with his wife Fanny and son Torbet in the background. (Esmé Gordon remembered the merchant Willie Mackie as always looking very affluent and smelling of cigars.[9]) Curiously, the painting on the easel is not the commissioned work but the better-known *Las Meninas* (*The Maids of Honour*). No answer to why this is the case has been found. A whole batch of watercolours also came home with him from this Spanish jaunt – the climate had proved much more conducive to outdoor work than his native land.

The tone of this final extant letter is warm – he wants to know when Hornel will be coming to Edinburgh and signs it off: 'Kindest regards to your <u>better</u> half', possibly in tacit recognition of all that had transpired in the interim. Their paths did cross again later, as Mackie and Hornel were both elected Vice Presidents of the Yorkshire Union of Artists in 1907. This was a link that Mackie established during his time at Staithes in north Yorkshire. Despite the earlier ructions in Edinburgh, Hornel was also minded to exhibit at the SSA. Mackie was a founder member, elected Chairman in 1900 and had always championed it strongly. However, it was not until 1911 that Hornel allowed himself to be proposed for election as a Professional member. Their records also show Hornel exhibited paintings at regular intervals in the exhibitions from 1898 to 1915. *The Wounded Butterfly* in 1909 was priced at a heady £500 but since there are no surviving sales records, it is not possible to know whether it found a buyer. By contrast, the total cost for all of Mackie's paintings that year amounted to a more moderate £135. Both men exhibited at the RGI and the RSA but Hornel did not attend Mackie's funeral in 1920, being abroad on a grand tour of Burma, Singapore, Hong Kong, Japan, Canada and the USA.

Their careers had certainly diverged by that stage, both socially and professionally. Hornel had immured himself in Broughton House with his Japanese garden, painting Japanese girls and chrysanthemums or, alternatively, depicting decorative young Galloway lasses in landscape or seascape settings. The raw and radical nature of the painting which both had produced in the 1890s had disappeared. In Mackie's case, he had sought to experiment in different media and travel further afield. Hornel seemed content to settle for the assured commercial success that had greeted his sentimental *oeuvre*, aided and abetted latterly by his sister Tizzie.

Hornel and Kirkcudbright had provided a synergy of person and place which had inspired the young Mackie. He did not easily loosen the ties of friendship but Hornel gradually retreated into crabbed isolation. By contrast, Mackie would make his mark on the wider world, with Edinburgh as his personal, social and artistic fulcrum. The love of Galloway and its landscape stayed strong, forging a link with his Edinburgh life that would leave a lasting mark on Ramsay Garden, in the heart of the Old Town.

NOTES

1 All quotations from Charles Mackie in this chapter come from the letters in the Broughton House archives, courtesy of the National Trust for Scotland and with the kind permission of Bill Mackie.

2 All this would be resolved in 1907 when the Scottish Education Department took over these responsibilities and the Edinburgh College of Art was created, housed in new premises at Lady Lawson Street from 1909. It has continued to evolve and is now part of the University of Edinburgh.

3 The Royal Assocation for the Promotion of Fine Arts in Scotland had been set up in 1848. It functioned as an Art Union, using public subscriptions to benefit artists and the general public alike. For their annual subscription members would receive engravings of contemporary Scottish paintings. Any remaining funds would be used to purchase pictures at the RSA Exhibition which would be allotted by ballot to the subscribers.

4 William Stuart MacGeorge (1861-1931) was a painter of landscapes, portraits & figure subjects in oil. William Walls (1860-1942) specialised in animal paintings, mainly in oil. William Burn Murdoch (1862-1939), lithographer and etcher, also worked in oil and watercolour.

5 *Old Statistical Account Vol. X*, p. 146, republished as *New Statistical Account Vol. XI*, p.113.

6 Both comments on Anne Mackie are from the Mackie-Walls family correspondence, courtesy of Bill Mackie.

7 Pabulum: 'food for thought'. Mackie's classical education at George Watson's had evidently proved useful.

8 John Keppie (1862-1945) would later go on to design Hornel's studio and picture gallery at Broughton House in Kirkcudbright.

9 Esmé Gordon, former President of the RSA, became a good friend of the Melbourne Mackies and his correspondence with Bill provided many such memories and anecdotes. His father had been one of Charles Mackie's closest friends in Edinburgh. Esmé himself had warm memories of visiting the painter's sister Annie when she lived in Howe Street.

Two
Not a single rowan berry

On a wintry day in March 2013 the National Trust for Scotland gave me access to an equally chilly 14 Ramsay Garden, bequeathed to them by the architect, the late Robert J. Naismith and his sister Annie Naismith, known to all as Nan. They had lived in the property for nearly three decades before it passed into the care of the Trust in 2004. I was on the trail of the Mackie murals which he had executed for Patrick Geddes in 1893-4. I confess to having experienced a frisson of excitement and anticipation at the prospect of seeing these unique Mackie murals in the flesh. The third-floor flat, designed by the architect Stewart Henbest Capper, occupied the whole of that level and it has seen some alterations since the days when Geddes and his family lived there.

This was where their daughter Norah was born in October 1887, followed by her brother Alastair in June 1891. Her vivid *Reminiscences*, housed in the National Library of Scotland, provide a first-hand description of the life lived by the family who resided in the flat until 1896. Her eye-witness description of the murals which Mackie painted for the flat are rich in detail.

The main rooms are much as she would have known them, apart from an insert panel, separating the two drawing rooms, and some layers of paint covering hidden Mackie treasures. In the former bedroom, where some other Mackie murals had been removed, Mr Naismith had commissioned Reinhard Behrens to fill the missing spaces with more modern landscape depictions. Was it coincidence that Behrens was at the helm of the Society of Scottish Artists one hundred years after Mackie's Chairmanship? Some attempt had been made at amateur restoration of two panels but it was the employment of skilled professionals which had brought the murals back to life. They are in what Norah knew as the red room and her description matches the fine pictures revealed: 'spring felling in a beech wood and taking up quantities of winter leaves.'[1]

The spring picture has the central figure of the woodcutter, attacking his chosen tree in the beech wood, while the Clydesdales pull away the felled timber along a path leading off into the distance (Pl. 3). It is depicted with strong, clear lines and pools of colour, surely reflecting Mackie's continued focus on applying the colour lessons he had just imbibed in France. The disposition of the green guides us through the wood and the remnant winter leaves add a brown contrast, picked up in the coat of one of the horses. Black and white horses complement the woodcutter's attire. In the companion mural, the winter leaves are being gathered up by two girls and a boy in that same wood, identified as Boreland Wood, behind Cardoness Castle and its Castle Cottage where the Mackies were staying at the time. The tall trees frame their toil and its impact is the stronger for the simplicity of the theme, possibly meriting the label of 'Gauguinesque' (Pl. 4). In fact, it would be the following year when Mackie would meet Gauguin in person. In October 1893 he was demonstrating his response to the ideas of the new French friends of that summer's sojourn in Paris. Without doubt, this group of painters had looked to Gauguin for inspiration and Mackie would have seen the evidence in their studios. Gauguin's imperative would have appealed to the Scotsman: 'the painter ought not to rest until he has given birth to the child of his imagination.'

Mackie's mural 'progeny' can be seen in Ramsay Garden and in one preparatory work. The small oil sketch in the Hunterian Gallery in Glasgow, *The Faggot Gatherers*, is similar in style and composition to the larger mural but its colours are much sharper (Pl. 6). It is further confirmation that Mackie was still drawing inspiration from his experiences in Brittany and Paris. They are markedly different to the naturalistic art he had exhibited at the RSA in the 1880s (Pl. 1). Mackie's new style has been likened to Pont-Aven symbolism by several art historians, a theme explored further in chapter 4. *The Faggot Gatherers* is the only surviving sketch for these murals and the more precious for that.

In Norah's day, the two rooms were divided by double curtains, allowing them to be drawn back when there were larger social gatherings. The rationale of the design underpinned this, since it had been planned for receptions, not dinner parties, the dining room being small. The Mackie murals would have been showcased in this setting, underlining how highly his talents were rated by Geddes. She goes on to describe the other two Mackie panels, in the yellow drawing room, dealing with high summer and early autumn. These are hidden treasures awaiting discovery, when further restoration can be carried out by the National Trust. All four *Seasons* had been dealt with on a grand scale in the two public rooms but the theme was also carried into another room, where Norah can be the guide.

She described her parents' bedroom as:

> spacious and beautiful. Its shallow box window looked to the Castle over the trees of the wooded slope far below and north-west over the Forth. Along one wall and over the fireplace were frescoes by Charles Mackie. The long wall showed a series of country scenes arranged in sequence according to season and time of day. To recall them gives me satisfaction still.

Alas, these panels have not fared so well. The room was converted into a dining room, some of the Mackie panels were removed (or, hopefully, covered over), to be replaced by the work of a more modern artist. Only two are currently extant and one is in quite poor condition. *The Drinking Pond* is very reminiscent of a Galloway landscape, although the colours are more muted than George Henry's, while *Age* is faint in outline and in poor condition. It is only the latter title which matches Mackie's own list. Clues to the themes of these panels can be found in letters to Geddes, updating him on progress. Mackie evidently also supplied two panels for the head of the bed, depicting cultivated and wild fruit. In the main drawing room there is reference to *The Daisy Chain*, which might well be the illustration *Summer*, revealed in a contemporary article. Executing this commission for Professor Geddes occasioned Mackie much worry, both in terms of overdue payment and problems with the weather in Gatehouse of Fleet. He refers to a practical reason for the delay in finishing one panel, since 'there was not a single rowan berry seen here this summer',[2] so he was going on with *the storks* instead. This is unidentified and does not match his own list, whereas *the wind scattering leaves* would be a good fit for his title of *autumn breeze* (vid. Mackie's accounts page 32). He also was anxious about his financial situation, telling Geddes in the same letter,

> I am glad to get my wages as my gunwale was under water, your last £30 being paid away after being received. Many thanks.

Keen to ensure that the murals were attached to the wall properly, he asked Geddes to check that Dott took special care, partly relieved when John Duncan 'offered to see them on to the wall'[3] Mackie's trust in Duncan was linked to the latter's first-hand knowledge of French murals. Duncan had seen the work of Puvis de Chavannes in the Pantheon in Paris. His first Notebook in the NLS details his praise of the colour, tone, simplicity of treatment and attention to detail.[4] In addition the Dott-Geddes family connection might also have helped ensure that the workman adhered to the instructions. Aitken Dott was an established art materials business in Edinburgh, situated at 24 Castle Street, and well known to Mackie. Peter Dott was married to Rebecca ('Bex'), the elder sister of the former Anna Morton who had married Patrick Geddes in April 1886. Like Mackie and his wife Anne, Mr and Mrs Patrick Geddes shared common ideals and sought to improve the lot of their poorer fellow citizens in the city Geddes later described in a Summer School lecture as 'the metropolis of dirt'.

At this time Mackie was using a French technique known as *marouflage*, whereby the painted canvas is fixed to the wall using an adhesive that hardens as it dries. The murals were not painted in situ. Thus, the artist enjoyed the freedom to work at these on canvas, in his studio, no doubt after preliminary studies *en plein air.* Mackie took particular care with the canvas, bought whole-sale and prepared by him personally. This allowed him to be confident in commending it for its qualities of durability, fitness and economy. He even assured Geddes that this would be a better bargain than buying the canvas from Dott directly. Diligent canvas preparation was worth the time, given the fact that these were to be murals. When the canvas panels were attached to the wall, even greater care had to be exercised:

> be most particular in seeing that the man does not go all over them with his bare paws but puts smooth paper between the panel and his hand when pressing them down.[5]

Mackie was concerned that the grease from the workman's hand would be transferred to the wall painting, to the detriment of the matt finish the artist was seeking to achieve. The instructions must have been followed, since those that remain have stood the test of time and fulfilled Mackie's dearest wish:

> I have no doubt that generations yet unborn will see these panels as you see them.[6]

The letters sent to Geddes contained in the archive housed in the University of Strathclyde all fall within the period October 1893–July 1894, sent from Gatehouse of Fleet, as Mackie was using his now familiar Galloway landscape as inspiration for the seasonal theme. Since the murals are currently incomplete and Norah Geddes does not identify them all individually, I was left wondering as to their individual content. By chance, I found a handwritten account drawn up by Mackie, itemizing all his work for payment.[7] It not only provides information on the cost, but also names all the panels, with their titles and dimensions. The amended number, reduced from eighteen to ten, indicates that the original scheme had been even more ambitious (Fig. 3). It is possible, using this document, to identify each individual mural, its location and exact size, since Mackie was quite specific. There is also a pencilled note from Geddes on the reverse of the account, noting that the two panels for the yellow room (referred to above) were still to come. The document is evidence of the mural treasures which once existed at 14 Ramsay Garden. It is worth quoting in full since it provides one of the clearest insights into Mackie's work and his attention to detail. He had to make a living as a painter and the Geddes commission had been his largest to date, as well as being one which had actually materialized. Mackie's guarantee to Geddes was that all his energies would be focused on this commission, saying in one letter 'I am working exclusively on your work'.[8]

Great care was also taken with the surrounding colour scheme. A contemporary observer, Margaret Armour, confirmed this, 'The tone, as always with Mr Mackie, is adapted to the colour of the wall'.[9] An intriguing comment, which

3 Accounts for the murals executed for Patrick Geddes in Ramsay Garden. In Mackie's own handwriting, detailing size, theme and cost, they provide the best guide to the commissioned work. T.GED 10/1/48. © The University of Strathclyde Library, Department of Archives and Special Collections

hints at some knowledge of earlier mural work by Mackie undertaken at the Royal Infirmary. At Ramsay Garden, the architectural details were downplayed, so that the impact would not be lost. Beads surrounding the areas of panelling were in plaster, rather than wood, and the whole scheme would have seen the murals at their heart, not lost amid uncomplementary colours. The artist had already costed 'colour consultations' in the accounts above, to ensure that an overall harmony was achieved. His collaborator in the overall scheme was a fellow Edinburgh Social Union muralist, Miss Mary Rose Hill Burton.

These murals would have looked down on many social gatherings, hosted by 'Pat', as Norah's father was known. The family lived in the flat for seven years, coincident with the period of the Celtic Revival and she remembers 'hearing so much interesting adult conversation'. She can remember the buzz even as she lay in bed at night; 'I could not but be aware of all this activity and felt it to be very important.' In April 1895, Geddes opened his flat for public viewing, so Mackie's murals would have been seen by many of his fellow citizens. Given that admission was free, the Edinburgh bourgeoisie would have been eager to see all that lay behind Geddes's front door (normally, they would have had to part with 6*d* for such a treat). In addition, 14 Ramsay Garden saw much entertaining of guests, British and foreign, and French would then be spoken at the dinner table. Unlike Hornel, whose French pronunciation was considered poor, Anne and Charles Mackie would have been at their ease in this situation. They had already acquired a number of French friends and had of course spent time in France itself, enjoying the sociability of their artistic circle.

Geddes numbered among his friends Henry Beveridge of Pitreavie Castle in Dunfermline, who must have also have viewed the murals at no.14. This wealthy linen manufacturer decided to commission his own but our only evidence is documentary since the castle no longer exists. Geddes did stay at Pitreavie in 1903 so he would have seen the new murals, but he left no description behind. Beveridge died in 1922. The castle was sold to the Air Ministry in 1938 and any decorative work suffered the indignity of being overpainted or whitewashed, in the interests of national defence. The remaining buildings now offer deluxe accommodation fit for the twenty-first century and no trace of their mural history is evident. There are some written references to Mackie's work, saying that these had been done in tempera and that his medieval frescoes flanked the great oak staircase. Our best knowledge of the Pitreavie murals is based on the article written by Armour on 'Mural Decoration in Scotland', published in *The Studio*, an influential art magazine, in 1897. She knew Patrick Geddes, contributed to *The Evergreen* and was a member of the Edinburgh Social Union. Fortunately, she also supplied illustrations of three Mackie murals, with the distinctive Celtic M monogram;[10] unfortunately, they are in black and white. Two illustrations are Pitreavie pictures: *O Lang, Lang May the Ladies Sit*, based on the ballad of Sir Patrick Spens and *The Call to Arms*, from the ballad of *Hardyknute*. Seemingly, there was another in the *Hardyknute* series entitled *The Battle* and a further two linked to Queen Margaret of Scotland. They were not shown in the article, so we can only speculate on their content. Beveridge had settled on these themes since they were directly linked to the history of the castle. According to Armour the two ballads had been penned by a former owner, Lady Wardlaw. She goes on to describe the composition as 'alive with old world romance'. One other Mackie illustration was shown – *Summer*, which was a Geddes panel, also carrying that distinctive Celtic M monogram.

Indeed, she celebrated the quality of the work he had executed on Castle Hill, commenting on the drawing room panels:

> Nobody with the slightest eye for art could be in Professor Geddes's study and miss Mr Mackie's two landscape panels. The audacious forms and colour schemes are justified by complete success.

She referred to the bedroom as having been transformed into 'a small art gallery through Mr Mackie's genius', enthusing about his 'human eye' and 'the sane and classic balance of all his work'. She concluded:

> Originally a painter of easel pictures and accustomed irresponsibly to assert his own vivid moods, he has now attained to the wider and more impersonal outlook of the decorator ... he has worked himself into a style individual and distinguished, and has achieved 'a grand manner' all his own.[11]

Praise indeed, and it must have been encouraging to Mackie after his earlier foray into the murals for the Edinburgh Royal Infirmary, dealing with Professor Geddes's accounting and the criticism of the modernness of his art.

In fact, the Royal Infirmary project had been his first mural commission, dated to March 1887 in the Edinburgh Social Union Minutes. As the chairman of the Union's Decoration Committee, Geddes was again the link and he reported that 'Mr Mackie had undertaken the work subject to the approval of the Decoration Committee of the Social Union and the Infirmary Committee.' As further confirmation, the recording secretary had noted on the facing page 'Decoration in Infirmary undertaken by Mr Mackie'.[12] As Geddes was a leading light in these proceedings, he would have seen Mackie's talent and reliability first hand. The Edinburgh Social Union had been set up in January 1885, an outgrowth of the Environmental Society, with the avowed aim of being 'a scheme for the organization of all benevolent enterprise'. It followed ten years after the creation of the Cockburn Association. The latter, then as now, saw itself as the civic guardian and watchdog of the urban architecture of Edinburgh. Its aim was to protect and enhance the beauty of the city. By contrast, the emphasis of the Social Union was more radical and interventionist. The members, including

Geddes, felt that it was important to try and bridge the class divide, by offering opportunities to the poor, of the sort that the middle classes took for granted. These would encompass art and access to recreation in creative evening classes. The Union differed in structure as well, encompassing an educational programme under James Oliphant, Geddes's brother-in-law; an Entertainment Committee providing musical performances and poetry readings; a Public Open Spaces Committee led in later years by his son-in-law, Frank Mears; and a Housing Guild which carried out active and effective remedial work in the Old Town. The Artistic Guild was one of the first to be set up and it was responsible for commissioning much mural work in the city. This related directly to their philosophy of the importance of art in the daily life of the poor. The approach to social and civic regeneration was holistic. Improvement in housing conditions was also to be matched to life-enhancing surroundings, combining the creation of gardens and open spaces with beautiful buildings and hygienic housing. The Social Union lay at the heart of what Geddes envisaged for the Old Town, in terms of producing a wholly new cultural environment — that was why he and Anna chose to live there.

Decoration projects were considered by a special committee, chaired by Patrick Geddes in person and the architect of Ramsay Garden, Henbest Capper, also served alongside him. Edinburgh's artists were encouraged to decorate the walls of public buildings, following in the French footsteps of Pierre Puvis de Chavannes (1824-1898) whose frescoes in Rouen and the Pantheon in Paris would have been known to them. Mackie might well have seen these during his own visits to those cities. Geddes held the French muralist in high regard and must have communicated this to his coterie. His 1888 pamphlet *Every Man his Own Art Critic* had been given to many of them, so Mackie and his friends would have been well aware of his predilections. Such was the enthusiasm with which these young men and women took up their paintbrushes that *The Studio* later reflected in its 1897 article that 'Edinburgh is busy making art history on her walls as Glasgow is busy making it on her easels', while Ramsay Garden was noted as 'one of the chief show places'.

Ten years earlier, under the aegis of the Social Union, Mackie had designed six mural panels on the history of corn. These were recorded in the RSA catalogue for 1887, featuring in the watercolour exhibition as *Six designs for panels in the Royal Infirmary, Edinburgh*. However, they were not mentioned in any of *The Scotsman* reviews of the exhibition. Its only comment on the water-colour room was that it contained 'no picture of an outstanding nature'. Mackie's designs encompassed all the seasons and the related rural activities: ploughing, sowing, harrowing, reaping, harvesting and grinding. They were described in the Social Union's 1888 annual report as 'an important series of six large original cartoons in oil colour ... at present in active progress'. Intended for the walls of one of the wards (possibly Ward 11 or 12) of the old Edinburgh Royal Infirmary, they were meant to nourish the urban sick with wholesome country scenes. Professor Baldwin Brown confirmed that Mackie was engaged in this philanthropic undertaking and the Decoration Committee had been pleased that they were receiving practical assistance from professional artists. The 1889 report confirmed that the work was well on track, with several panels 'already completed' and by 1890, all that was needed was committee approval before they were fixed in position in the infirmary. The final reference to this work in the minutes is dated June 1891 and states: 'Mr Mackie had forwarded one of the set of panels undertaken by him in 1889 with the request that it be hung in Dr Duncan's Ward.'

A wide range of artists were involved in such decoration schemes, including students and noted female artists such as Phoebe Traquair and Mary Rose Hill Burton. Under the aegis of such luminaries as William McTaggart, Professor Baldwin Brown and Henbest Capper, brushes were wielded far and wide, improving many walls in Edinburgh. *The Scotsman* judged these emissaries of the Social Union to be fitting 'missionaries of civilization'. Unfortunately, we cannot view Mackie's earliest murals. The old infirmary no longer exists and the buildings have been extensively remodelled into luxurious flats, known as the Quarter Mile. Even the National Health Service records did not yield any further reference to the fate of these mysterious murals.

The fact that some of Mackie's murals in Ramsay Garden have survived while the rest have disappeared is the serendipity of history. The flat is located at the heart of a World Heritage Site and Mackie's art is equally deserving of iconic status. The polymath Geddes was to give Mackie another commission, albeit of a somewhat different nature. Place and person remained the same, but this time he was able to demonstrate different skills, in furthering the Celtic Revival.

NOTES

1 All extracts are taken from Norah Geddes's *Reminiscences* in the National Library of Scotland, MS 19266, quoted by kind permission of the National Library of Scotland.
2 University of Strathclyde Library, Department of Archives and Special Collections, Geddes archive, T.GED 9/77/.
3 Ibid.
4 National Library of Scotland, ACC 6866.
5 University of Strathclyde Library, Department of Archives and Special Collections, Geddes archive, T.GED 9/76.
6 Ibid. T.GED 9/77.
7 Ibid. T.GED 10/1/48.
8 Ibid. T.GED 9/76.
9 *The Studio* 1897, Vol. 10, p.105.
10 He only used this monogram in the 1890s during his Celtic Revival period; all other work is signed or initialled conventionally.
11 *The Studio* 1897, Vol. 10, pp.104-6.
12 Edinburgh Social Union Minutes and Annual Reports, HV250 E23 S; Edinburgh and Scottish Collection, courtesy of Edinburgh City Libraries and Information Services.

Three
It is bad from cover to cover

This negative review of the first edition of *The Evergreen* in 1895 added 'and even the covers are bad'.[1] It was Charles Mackie who had designed and produced them, as well as contributing several illustrations and prevailing on other artist friends to provide additional material. The concept of this publication lay at the heart of the movement known as the Celtic Revival, which a number of artists, such as John Duncan and Mackie, embraced with enthusiasm. Mackie's patron and friend, Patrick Geddes, was its evangelist. *The Evergreen* was to be its mouthpiece.

Geddes saw the publication as an organ for the dissemination of his philosophy and ideals, combining Literature with Art (sic), designed for everyman and all men. It was to provide a platform for younger Scottish writers, students, painters, men of science and all those in sympathy with this fusion of history, nature, humanity and Celtic design and ornament. Indeed, it was a heady mixture and the lofty synthesis which Geddes outlined in his preface showed that he saw himself as heir to the Scots poet, Allan Ramsay. The latter had published a poetry anthology, *Ever Green*, in 1724, in an attempt to revive local tradition, Scottish history and an interest in the natural world. Geddes, an avowed Francophile, was trying to go further, lauding the Celtic Renascence (sic) in literature and art, as well as the revival of Scotland's auld alliances. Edinburgh, he argued, was not just a city of culture, history and colour but it was also a European city: 'one of the European powers of Culture'. The social life of the city was to be in harmony with nature, science, literature and art. In the past, he argued, art and literature had been associated; now the parallel was to be natural history and social studies. Science and the humanities were to be seen as a whole, since this was the path to understanding life and the real world, where no such artificial divisions existed. Geddes may have paid homage to the past but this was allied to a vision for the future, and *The Evergreen* was in the vanguard.

Where did Mackie fit in to his scheme? He was central to its initial impact, since he designed and produced the embossed and tinted leather cover for all its editions. This would have been the first impression, conveying the nature of the new publication. One cannot always tell a book by its cover but, in this case, the cover was integral to the concepts enshrined in *The Evergreen* (Pl. 5).

The seasons of the year provided the continuity and the contrast of the publication's structure, and the editions which materialized matched the chronology of the natural cycle. Part One covering *Spring* appeared in April 1895; Part Two was *Autumn*, in October of the same year; Part Three was *Summer*, in May 1896; and the final edition was *Winter*, in November 1896. The experimental approach was original, since the content of each volume would reflect the season denoted on the cover, both in mood and thought. The art, prose, poetry and design would all harmonise with the particular time of year. When the first edition reached the critics in 1895, *The Art Journal* was impressed:

> This publication has been so well thought out and is so well-produced, that it ought certainly to have a lengthy life ... the writers and illustrations are all of the northern soil ... ([it is]) sufficiently original to be promising.[2]

The Manchester Guardian concurred, seeing it as 'an indication of the vitality of young Edinburgh.' C.H. Mackie is credited with the 'coloured covers, varying for each season, fashioned in leather.' Each edition was enclosed within rough-edged calfskin with beautifully embossed designs in tooled leatherwork. Each front cover differed slightly in its layout, with the first, *Spring*, being the most colourful and complex.

With the one critical exception noted at the outset of the chapter, there was fulsome praise for both the design and its execution. Geddes cut out and kept a meticulous record of press cuttings, of all shades of opinion and nationwide. Some of these contemporaneous comments include: 'A book the mere externals of which make it a delight to handle'; 'beautiful binding'; 'beautifully embossed'; 'the leather-embossed cover is quite admirable'; 'the best part of *The Evergreen* is its leather cover'; 'a fine piece of design and colour'; and, damning with faint praise, 'the lone thing to whom nobody will take exception.' One verdict is worth quoting at length, since it is the most descriptive, comprehensive and positive:

> The tan leather cover stamped with light green, with the lion and thistles behind and conventionalized flowers in front, is a real work of art, much the best thing of the kind I have seen lately.

Geddes was clearly assiduous in collecting these press reviews of his new publication and he must have felt that his input into the cover had been fruitful. The papers in the archive do reveal his keen determination to ensure its quality. In the margin to the minutes of an *Evergreen* business committee meeting, held on Monday, 2 December 1895, there is a handwritten note to the effect that: 'Cover as formerly is still directly under control of Mr Geddes personally.'[3] While he might have agreed with the artist on the choice of *arbor vitae*, the tree of life

(*Aloe plicatilis*), he still wanted to ensure that the whole continued to reflect his vision. Since there had been initial technical problems with the leather work, the Business Committee recommended economy of design (*Spring* could double as *Summer, Autumn* could double as *Winter*) while allowing for a change of colour. The Committee wanted to avoid an over-ambitious design since the process of staining the leather had occasioned difficulties. On the first print-run, it had resulted in some blotchy, unsaleable editions, which could be ill-afforded. For the future three editions, Mackie kept his front cover variations to the minimum and the back covers were virtually identical, so he had listened to their concerns. No two front covers were the same but standardisation was evident in the inside lay-out. Geddes had retained control of the product and the artist but allowed him some freedom to experiment with design and technique. After all, he had already seen what Mackie could produce.

I had not been aware of any precursor to *The Evergreen* until I made an exciting discovery in the Scottish Arts Club in Rutland Square. They had kindly given me access to their basement archives and it was in one of these boxes that I found three copies of the first hand-tooled leather book produced by the hands of Charles Mackie. It was an exciting discovery since there had been no mention of this in any other reference work. The design is very much in sympathy with the Celtic Revival and would have won the approval of its many recipients. The cover motif depicts stylised lions rampant, rearing to right and left, surmounted by thistles and, angled across the front, in Celtic script, is *The Scottish Arts Club. Opening Ceremonies 1894*. On the back, there is a distinctive roundel, containing a flower (possibly a rose?) and 'Charles H. Mackie: Del et Imp. Edinburgh.'[4] The contents include details on the opening ceremony, the reception, toasts, speeches and musical programme. All the great and good of Edinburgh society were present. The archives described these participants as 'representative', including 'numerous ladies'. The reception was hosted by Sir George Reid, the President of the SAC and the RSA. It all augured well for the promotion of art and the welfare of the member artists. However, the glitter of the occasion was not allowed to obscure the true purpose of the Scottish Arts Club.

Their first Annual Report hoped that 'the Modern Athens' (sic) would welcome the establishment and promotion of such a club for all those convinced of the need to support art. The opening ceremony had been very well attended, with the smoking room 'crowded to excess'. The booklet had been produced to commemorate this auspicious occasion, marking the move to its present location in Rutland Square. The building at number 24 was purchased for £2,100 and the cost of alterations resulted in a total outlay of £2,668.2s.3d. Geddes had tried to interest them in acquiring a plot in Ramsay Garden but although this had fallen through, there were no hard feelings and he had accepted honorary membership in 1891. Given his social prominence, he would have been an honoured guest at the inaugural dinner and thus received a copy. Unfortunately, the archive evidence does not confirm his attendance, but given the closeness of artistic circles in Edinburgh, he would surely have been aware of Mackie's work.

In addition, Geddes had already praised Mackie's art and established strong connections with other Edinburgh artistic circles. After the foundation of the new Society of Scottish Artists,[5] Geddes was not only present at their well-attended opening banquet on Friday, 22 April 1892, but gave a speech. He would have been sympathetic to their publicly professed wish to win 'the support of all classes.' This would reinforce and strengthen his relationship with youthful and talented Scottish artists. It was no surprise that Mackie would be found hard at work on the Ramsay Garden murals by 1893. Having shown in 1894 that he could turn his hand to leatherwork, he was in prime position to take on the cover of *The Evergreen*. After all, he already had his design for the reverse – lions rampant and thistles.

With regard to content, Geddes also relied on Mackie for a major artistic contribution in terms of illustration. Since the theme of the seasons matched the mural work in Ramsay Garden, it is a distinct possibility that some of the pictures contained within the covers of *The Evergreen* supply an answer to the missing murals. The cover of the *Spring* edition was surmounted by a roundel showing girls picking flowers and this was replicated as a woodblock print on the frontispiece. The contents also contained two black and white woodblock prints: *Robene and Makyn* and *When the Girls come out to play*. The former was a direct reference to the Scots poet Robert Henryson ('the Scots Chaucer' who hailed from Dunfermline), with its tale of unrequited love and the moral taught therein. The latter print is unashamedly modern in its heavy line and cursive shapes, in tune with the contribution from Mackie's French friend, Paul Sérusier. The latter had contributed *Pastorale bretonne* to the same volume.

These last two pictures vied, in the eyes of one critic, for the award of: 'the worst picture in the book.' Mackie's girls are described as: 'lumpy and lifeless; the skipping rope is nearly as thick as a weaver's beam. What the Red Indian Squaw is doing behind the tree passes our comprehension.' The local press were equally scathing, with the *Edinburgh Evening News* recommending that: 'Mr Charles H. Mackie and Mr Paul Sérusier should go back to their drawing blocks before thrusting such abortions of black and white work upon the market.' Undeterred, Mackie provided two more black and white prints for the *Autumn* edition: *Hide and Seek* and *Lyart Leaves* (lyart is a Scots word which refers to the variegated colours of the fallen leaves in autumn). The latter would later be republished in *A Celtic Miscellany*, in 1922, after Mackie's death, to raise funds for the Outlook Tower.[6] Viewed as 'strong and beautiful' by *The Glasgow Herald* at the time of its original publication, Mackie felt sufficiently pleased with the result that he sent copies of both prints to two other French friends, Monsieur and Madame Ranson. (They are still in the possession of their descendants in present-day Paris.) They might have provided the reassurance missing in the mixed critical reception that had greeted his drawings. (Pls. 7, 8). The *Edinburgh Evening News* was to the fore again: 'illustrations childish to a degree' – while another magazine was blunt: '*Hide and Seek* is downright bad.'

But worse was to come for *Chucks* in the *Summer* book, since it was dismissed as: 'ink daubs and meaningless curves'. In *Winter*, Mackie finally received some praise for *Felling Trees* as: 'decidedly the best' of the illustrations. This was the same as the mural he had painted for Geddes in the flat, and lends further weight to the theory that other illustrations might be lost mural designs. The *Winter* volume also contained the woodblock print of *By the Bonnie Banks o' Fordie*, though this would be altered in detail when it was worked up into a full-scale oil for exhibition at the RSA in 1897. (PL. 16). In this final edition of *A Northern Seasonal* (the subtitle of *The Evergreen*), Mackie's younger sister Annie contributed a number of headpieces and tailpieces, of Celtic design. Several of his friends such as James Cadenhead, Robert Burns and William Burn Murdoch were also regular contributors. Cadenhead and John Duncan, Mackie's erstwhile mural collaborator at Ramsay Garden, contributed to all four volumes.

Much of Mackie's creative energies and practical application had been at the service of Patrick Geddes over these years and he was one of the foremost artists enrolled in the missionary enterprise. His talents were further employed in the other main venture of Castle Hill – the Edinburgh Summer Schools. These began in 1887 and were held every August until 1899, and then intermittently until 1903, though Mackie seemed to end his participation well before that date. He might have been tempted to rejoin the Summer Meeting in 1900 when Geddes relocated to Paris. It called itself the Paris International Assembly and was an educational adjunct to the *Exposition Universelle* of that year. There was also the added attraction of the Durand-Ruel Exhibition of twenty-seven Monets and twenty-one Renoirs. One would expect an ardent Francophile like Mackie to have visited the Paris of 1900 but, unfortunately, there is no confirmatory evidence.

The Edinburgh meetings consisted of lectures and seminars, wholesome activities, practical work and excursions to places of historic or natural interest. Targeted at those with an educational vocation as well as the Edinburgh *cognoscenti*, many practising teachers found the timing ideal. The programme included lectures and seminars on contemporary social evolution, history and practical economics, as well as literary and musical recitals and visits to museums and galleries. Norah Geddes recalled the 'stir and bustle' of these summer months. She says that her father tried to bring the past alive by organizing a mock Viking raid on Inchcolm Island in the Forth and celebrating the Beltane Festival at midnight on Arthur's Seat. The longer excursions took place on Saturdays and they visited a variety of attractive locations including Stirling, Melrose, Abbotsford and St. Andrews. The other highlight which she remembered was a performance of *The Gentle Shepherd* by Allan Ramsay. Geddes was, after all, literally following in his footsteps in Ramsay Garden. (The ground on which Ramsay Garden stood had been bought by the self-same poet in 1733; he built Ramsay Lodge in 1734. Geddes, in turn, had purchased the property from Lord Murray of Henderland, one of Ramsay's descendants.)

Without doubt this educational enterprise represented the synthesis of science, history, art and creativity that lay at the heart of Geddes's philosophy. In 1893, one hundred and twenty people attended and there was a core group of regulars, who relished the radical, relatively 'liberated' and heady cosmopolitanism on offer in the normally strait-laced capital. There was a wry comment on the number of romantic attachments and ensuing marriages that resulted from this congregation of such spirited and high-minded participants. Following the death of his much-loved Anna in 1917, it was perhaps fitting that Geddes's second marriage in 1928, in the twilight of his life, was to a former summer school participant, Lillian Brown.

Did Mackie play any part in these summer schools? His importance was captured by the photographer who has given us the visual record of participants. (Fig.4A,4B). Mackie's place is right beside Geddes in these photographs. In 1891, in front of New College, Charles Mackie stands behind him, while their wives are to be found in the fourth row; in 1896, he is seated right beside him, albeit with a troublesome child on his knee, and Anna Geddes is seated beside her husband, while Anne Mackie stands directly behind Charles. The position he occupied in these photographs is visual testimony to the high rank Geddes accorded him — they were seen to be brothers-in-arms. However, there are only scattered references and hints as to his actual hands-on activity, which had to dovetail with the demands of being a professional artist.

The timing of these meetings covered virtually the whole of August which would render them accessible to teachers, but they robbed the working artist of the time to engage with the landscape at a more clement season in the Scottish year. It had to be a juggling act, both financially, artistically and logistically. Total commitment to Geddes and his projects occasioned much worry for Mackie. In a letter dated 26 October 1893, there was a heartfelt plea:

> If you have work for me when I have finished your present commission I will go on with an easy mind but if there lies nothing beyond I must turn aside to picture making between times. [7]

Mackie had to make a living and he felt that some of Geddes's plans lacked clarity: 'You spoke to me of the Municipal decorations. Am I to go on with them?' Nothing seems to have resulted from this but his other query had produced an outcome: 'And what are your proposals regarding the School of Art. Duncan gives me a

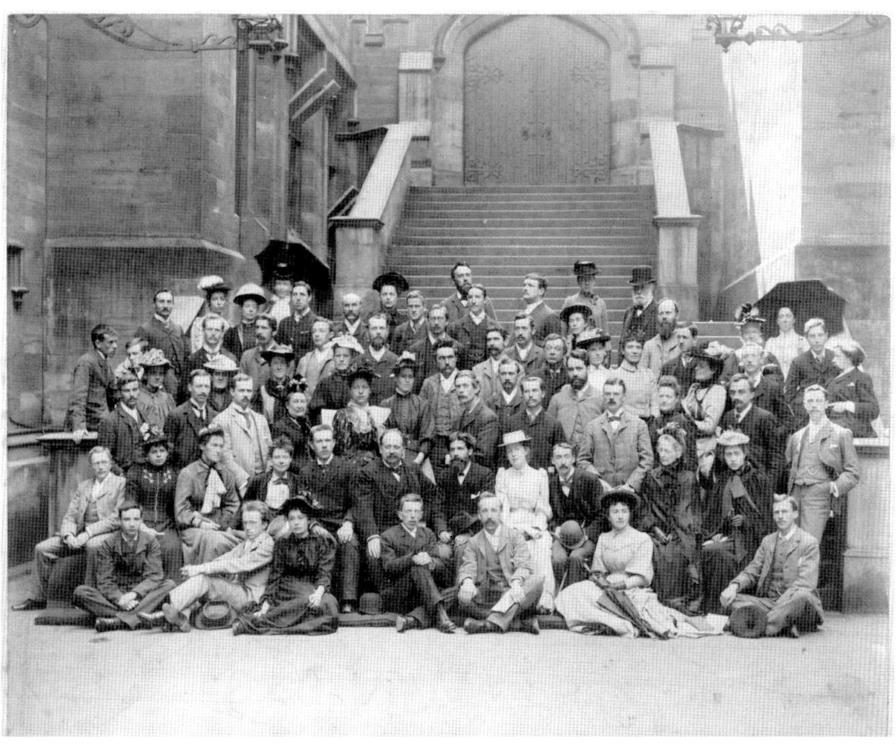

4A Edinburgh Summer School 1891. Photograph of participants taken in front of New College, Edinburgh. Patrick Geddes is seated in the middle of the second row from the front, with Charles Mackie standing directly behind him. Anna Geddes and Anne Mackie are both standing in the fourth row, third and first from left respectively. John Duncan is seated second from the left in the front row.
T.GED 22/3/42.2 © The University of Strathclyde Library, Department of Archives and Special Collections

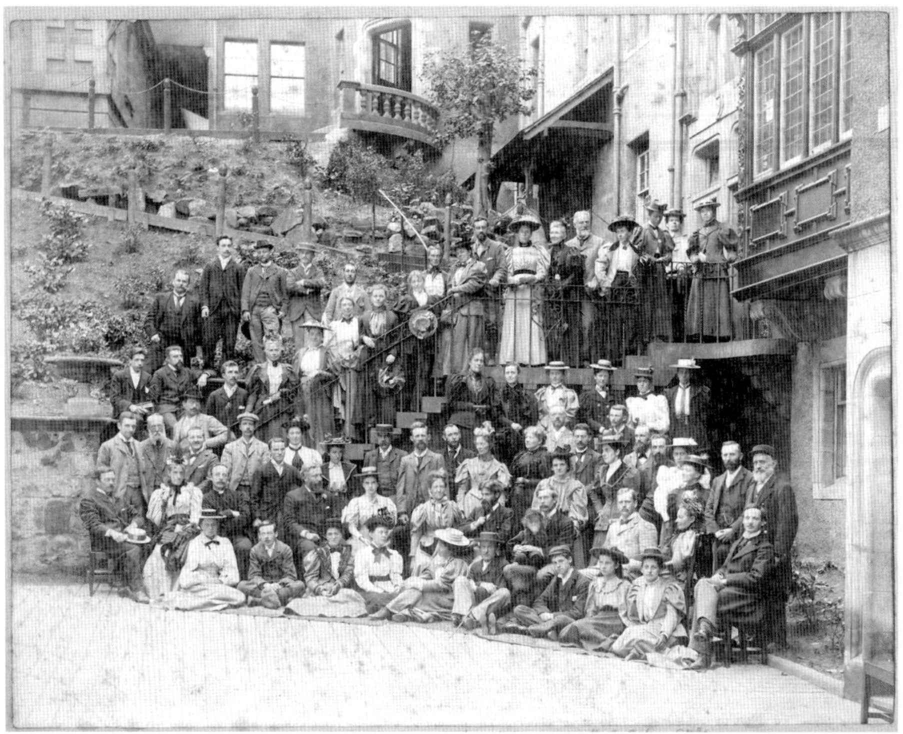

4B Edinburgh Summer School 1896. Photograph of participants in the courtyard of Ramsay Garden. Anna and Patrick Geddes are seated side by side in the centre of the second row. Charles Mackie is seated to the right of Geddes, with his wife Anne standing directly behind him. The small child sitting on his knee could well be one of the Geddes's children. Alastair Geddes would have been aged five at this point while his sister Norah was aged eight.
T.GED 22/3/27.2 © The University of Strathclyde Library, Department of Archives and Special Collections

most hazy idea of it.'[8]

Mackie undertook some specific teaching under the aegis of this summer school of art, working with house painters on the harmony of colour. The confidence he now had in two of his protégés, Archibald and Wilson, was conveyed to Geddes. The pair, in Mackie's opinion, more than rivalled any master painters of his acquaintance in Edinburgh, since they could devise their own new colour combinations. The link between the house-painter and the artist was already known to Mackie. William Mouncey, Hornel's brother-in-law down in Kirkcudbright, had started as a house painter before becoming a full-time landscape artist. There was a typically self-effacing verdict on his teaching: 'not a bad result to arrive at in three months'.[9] But he must have been gratified that his students had progressed so well. Such direct input into the summer schools is referred to only intermittently in Geddes's papers and these scattered mentions provide an incomplete picture. A few tantalizing glimpses suggest that Mackie was fully involved in the delivery of the art programme. An undated 'Art Lecture 2' was on Mackie Woodblocks.[10] In the 1893 programme for the studio, after mention of Burn Murdoch and Duncan, it reads: 'and Mr C.H. Mackie (who will respectively direct other schemes of work)'. In the 1894 summer school: 'Mr C.H. Mackie kindly gave some evening chats (sic) on art.'[11]

Prominence was given to the School of Art, since it provided the synthesis of decoration and education. The aim was to encourage creativity and intelligent enthusiasm, so that these evangelists would ignite the fires of the Celtic Revival in the douce city of Edinburgh and beyond. In the eyes of Geddes and his supporters, like Professor Baldwin Brown at the University of Edinburgh, artists had a moral responsibility to society. As such, they had to play their part in social improvement and civic regeneration. Such ideals would have appealed to Mackie, since they fitted well with his Christian beliefs, where action had to match principle. As a young man he had lived in the Old Town himself and worked among the poor. But now he was to be paid for his services – an undated handwritten note from Geddes refers to £15 as the half-fee for the summer meeting.

Geddes was very keen to stress 'the French Connection', as the ideas and aims of certain French artists accorded with his own.[12] He wanted to secure a Continental input to the summer schools. Here Mackie could be of direct assistance, since he had formed his own circle of personal friends and fellow artists during his time in France. His note to Geddes urged him to write to Paul Sérusier directly to secure his contribution. Although Mackie already knew from an earlier letter that the summer period was unsuited to the Frenchman's schedule. There was an additional caveat from Mackie: 'I don't care to be responsible in any way for the introduction of his work as it might not give satisfaction to most people.'[13] Mackie was well aware of the caustic conservatism of his domicile, where artistic experimentation was not always well received.

Sérusier's reply to Mackie's initial enquiry had indeed been non-committal.

The Frenchman was clear that he did not wish to interrupt his work in August and September, the most productive time. The apparent reluctance to lecture or teach was another negative, since he indicated a preference for painting decorations. Although he expressed the hope of tapestry work: 'dans le manière de Gobelins' if there was an interested British manufacturer, the date on offer would not fit with the Geddes's schedule. The invitation from Mackie's 'esteemed friend' (Geddes) to contribute to the 1894 summer school apparently never materialised.[14]

This brief missive does, however, confirm the close bonds that had formed between the two artists. Sérusier wanted to elicit from Mackie his opinions on the 'Art Moderne' which he had seen in Paris, greeting him as 'Mon cher ami'. The time Mackie had already spent in France had helped him to forge these friendships across the auld alliance. Gallic influence and inspiration would fire his art and a life-long fascination with colour. The French countryside and its people would furnish him with fresh scenes for his painterly eye — and this love affair would last until he could paint no more.

NOTES

1 University of Strathclyde Library, Department of Archives and Special Collections, Geddes archive: T.GED 8/1/8.

2 All quotations from contemporary publications in this chapter are taken from the Geddes scrapbook in the University of Strathclyde Library, Department of Archives and Special Collections, Geddes archive: T.GED 8/1/8.

3 T.GED 8/1/1-7.

4 Del et imp: delineavit et impressit. He drew and printed it. (Imp = imprimatur, it was printed by him, was also used: CHARLES MACKIE IMPRIMATUR EDINBURGH). He re-used this logo on later book productions, though varying the front design, e.g. 'John Knox, with two illustrations by C.H. Mackie ARSA' by John Barbour. Printed by T. & A. Constable, 1905, this book was drawn to my attention by the ever-helpful Dr Elizabeth Cumming

5 The SSA is addressed in detail in Chapter 7.

6 The location of the current tourist attraction, the Camera Obscura.

7 University of Strathclyde Library, Department of Archives and Special Collections, Geddes archive: T.GED 9/77.

8 Ibid.

9 University of Strathclyde Library, Dept. of Archives and Special Collections, Geddes archive: T.GED 9/2173

10 T.GED 5/4/28.

11 T.GED 12/2/48/2.

12 *Patrick Geddes: The French Connection* edited by Frances Fowle and Belinda Thomson is an excellent examination of this aspect.

13 University of Strathclyde Library, Department of Archives and Special Collections, Geddes archive: T.GED 9/2173.

14 T.GED 9/2280.

Four

Very clever people, the French...very clever artists

Mackie would have endorsed the above observation made by Geddes in 1887, finding it confirmed by the personal contacts and French friendships he later forged in that country. In the year after their marriage, Anne and Charles crossed the Channel, to enjoy an artistic pilgrimage combined with a delayed honeymoon. The daughter of Provost Walls of Dunfermline and sister to William Walls, Mackie's artist confrère, Anne was to embark on many journeys at the side of her painter husband. She was described as being classically beautiful and spiritually very high-minded: 'to an altitude almost too great for the unacclimatised to breathe.'[1] She was a Francophile and often expressed herself in French in her letters when the emotion could not be matched to adequate English. Even in early letters to her brother William in Antwerp she would sign off 'ta soeur qui t'aime, Annette'.[2] Although she had travelled abroad before, the excitement and novelty of this extended sojourn was never forgotten by the impressionable young woman. Many years later, in her long widowhood, she looked back on the happy interlude and penned a journal, piecing together the main events in her husband's life, thereby providing us with valuable details on their French travels. Her memories have to be matched against the true historical record since her dating was unreliable but it is the most valuable first-hand account of this formative period in Mackie's development as an artist.

In April 1892, they were in London visiting the National Gallery. No doubt they looked at the Old Masters and the Turners, soaking up all that the imperial metropolis had to offer. It was a place that Charles knew well from the earlier visits to see his brother Willie in Barnes. A successful timber merchant in the Baltic, Willie also had an office and apartment in Paris but Charles and Anne chose to stay resolutely independent in their own *pied à terre* when they later lived in the French capital.

Having made the crossing to Cherbourg, their initial destination was Gréville, the birthplace of Jean-Francois Millet, whose paintings had inspired Mackie as a student. Millet's subject-matter would be replicated by him, since both painters were attracted to depictions of peasant life, incorporating the animals at its heart, such as sheep. Millet was actually born at Gruchy in Gréville-Hague but they did stay a fortnight in the area, so the pilgrims no doubt found the hamlet of Gruchy itself. The healthy outdoor exercise suited them both, as the 'long, happy tramps'[3] included a five-mile barefoot trek across the sand, against the force of the wind.

No wonder they had a healthy appetite for the mouth-watering food on offer in Normandy. After the legendary dullness of a Scottish diet, Anne revelled in the richness of the cream, delicious bread and coffee. Her finest praise was reserved for the sculptured towers of butter that had greeted her at one hostelry, which astounded her afresh each morning:

> the butter standing at least a foot and a half high on the table, made up to resemble a castle with turrets and battlemented walls. I was afraid to put my knife in but each day the walls reared themselves afresh at each end of the table.

The modern reader can spot an important omission in her description of these culinary delights. When I first read the manuscript, my reaction was to note that there was no mention of wine. However, once I learned that she was a 'Wee Free' i.e. a member of the Free Church of Scotland, with all the lifestyle restrictions attendant on that belief, such abstemiousness seemed understandable. As Hamish Walls commented, 'it was an idyll of art and castellated butter'.[4]

They evidently had not booked their accommodation in advance, finding on one occasion that there was literally no room at the inn. A house was opened up for them specially, despite Anne's willingness to lie on straw in the barn. The memory of that mishap had stayed sufficiently strong in her memory for her to recount it over thirty years later. They delighted in the pretty French inns, with their four-poster beds, panelled walls, cleanliness and appetising food. It was an adventure for them both since they travelled light, 'carrying little but a comb and a toothbrush' and trusting their bodies to the perils of nineteenth-century travel. One can imagine them hanging on for dear life in one 'ramshackle diligence with two horses which tore down precipitous hills'. Anne thought that the harness seemed to be about to give way, secured as it was by string.

They sought out quaint and beautiful old French towns and their journey eventually took them from Normandy into Brittany. They had an idea of a little town, known for its waterfalls, wooded gorges, rocks and pools. It was located on a large lake, next to an immense green forest and this surrounded a natural grotto of gigantic, lichen-covered boulders. Even then it was a resort village, popular with British tourists. They had read a description of its scenic charms but had forgotten its name until a fellow guest, a commercial traveller staying with them in one inn, answered their query. The place was Huelgoat, located in central Brittany, en route to Pont-Aven, though they do not appear to have made it that far. Huelgoat was to prove a life-changing destination.

It was here that the Mackies were to meet 'les symbolistes', a group of French artists, who included in their number Paul Sérusier, with whom Mackie was to forge a strong bond (as discussed in Chaper 3). Only two years younger, he matched the Scot in ability and intelligence. Anne's initial reaction to their strange art was puzzled fascination, as she tried to work out 'the misshapen peasants and pink ploughed fields', but she acknowledged that this was at the cutting edge, calling it 'the most advanced French art'. Their conviviality in Huelgoat was cut short by the sudden death of Madame Clemence Sérusier, Paul's mother. Anne attributed it to a kind of cholera, following her consumption of lobster and strawberries. Given the known symptoms of cholera, further research established the probable cause of death as a heart attack. Maurice Denis, in his biography of his good friend Paul Sérusier, says it occurred on 18 July 1892 and that the heart attack was due to her distress at losing a favourite piece of jewellery in her son's room. This does seem a more plausible explanation and, amid all the upset, Anne could easily have been mistaken. In fact Sérusier did not accompany his mother's coffin back for interment in Paris but stayed on in Huelgoat, since it offered greater peace and solitude for painting, as well as mourning. They had been particularly close. The distress, bureaucracy and expense of arranging the transportation of the body made him adamant that he would not wish this to happen to anyone else. He asked to be buried where he died and his wishes were carried out at Morlaix in October 1927.

Before his Mother's coffin left Huelgoat, a service was held and both Mackies attended. For Anne this would have been a marked cultural contrast to her own religious experience and she commented on the emotional atmosphere in the dimly-lit chapel, with the smell of incense and the sound of chanting. It was a sad curtailment of their stay but one of the group travelled back with them to London – Clement, a Dane.[5] He was to exhaust their patience and their funds, but he had been encouraged to come and view the Turners in the National Gallery. Charles must have felt that his enquiry, 'Who is Turner? Est-il bon?', could only be answered by seeing the pictures themselves. Sérusier's lack of enthusiasm was forgiven and forgotten since Clement's emotional response matched their own. The highest compliment that he felt able to pay was 'Il est Wagner', as he was a passionate musical devotee. The Mackies stayed on for another month in London after his welcome departure, using it as an opportunity for in-depth and devoted study. Every day was spent in the National Gallery and every evening in the British Museum. Charles was mulling over what Anne described as a chance remark by Sérusier: 'cherchez le gris'. He was to embark on a long quest for the answer and how to apply the theory to his colour palette in practice. As she explained, 'after making endless experiments that simple remark became the foundation of C.H.M.'s colour theories.'

Sérusier gifted two of his Breton studies to his new Scottish friend: *Paysanne bretonne* and *Louise* or *La Servante bretonne*, possibly to act as a reminder of that momentous meeting in Huelgoat. Although there is pencil overwriting *Gauguin* they were undoubtedly executed by Sérusier during this Breton sojourn. The superscription in fact bears a remarkable resemblance to Mackie's own handwriting. The atmosphere he encountered in Brittany would have appealed to the Scot, sensing similarities to his own homeland. Rain, mist and looming grey skies could be present in summer as well as winter in both places. These gifts must have been much studied on the journey back north and undoubtedly had an immediate impact on his approach to colour. The muted tones of the one verified Mackie painting from this period of Celtic-Breton exchange reflect his response. *Breton Girl Crocheting* was Mackie's first foray into Nabi style, with its simplicity and emphasis on forceful colour (Pl. 10). Currently in a private collection, its owner was kind enough to remove it from its frame so that we could study it in detail. The Mackie monogram is clear and still visible in the right-hand corner and the style of colour and execution are testament to Mackie's initial response to Nabi ideas. Charles and Anne were both eager to return to France to follow up these exciting and stimulating artistic contacts. He was hoping to find more answers or, at least, new questions to pose for his paintbrush. The journal says that they went to Paris the following May but some of the events described could only have occurred in 1894. Anne's recollections might have been confused by the passage of time so that she conflated the timing and thereby got the dates wrong. Hence, one must rely on external evidence to verify the events of these years. In May 1892, there had been an *Exposition Renoir* and in April 1893, forty-three Manets were exhibited in a retrospective show. Anne does mention taking in a Renoir exhibition but does not identify which Manet exhibition they visited. Charles's own letters to Geddes in March and October 1893 allude to another visit to France that year, although the two couples had not been able to meet up:

> We were sorry you didn't join us for your last holiday, we could have talked so many things over for the future. I hope you had a good time of it on your walking tour.[6]

Helpfully, Anne also mentions meeting fellow Scots, Glasgow Boys James Guthrie and John Lavery, who were in Paris to see the *Exposition Manet* at Durand-Ruel, the famous art dealer. It contained sixty-five works by this one painter and Sérusier urged the Mackies to see it before it closed in two days time. Since the exhibition was held between April and May 1894, this would place the visit she describes in detail in that year, 1894. They might have found time to take in the lithographs of Toulouse-Lautrec, shown in May 1894 and the 122 works of Caillebotte shown in June of that same year. Visits to the Louvre and artistic camaraderie were also packed into this busy time. The surviving facts all point to follow-up visits in both 1893 and 1894, despite Anne's inference.

Sérusier had introduced the Mackies to his friends at a lunch party before he set off for Brittany. They met a number of French artists including Paul Ranson, Edouard Vuillard, Maurice Denis, Odilon Redon, and others whose names Anne had forgotten. This was a community of young painters, brimming with ideas and enthusiasm, happy to discuss them with their new Scottish guests. The group also included Pierre Bonnard and Ker-Xavier Roussel. Collectively, they gave themselves the name 'Nabis' (the Hebrew word for prophets), and Sérusier was their acknowledged leader. They met once a week in Ranson's studio to share their ideas on poetry and literature and expound their philosophy of artistic brotherhood. They regarded themselves as the disciples of a new faith, waging war against entrenched Academic art in the name of Symbolism.

Since they saw themselves as artists rather than painters, they would go beyond easel painting to embrace decorative arts, prints, monumental murals, theatre work and much theorising. There was a quasi-spiritual intensity at their weekly dinners, with the creation of a special language, Nabi costumes and ritual in 'The Temple', Ranson's studio on the fourth floor at 25 Boulevard Montparnasse. In true symbolist spirit, poets, writers and musicians were invited to attend and the bonhomie was marked by gales of laughter as well as serious discussion. Sérusier even painted Ranson in his Nabi costume. Fantasy and imagination were given primacy. In this all-male fraternity they did make allowance for Madame Ranson as 'La Lumière du Temple', since she provided them with such necessities as mugs of beer, cups of tea, sandwiches and tobacco. They then repaired in the early evening chez Vuillard to consume a more substantial 'pot-au-feu', accompanied by wine, before ending the Saturday at Le Chat Noir. They were dedicating their lives to the pursuit of beauty and the practice of their new art, but this did not rule out enjoying the good things of French life.[7]

It was a few years earlier that the first spark had been struck in Pont-Aven, a small village to the east of Concarneau, ten miles inland in the Breton countryside, which had become an artists' colony by the 1880s. The Breton peasants still wore their native costumes and would pose for the artists. The atmosphere there, simple, pious and almost mystical, had attracted Paul Gauguin whose *Vision après le sermon* reflected all this. Its emphasis was on limited, flat colour, simplicity of composition and free form. It meant that the artist felt at liberty to change the shapes of nature to accord with his own interpretation. This was the artist's personal response to the overt visual world and it was projecting an inner reality. It is difficult to convey in words what is evoked on the canvas but the effect of seeing Gauguin's work changed the direction of Sérusier's career. It would help the reader, as it helped the author, to study this Gauguin masterpiece, currently in the collection of the National Galleries of Scotland. In 1888 Gauguin gave Sérusier painting lessons and this resulted in *The Talisman*, with its vivid and limited colour palette. This was a conscious choice of title for Sérusier and his fellow Nabis. A talisman is a revered object, believed to contain magical or sacra mental properties, thus bestowing good fortune on the owner. Executed on a small cigar box panel, this painting was never publicly exhibited but, painted under Gauguin's direction, it demonstrated the working method to be employed in the artistic movement known as Symbolism. Sérusier was relatively affluent and had no pressing financial need to exhibit, unlike many of his friends. Since it was not a single style but more an attitude of mind, if one is not an artist or art historian, the ideas of 'les symbolistes' can appear challenging.

Their movement was short-lived but influential in the last decade of the nineteenth century, reaching into philosophy and literature as well as art. Even Mackie found he needed time to accept and engage with this vital new force and its visually discordant format. He was supremely fortunate to have met the brotherhood and be welcomed into their studios, homes and hearts. The absorption of their ideals would take longer. Its emphasis on the freedom of the artist to experiment, to feel free to distort what he saw in front of him, in the interest of the overall composition, and the key role of the juxtaposition of colour would be the lessons he would take home to Scotland. Symbolism emphasized the appeal to the viewer's feelings, through the artist's choice of colour and form. It was not a straightforward documentation of observed reality but used colour to evoke emotion. Sérusier himself was to move away from Gauguin, 'the master', and to develop ever more complex colour theories, since he believed that art abided by its own laws and was not bound to copy nature slavishly. His own experimentation with colour wheels in the years 1892-94 had seen him move from grey to brown as his base. Mackie would have been able to observe this in the paintings he saw during his French visits. (Sérusier's final verdict was elaborated in a challenging work *ABC de la peinture,* with its complexity of colour wheels, published in 1921 after Mackie's death.)

In Paris, though she could not provide wine or French cuisine, Anne Mackie felt she had to do her Scottish best by returning the warm hospitality shown to her and her husband. She hosted afternoon teas in their Rue Bara apartment, with lashings of bread and butter to accompany the weak tea and Paris cakes. Hungry artists meant she had to make many journeys into the kitchen to replenish the supplies. There was fun to be had chez Ranson, since they went there on Saturday afternoons for tea, brioche and games. The latter was possible since his studio was much larger and Ranson's wife, Marie-France, was willing to play her part. Anne recalled how a cricketing term, translated into a French approximation, was the occasion of much hilarity. Charles had declared Madame Ranson, a southern French beauty of goodly proportions, to be out 'l.b.w.', since the game of the moment was cricket and she was batting. 'Qu'est-ce que c'est l.b.w.?' Charles's reply fitted the shape of the lady and her leg in front of the wicket: 'jambon devant wicket'! Anne remembered:

> Nobody smiled but I was less polite and wept with laughter, much to the relief of the others who joined in heartily. One had to see Mme. Ranson to get the full significance of 'jambon devant wicket' with her skirt tightly swathed round her somewhat sumptuous leg.[8]

Of such innocent remarks are friendships forged and the Ransons became their good friends.

The other event which is most often cited as singling Mackie out among his Scottish contemporaries is the visit to Gauguin's studio, which could only have taken place in April 1894. Gauguin was in Tahiti in 1893, only moving in to rent this studio from the New Year of 1894 until his late April departure to Brittany. The introduction had been effected by Paul Sérusier and the Mackies visited Gauguin in the Rue Vercingétorix at the artist's invitation. Living in the Rue Bara, near the Seine, they would have found it was only a fifty minute walk in the Parisian spring air. What greeted their eyes must have appeared like a symphony of sunshine, compared to the grey buildings outside. The walls of the upstairs apartment at number 6 had been covered in chrome yellow paper, edged with a saffron border, while the west-facing window had been painted with the same yellow. Gauguin had also filled his studio with exotica from Tahiti, savage-looking wooden sculptures, shells from the South Seas, multicoloured frames round his pictures, primitive prints and even a bell-jar containing a humming-bird on a branch. Anne was not exaggerating when she said that they spent there 'one of the most interesting afternoons of our lives'. The colourful flamboyance and charm must have blinded the somewhat sheltered Scotswoman to certain irregularities in his domestic ménage. His mistress, Annah the Javanese mulatto, was not in evidence and neither was her monkey. The inscription on the painted glass entrance panel was 'Te Faruru' (here one makes love) — thankfully, an invitation not understood by the Scots couple.

Gauguin himself made a lasting impression: 'an enormously fat man clad in a thin white silk undervest and a pair of trousers, for all the world like a Great Chinese God.' But it was the art as well as the artist that they had come to see and they were not disappointed. Anne's words capture their excitement at what greeted their eyes:

> Strange, weird things we saw — wonderful pottery and wood carving, extraordinary paintings ... of beautiful colour and intensely interesting and sincere.

All this, in tandem with Gauguin's personality and charm 'made a deep and lasting impression'. It made her more critical of the Sérusier paintings as being insipid and unoriginal by comparison but she acknowledged that Charles was more generous in his judgement. After all, he was the practitioner and understood that the quest for identity and originality was no easy matter.

The painter who aroused their joint sympathy was Edouard Vuillard who also invited them to his studio. The contrast to Gauguin could not have been greater but Scotland is in his debt, since this was to be the means by which the Modern Art Gallery could claim to exhibit the first Vuillard ever brought to Scotland. Anne had thought Gauguin's studio beautiful but she thought that it was poverty that was the hallmark of Vuillard's garret. He had a large stack of unsold pictures and urged his Scottish guests to select one as a gift. In typical self-effacement and out of concern for his circumstances, they picked the smallest one they could find, an oil painted on cardboard, *Ouvrières dans l'atelier de couture* (seamstresses in the workroom). Vuillard's mother was a seamstress and since he lived with her for sixty years, it would have been a familiar enough scene. Painted in 1893 when the artist was scarcely known, it stayed with the Mackies until the widow parted with it. An early Nabi work, it is a good example of his emerging, experimental style. When she wrote her journal Anne could say with feeling, 'that painting is still a joy.' It was sold to Stanley Cursiter and finally was acquired by the Scottish National Gallery of Modern Art in 1990.Carried back in their luggage, it could be argued that it acted as a source of continued inspiration for Mackie, showing the influence of Vuillard on his art. The Hunterian oil sketch *By the Bonnie Banks o' Fordie* carries a place name 'Rouen' beside Mackie's signature (Pl. 9). The date could be 1894, following the visit described above. It would have made sense for the Mackies to have stopped off in Rouen en route home, since the city had acquired a number of artistic attractions by that date. They would have been able to view the recently installed Puvis de Chavannes murals in the Museé des Beau Arts. Possibly they combined lunch and artistic appreciation in the Hotel d'Espagne, whose owner had covered its walls with contemporary Impressionist works by Sisley, Cézanne, Pissarro, Renoir, Manet, Morisot and Van Gogh. A city known for Impressionism, it should be no surprise that Mackie recorded the visit on his oil sketch. He would go on to use it as the basis for a woodcut and a later larger oil painting.

They had loved their time in Paris and, like tourists now, they would search in the bookshops and art dealers for items that could be transported back to Scotland in their luggage. Paris was awash with Japanese knick-knacks, ceramics, screens and textiles after several successful exhibitions of Japanese art in the French capital. The walls of Sérusier's studio in Huelgoat had also been covered in a profusion of Japanese art. The young couple would be given huge bundles of similar Japanese prints to take home on trusting approval, from which they would make their selection. However, money was tight and later in life Anne regretted not having purchased more. They became very fashionable and sought after, so the investment of a few francs would have resulted in ample pounds later. Charles used these Japanese purchases in several of his pictures and his models can be seen scanning the Japanese prints he and his wife had brought back from Paris.[9] (Pl. 13).

After the Scots returned home they did not lose touch with their friends. Mackie responded with personal gifts, as well as urging them to collaborate in his work for Geddes. As mentioned earlier, he urged the latter to write in person to Sérusier, to secure his presence in Edinburgh. Sérusier's caution and lack of interest in a major mural undertaking were understandable, since he had a new mistress, Gabriella Zapolska. Scotland was a long way off. Vuillard and the Ransons were also not forgotten.

Belinda Thompson has shown that the painting known as *La Poursuite*, formerly attributed to Edouard Vuillard, was in fact a gift to him from Charles Mackie. The surviving photographic evidence confirms the clear link with Mackie's subject matter and style at the time. The original print in *The Evergreen* was known as *When the girls come out to play*, with Scottish pinafores on display. There are some slight differences of positioning between the two but Thompson is in no doubt that this was a painting given to Vuillard as a thank you for the seamstress painting they had selected in Paris. She also points out that Mackie sent three works to Paul and Marie-France Ranson over the festive period 1894-95. He had made a copy of a Botticelli Madonna and Child, which he had seen in the National Gallery; the other two presents were woodcuts from *The Evergreen*: *Hide and Seek* and *Lyart Leaves* (Pls 7, 8). Although the whereabouts of the Vuillard gift are currently unknown, the Ranson family still have their two prints, with inscriptions thereon from Mackie to his friends: 'best wishes for the coming year.' This exciting period of French cultural interchange was also the time when Mackie was being encouraged to experiment in his art. As discussed in the previous chapter, he was engaged in all manner of work for Geddes – murals, woodblock prints, *The Evergreen*. The few works from his easel during this period reflect that same eagerness to throw off the shackles of his academic training and defy the current Scottish conventions. *The Pool of Ness* (Pl. 2) is a good illustration of how far he had succeeded. He had seen what could be done with form and colour if the artist broke free from the straitjacket imposed by the society of his day.

Those initial encounters with the Nabis and the artistic energy of Brittany and Paris meant that, once again, a fortuitous conjunction of people and place would have a lasting impact on Mackie's development. In many ways, he now stood at a crossroads and the finger post would point him down the road less travelled. It would not be an easy journey.

NOTES

1 Walls–Mackie family correspondence, courtesy of Bill Mackie.
2 NLS Walls family papers, ACC 10448, quoted by kind permission of the National Library of Scotland.
3 Except where indicated, all quotations from Anne Mackie in this chapter are from her handwritten journal in the NLS, ACC 9177, quoted by kind permission of the National Library of Scotland.
4 Walls–Mackie family correspondence, courtesy of Bill Mackie.
5 Clement, Gad Frederik (1867-1933) was a Danish painter. After his time spent with the French Symbolists, he studied Italian Renaissance painting and then settled into a Naturalist style.
6 University of Strathclyde Library, Department of Archives and Special Collections, Geddes archive: T.GED 9/77.
7 Maurice Denis in his *Homage to Cézanne* painted in 1900, now in the Musée d'Orsay Paris, captured many of them in oil on canvas.
8 Maurice Denis painted *Madame Ranson with Cat* c.1892. The painting is in Saint-Germain-en-Laye, Musée Départmental du Prieuré.
9 *A Japanese Album* held in the National Gallery of Art, Sydney, Australia, is one example. The model is thought to be Charles's sister, Annie. Esmé Gordon, former President of the RSA, had known her well and had fond childhood recollections of 'my dear Annie' who had befriended him as a young boy (Pl. 13).

Five

Cabbages and sunsets

If we look back with Charles Mackie to reflect on his life up to this point, it will help us to understand him better as a person and an artist. He was very much a child of Empire. His Father, Captain William Mackie served his sovereign for thirty-two years in the wars of conquest and retribution which were the hallmarks of that imperial era. He had enlisted at Glasgow in 1841 as a private, aged twenty-three, in the 1st Battalion, 2nd Queen's Royal Regiment of Foot. According to his grandson Donald, William had run away from his home in Caithness to join the army and see the world. Initially sent to fight in India, in 1851 the regiment was transferred to South Africa to engage in the Third Kaffir War. By 1854 he had risen through the ranks to be a quartermaster sergeant and his future family was destined to travel with this serving soldier. He married an Edinburgh woman, Anne Young, who had travelled on her own half way round the world to marry him at Fort Hare in 1854. Charles's older brothers, Willie and Copland, as well as the elder sister Helen (known as Nellie) were all born in South Africa, at two year intervals, 1856, 1858 and 1860 respectively. The family history proudly records that Nellie was born in the back of a bullock cart. Mrs Mackie must have been made of stern stuff! Mackie senior's time in China was equally eventful, though the family do not seem to have accompanied him. The Melbourne branch of the family still possesses part of the loot from the sacking of the Emperor's Summer Palace in Peking in 1860. It had been 'liberated' by the quartermaster's batman and then used by William Mackie for his ablutions. His children were told that he had 'won' it. His grandson Donald claimed that it had originally been filled with gold and jewels, returned by the 'honest and upright' Scotsman, no doubt to be filched by some other soldier with a less tender conscience. This large cloisonné bowl had succumbed to an ignominious fate at the hands of the Mackie children, being used for various games, since it was large enough to fit a small child. Apparently, Charlie (aged four) and Annie (aged two) would sit in it and bounce about the room, treating it like a boat. It still bears the dents. When Bill's Aunt Gladys died in 1979, he bought it from the estate for £30 since it was deemed to be in a 'distressed condition' (Pl. 14).

Cloisonné bowl stowed safely in his baggage, Quartermaster Mackie returned to Britain in 1861 with his regiment and his family. It was this year that saw his commission to officer rank. Charles was subsequently born at Aldershot, before the family decamped to Plymouth where their last child, Annie, was born in October 1864. Garrison duty at Cork followed in 1865 and it is at this point we can track the family again, since the senior sibling Willie possibly attended the Royal Hibernian School in Dublin, a military style boarding school. There seemed to be a matrilineal family link — one William Torbet Young was a resident master at the school. The surviving photographs show serried ranks of unsmiling boys in Eton collars. The Luftwaffe put paid to any chance of checking any details of his time there. After the school closed in 1924, the records moved to Walworth and were destroyed in the Blitz in 1940.

When the regiment was posted to Aden in 1866, to fight in the war against Abyssinia, Mrs Mackie and the family returned to Edinburgh, to stay with her parents. Presumably it was time to think about the boys' schooling. Charles's paternal Copland ancestry has already been mentioned and his widow claimed in her journal that the maternal line was of interest too. Herein lay the unconfirmed claim to gypsy blood. His Mother's maiden name was Anne Torbet Young. The Youngs of Kirk Yetholm in the Scottish Borders are still considered to be the oldest Romany tribe in Scotland but it has proved impossible to trace a direct gypsy lineage for Charles Mackie. Perhaps it was one of those tales that grew in the telling? One background fact has been confirmed — Portobello potters were in his ancestry, on the male side.

After completing his service in India, Captain Mackie rejoined the family in 1873. He purchased a number of different properties in Musselburgh and Edinburgh. The final decision to buy 28 Buccleuch Place proved to be an ideal choice for both secondary and tertiary education, since it is near to the university and the site of the old George Watson's School. Charles was admitted to this school on 14 May 1871 and he was followed by his brother Copland on 2 October 1872. Sad to say, that seems to be their only mark on the school's historical record since absolutely nothing else appears to have survived. It was an important rite of passage and no doubt his parents thought being a Watsonian would open further doors. Then as now, the Edinburgh school structure has been compared to the gradations of the Hindu caste system. Assignation, almost at birth, denotes rank and membership of a carefully defined elite. The experience of his school days stayed with him. It was not entirely positive. He would not allow his only son Donald to attend, citing 'the corruptive influences' of a boys' school environment. This remark was never elaborated further and I leave it to the reader to speculate. It should be remembered that Charles and Copland were day students and were not exposed to any after-hours activity. Prior to their entry, the school had moved from the semi-monasticism of the hospital model and had changed into a day school, in the interests of reform and efficiency. The Merchant Company was keen to protect its funds from government interference and to insulate itself from public criticism. They sold off their old building in Lauriston Place to the Royal Infirmary and relocated to Archibald Place, close to the Mackie home. Its doors opened to eight hundred boys in September 1870.

The one positive outcome from this period seems to be that he acquired his lifelong love of sport. Teaching his French friends the rudiments of cricket has already been described, but the real passion of his life, as is true for many Scotsmen, was golf. Anne Mackie alludes to this in her journal, saying that he practised for many hours on the links at Musselburgh. The academic curriculum he would have followed at Watson's would have been the standard mixture of the day and the prospectus lists the subjects taught as English, Latin, Greek, French and German languages, Writing, Arithmetic, Book-keeping, Mathematics, Drawing, Vocal Music, Botany, Natural History, Natural Philosophy, Chemistry, Dancing, Fencing and Gymnastics. Dancing was abandoned in 1875, during Charles's time there. Given the age recorded on entry as ten, he would have joined the Junior School while Copland went into the Senior School. The latter prepared the students for university (classical) or the professions (commercial). Classrooms were heated by open fires — never very efficient in the depths of a Scottish winter. The boys did not have a set uniform at this stage and would sit together at long benches, which served as communal desks. In the 1873-74 prospectus, drawing merits a mention and three masters are named: Robert Frier, Harry Frier and William Carmichael. The Mackie boys would have received a sound education of good quality in a school that prided itself on being very Scottish. The complimentary comments of Her Majesty's Inspectorate were quoted in the prospectus:

> great satisfaction with the organization, discipline and instruction ... admirably managed and efficiently taught.

In 1876-77, just before Charles left, provision was made for a park for 'cricket and other scholastic games'. In May 1876 the first sports day was held and a professional coach for cricket was also engaged.

With all this on offer the Edinburgh bourgeoisie were further convinced of their good fortune by the Merchant Company policy of keeping the fees moderate. It was affordable for them, but sufficiently prohibitive to deter the working class. The boys would have been happier with the knowledge that the headmaster George Ogilvie was no fan of the tawse (the Scottish leather strap) and discouraged its use. Apparently, the students liked him and he tried to get to know them individually. In his excellent history of the school, Les Howie does record some rough and ready behaviour with occasional classroom disorder and a tendency to resort to fisticuffs to settle any dispute. Was it not ever thus in a boys' only environment?

It is often said that the boy is father to the man and one's school days should be the happiest days of one's life. This was not borne out in Charles's recollections. The education he received was not to his liking. Anne's journal says that he spent all his time sketching in his work books as well as spending all his pocket money on artist's materials. She says he was 'wayward' but since it was not overt disruption, it was tolerated. He could already discern the path he wanted to follow but his father had other ideas.

At the age of sixteen he enrolled at Edinburgh University to study medicine. This career was not his true vocation but he did attend some of the anatomy classes. He could see that an understanding of the body would be useful for a painter. According to Anne, he would rise early in the morning to draw in his sketch book and to work on the human figure. Although he truanted from the bulk of the lectures, spending his time in the galleries, he absorbed a range of ideas and persuaded his father to pay for some painting lessons from Robert Hepburn Frier. His teacher was known in Edinburgh circles as a minor landscape and figure painter, having had five works exhibited at the RSA. His sisters had painted in Normandy but he preferred the scenery of Loch Tay, Fife, the Lothians and the Highlands. He probably met the eager young artist when teaching art at Watson's. He informed Captain Mackie that his son did indeed have talent and argued the case for allowing him to pursue his studies further. The professional soldier did have reservations, saying that he worried for his son's future, telling a friend that he 'would doubtless spend his time sitting among cabbages painting sunsets'. But he supported him in the lean years at the outset of his career, when he was studying at the Trustees' Academy, followed by the Life Class at the RSA.

In August 1900 the proud parents must surely have been relieved and happy when they saw their fine portrait grace the walls of the Royal Scottish Academy. Their friends and neighbours would also have seen it featured in the August edition of *The Scots Pictorial*. The photograph shows the artist, their son Charles, take pride of place as the newly-elected chairman of the Society of Scottish Artists (Fig. 7). The portrait is clearly discernible. It was just in time for the old soldier, who died on the 9 October 1901. He must have been secretly pleased that his dire prophecy had not been fulfilled. That portrait is still impressive (Pl. 11). Their formidable gaze returned mine when I studied it in Bill Mackie's dining room in Melbourne in November 2014. Like the Mackie family it had been on quite a journey.

The whole family helped Mackie in these early years before he became well known. There is a touching portrait of Charles's younger sister Annie, RSA Exhibition catalogue in hand. Since it was both signed and dated 1880, he would have been aged eighteen when he first exhibited this delicate study at the RSA (Pl. 15). The following year three of his works were accepted. They formed a very small part of the 1047 acceptances from the original 3000 plus submissions. Making his mark would not be an easy process for any young artist. In 1882 he enjoyed some time with his brother Willie in London, where his spending money was rationed but not his time. He would pass whole days visiting and studying in the London galleries and going to exhibitions, even if it meant parting with his last shilling and having to walk a long way home.

Some of his London paintings have survived. Unfortunately they are in private hands and are not easy to locate. They do not date from this period but from a later visit in 1905. That year London was hosting the largest and finest exhibition of Impressionist painting ever seen in Britain. The French art dealer Durand-Ruel had mounted a blockbuster of a show at the Grafton Galleries. There were 315 works, including 196 from his own private collection. Included in the exhibition were thirty-eight pictures by Boudin; thirty-five by Degas; thirty-five by Monet; forty-nine by Pissarro; fifty-nine by Renoir; thirty-seven by Sisley; ten by Cézanne; nineteen by Manet; and thirteen by Morisot. All these riches would have acted as an irresistible magnet for Mackie, who must have been one of the large number crowding in to view this unique spectacle on offer in January and February 1905. Included were a number of views of London including a *View of the Thames* by Alfred Sisley.

Mackie had earlier completed thirty sketches during his first journey when he had walked the streets of the capital as a young man. Sisley's vision might well have provided further stimulus. The River Thames and the views from its Embankment also drew Mackie's eye and these later oils show scenes that have attracted painters over the centuries. They could have been based on his preliminary studies, but we have no way of knowing. *Barges on the Thames, Looking towards St Paul's, Westminster from the Thames* and *The Thames at Dusk* are all the works of a more mature hand. In the latter, the arch of the bridge frames a view where dusk and gaslight add charm to the working river traffic, whose smoky funnels spew into the twilight sky. Those first visits to London had allowed him to study the Old Masters and pay attention to the lessons of 'the Antique'. We know that he particularly loved the works of Turner and would take his new bride to see them when he revisited ten years later in 1892.

But it was to be Scotland's land and people which provided his subject matter at this early stage of his career. He concentrated on landscapes since they had the added attraction of saleability. The works that were shipped to Melbourne were mainly Scottish landscapes which must have made the migrants think of home. He loved Perthshire and the River Tay, contributing three illustrations to a book entitled *The River Tay*, published in 1891. The technique employed was photogravure,[1] a process that had recommended itself to Walter Crane. Mackie executed three highly competent illustrations: the Source of the Tay; the Tay above Aberfeldy; and the Tay below Aberfeldy. His handling and touch were sure, with the tonal variations hinting of the distance and light of each scene. One comment suggested that they verged on the 'Turnersque', a compliment which Mackie would have appreciated. As a native of the fair city, I can see his attraction to the silvery Tay. It is perhaps fitting that it was Perth Museum and Art Gallery which benefited most from his son's bequest in 1970.

Closer to home, he painted scenes at Craigmillar Castle, the Braid Burn, Peffermill and Inveresk, exhibiting some of these at the RSA in 1880 and 1881. As we know from Chapter 1 he was an early visitor to Kirkcudbright, exhibiting those rural scenes in 1884. The Borders and the East Neuk were the next ports of call for the young painter. His depiction of *Busking the cross at daybreak* in Culross had won him the Stuart Prize at the RSA in 1884 and featured in the 1885 Exhibition. He now travelled further afield to capture scenes of Highland life in the Western Highlands, Benderloch, Portnacroish, Colonsay and Appin. The clarity and purity of the Highlanders' Christian faith also appealed to his nature. He never forgot the admonition he received when he picked flowers on a Sunday. According to Anne, his Colonsay landlady reproached him, 'Don't you think, Mr Mackie, that you might leave them to look up to the Lord on His day?' He found an inherent nobility and honesty in the simple life of the highland crofter and captured this in paintings such as *A Colonsay Cowherd, Boy, with a strayed lamb, Benderloch* and *Girl weaning a calf* – to mention a few examples of his exhibits in the years 1886-88. His landlady regarded money as the source of sin, since it had done away with the natural instinct of hospitality. She disliked accepting it from him for that reason. He was learning lessons about life, its values and the strong bond with the land. There is a phrase in Gaelic, 'the blood is strong'. Though Scotland's Gaels have never fared well at the hands of history or politics, the scenes Mackie saw and the people he met left a lasting impression.

Mackie's only public recognition in these years appears to have been in the 1886 satirical SKITS on the *Exhibition of the Royal Scottish Academy price 6d*, where *Shepherd bearing a wounded ewe* is shown as *Coals*. Satirical acknowledgement is better than no acknowledgement at all (Figs 5A, B). *The Scotsman* had made no comment on anything shown by Mackie in the years 1880-86. His sales had been equally paltry, amounting to about £30. It can be no surprise that for most of these early years he lived with his family, who had now taken up residence at 16 Lee (sometimes spelled Lea) Crescent in Portobello. His exhibition submissions were entered from there.

He did make a breakthrough in the 1888 RSA Exhibition, achieving public recognition for two works painted at Appin: *Weaning time* and *E'ening brings a' hame*. They were extolled in *The Scotsman* in its very First Notice on 17 February. It praised the two landscapes as 'aglow with golden light' and 'full of the poetry of the evening', describing him as 'a young artist who has come rapidly to the front'. But the reviewer was not finished and, in the Sixth Notice on the

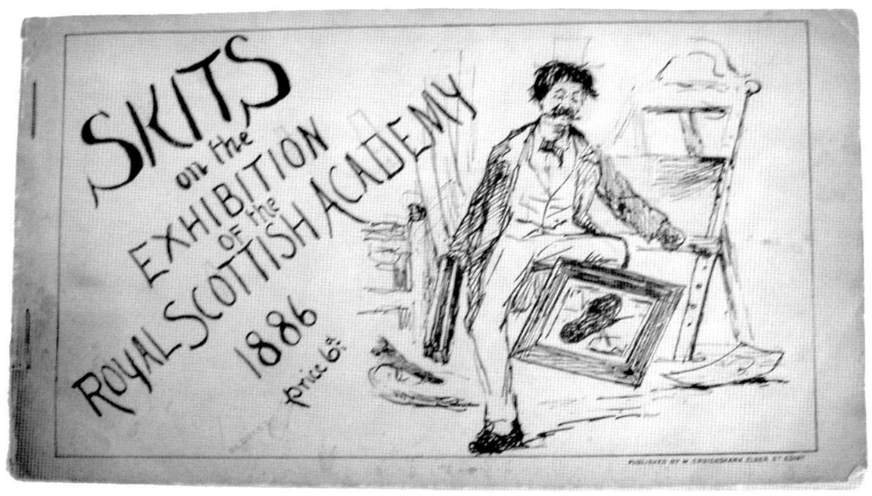

5A SKITS on the Exhibition of the Royal Scottish Academy 1886: satirical pamphlet priced 6d.
Courtesy of the Royal Scottish Academy of Art and Architecture

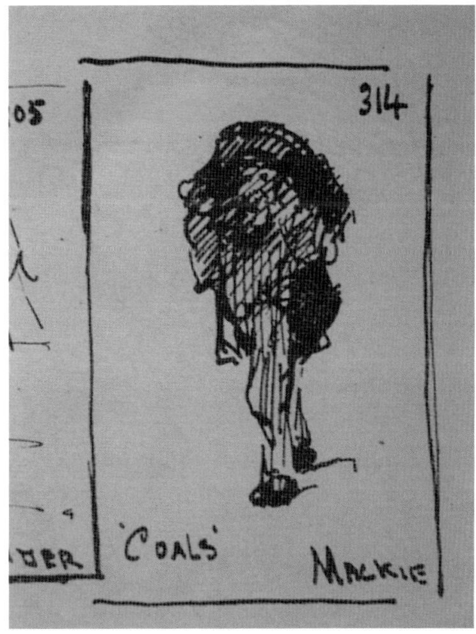

5B Sketch no. 314 shows *Coals*, attributed to Mackie.
This was shown in the 1886 RSA Exhibition as *Shepherd bearing a wounded ewe*. Courtesy of the Royal Scottish Academy of Art and Architecture

29 February, devoted a further twenty-seven lines of critique to these two pictures and the painter. He praised his 'high technical accomplishment ... true poetic feeling' and emphasized the artist's skill in managing 'strongly contrasted effects of light and shade' concluding that it had all been 'excellently realized'. By contrast, in the same notice his friend Hornel only had six lines and a brief comment on 'a certain artistic quality'. How fortunes would change.

In 1889, he found himself a studio at 15 Queen Street[2] and did merit a mention in *The Scotsman* for 'a thoughtfully treated landscape'. More significantly, Mackie's work had also come to the attention of Patrick Geddes since he reviewed it (and him) favourably in *The Scottish Art Review* (a short-lived publication of the period), accompanied by a black-and-white illustration of *Reapers returning at sundown*. He commends him for having imbibed his landscape lessons from Wingate, 'a spiritual father', but says it was important for his development that he avoided repetition. This he had achieved by forging on to 'new experiences', a fact that Geddes deems 'very praiseworthy' since external recognition of success is not always forthcoming when an artist changes his style and unsettles his public. How perceptive and true these words would prove to be in the future. Geddes was sure that the young artist would achieve success and would look back to value the years when he 'had time and peace to paint so varied a compass of subjects as his midsummer fields and sparkling frosty dawning'. Geddes, William Morris and Walter Crane were involved in the Art Congress that was held in Edinburgh in the October of that same year 1889. It was reported in *The Scots Observer* that Mr Crane had stayed with a banker in Murrayfield[3] and had also observed ongoing mural work in the Royal Infirmary. Crane was quoted as saying, 'I was much struck with the City of Edinburgh.' Given their shared interests, I would like to imagine that Mackie met them all there. I have no evidence for this but his eagerness to learn and his consistent engagement with the wider world would point to his attendance.

After his marriage to Anne Macdonald Walls in April 1891 the young couple set up home at 2 William Street. The same year his parents relocated from 16 Lee Crescent to 31 Durham Road, Portobello. No doubt this occasioned a 'spring clean' when he cleared out a lot of paintings from his former home and dispatched them to his brother Copland in Melbourne, in 1891-92. Bill Mackie thinks this was the main reason for these works finding their way to the opposite side of the world. It would have freed up room for the young couple and possibly provided them with welcome remuneration. The pictures in Australia all date from this early period in his art and reflect his interest in all things pastoral. A thoughtful *Colonsay cowherd* resides with Bill's sister-in-law, Maggie. The art gallery in his Melbourne home has some exquisitely rendered early Mackies, displaying a sensitivity to the differing tones of the Scottish seasons and the poetry contained in the often harsh reality of country life. His 'guard dog' at the door is *Snipe* (undated), a portrait of Alexander Roche's dog (Pl. 12). Bill related the Mackie humour which explained the genesis of this particular picture (Esmé Gordon had been happy to supply the background). When visiting Mackie's studio, Alexander Roche found a notice pinned on the door outside: 'Beware! Ferocious dog inside.' Entering with trepidation but hearing no bark, he was met by a picture of his own dog with an attached note. This stated: 'For Roche's dog'. Bill managed to purchase this picture in 1977 while on a visit to Edinburgh and it is now firmly restrained inside his front door! In addition to the family portraits mentioned earlier, his collection also includes ten other paintings executed by Charles Mackie.

The rural and pastoral themes reflect his early encounters with the landscape and people of his native land. Most are undated but were probably painted in the decade 1880-90, if matched against his travels and subjects from that time.[4] My personal favourite was *Landscape of a brook with a girl and frost on the ground at dawn* (signed and dated 1888). Bill thinks this is the painting exhibited at the RSA in 1889 (cat. 620) entitled *An Early Frost at Sunrise* (Pl. 17), as the subdued white landscape suggests a harsh overnight frost, captured on the spider webs, and the lighting of the sky is in tune with sunrise, not sunset. The girl is not heavily clad, so it was not snow, and she appears to be testing the ice with her toe, before filling her pail. For safety, she is holding on to the branch of a tree. It is an exquisite picture and it is sad it cannot do a return trip to its native land, where she would find the same weather conditions prevail.

In these early paintings his colour palette was restrained and the shapes were clearly defined with superb attention to the actual detail of nature. His skies are particularly fine in their rendering of the different times of a Scottish day or season. Mackie was following the Pastoral Realism shared by many of the leading Scottish painters of the day such as Lawton Wingate, cited by Geddes in the article quoted above. This is what he would have seen on the walls of the Academy and, at this stage, he sought to emulate his teachers. He needed to make a living from selling his work and the RSA sales records show that he only started to enjoy some significant income after the 1888 review, selling those two pictures for £75. 1889 saw no recorded sales and the Walls family helped out in 1890 by buying *Crofterland* for ten guineas. After that lean year his fortunes improved in 1891 with an encouraging £113. 1892 saw a reversion to scant sales – £17 in total; in 1893 nothing sold. That same year he had figured, alongside his friend Hornel, in the long leet of forty-seven under consideration for the ten ARSA places being awarded. Though both were deemed 'worthy of inclusion' by the *Edinburgh Evening Dispatch*, neither succeeded. Mackie might also have sold some work direct from his studio but since he did not have a secure base in that regard until later, there cannot have been much extra that year.

The commissions that we know would come from Geddes in the years following would prove to be a financial lifeline. He would exhibit nothing at the RSA in 1894 or 1895, busy as he was with that work. He certainly felt secure enough by 1895 to move to his final home at Roseburn, naming it the Coltbridge Studio. This would be where he would serve out his self-imposed apprenticeship as a painter. The studio and the art he produced would be the evidence of his embrace of new ideas and challenges.

NOTES

1 This process was invented in the nineteenth century and combined photography and etching, to produce a high quality print. The prior use of film gelatin on the then deeply incised copper plate produced a print with the detail and smooth tones of a photograph.

2 Anna Geddes's address book in the NLS actually records him as living at 18 Queen Street. Despite the numerical discrepancy, this shows that he was known to them before he embarked on the Ramsay Garden murals. NLS Geddes archive, MS 19997.

3 John James Cowan (1846-1933) was a wealthy accountant who lived at Wester Lea, Murrayfield. The family money came from papermills in Penicuik and Cowan was an avid art collector and future patron of Mackie.

4 *Potato Gathering* (1881?); *Still Waters on the Black Devon* (1888?); *Raking the Stubble* (no date); *Harrowing the field* (undated); *Crossing the Ford* (undated); *Landscape of a Lakeside view* (undated and I told Bill that I thought it was the Tay!); *Cattle grazing beside a farm pond* (1890); *Round the old ash tree* (undated but uncannily like the painting in Kelvingrove); *The Tay below Aberfeldy* (watercolour, c.1890, possibly for the book entitled *The River Tay*).

Six
Cherchez le gris

The above remark had lodged in the mind of Mackie after his time in France. Now that he stood at a crossroads in his artistic and professional life, he determined to find the answer to his quest. What did Sérusier's phrase actually mean? In simple terms it can be explained by looking at the artist's palette. To search for the grey elevated that colour to an importance in relation to the rest, since it would provide the keynote for all the other colours he would use. To be truthful, I puzzled over what this meant in practice until I visited an exhibition of the work of Dame Laura Knight in the Laing Gallery in Newcastle. The enlightening explanation of Laura Knight's biographer, Dr Barbara Morden, helped me understand the part played by 'le gris' on the canvas. As we shall see in Chapter 8, Mackie was to play a crucial role in Knight's development as an artist.

Mackie's quest was harder since he had to work out his own colour theory and apply it to his practice, while continuing to make an adequate living as an artist. Having moved into his new Coltbridge Studio in 1895-96, he soon had another mouth to feed. His son Donald was born on 30 January 1897.

Given these circumstances, many of Mackie's contemporaries were puzzled by his diversion into abstruse colour theory, since the young man had seemed to be on course for a flourishing career. He had exhibited regularly at the RSA in Edinburgh, the RGI in Glasgow and even further afield, at the Royal Hibernian Academy in Dublin and in London, at the Royal Academy. Furthermore, he had successfully completed impressive mural decoration in Edinburgh and Dunfermline, with both schemes meriting acclaim and recognition among a wider public. He had already demonstrated an impressive proficiency in other media, such as woodblock printing and embossed leather work. Well-known and respected in Edinburgh artistic circles, he had been elected as a professional member of the Scottish Arts Club in 1896. He now seemed willing to endanger all this on a whim or caprice?

His wife was much more forgiving when she looked back on this time. She refers to 'these lean years' very briefly, defending him for seeking to broaden his outlook and refine his ideas in the pursuit of artistic perfection. She was much

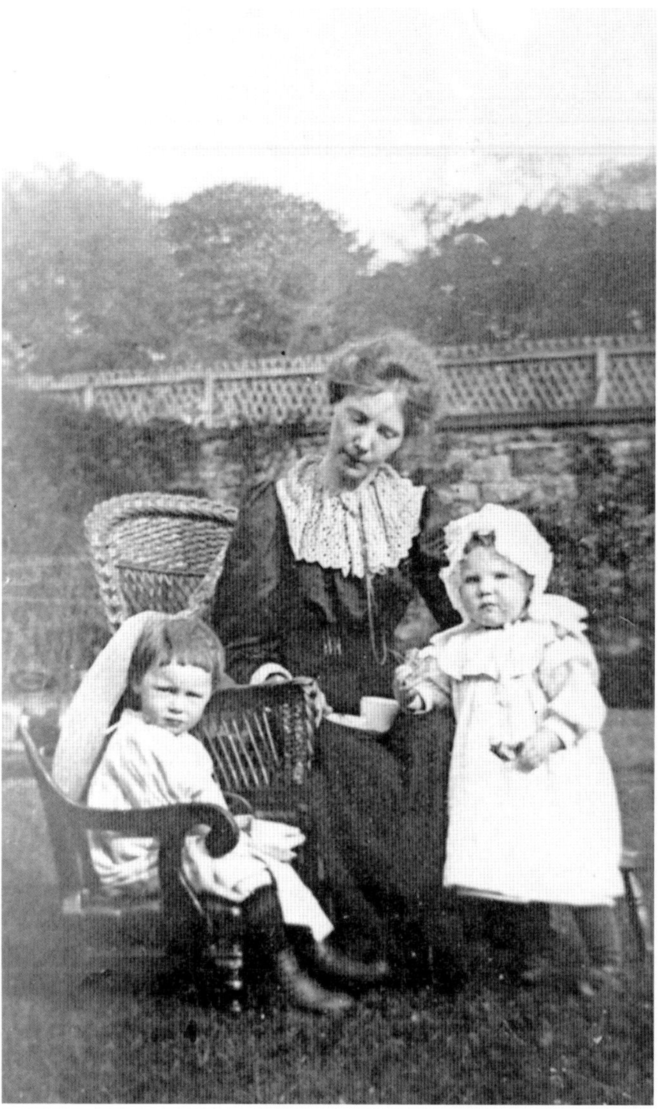

6 Photograph showing Anne MacDonald Mackie, wife of Charles Mackie. With her are two children: her son Donald is on the chair and the young girl standing is Anne Walls, daughter of William and Elizabeth Walls. Donald was born in 1897 and Anne in 1899, so this undated photograph was probably taken c.1901/2. The location is not identified but could well be the garden of the Walls' family home at Kaimes Road, Corstorphine. NLS ACC 10448 Reproduced by permission of the National Library of Scotland

more scathing in her summary of the abuse he received at the hands of his critics:

> Contemptuously dubbed a faddist, a crank, an experimentalist, little encouragement was given in Edinburgh.

The sting of those words shows how much it must have hurt at the time. The Walls family's view was that these years were spent perfecting his craft, even if that meant he went 'unrecognized and unrewarded'. Even the most sympathetic of contemporary commentators found his new direction hard to follow. James Caw, in his survey of Scottish painting published in 1908, felt that the problem lay not just in Mackie's obsession with an idea — that of an ideal of colour harmony — but the fact that he pursued it to extremes. This had the result that he tried to plan his pictures in a systematic and analytical way. Thereby, in Caw's opinion, Mackie had lost the pictorial qualities and emotional content that had made his earlier art so appealing. His spontaneity had been curbed by his intellectual pursuit of colour theory, to the detriment of his art.

Unfortunately, we do not have any explanation from the artist himself since there is no Mackie equivalent of his colleague John Duncan's thirteen notebooks. Lodged in the NLS, these outline all the copious details of his experimentation with varnish, adhesive, tempera and oil, as well as recording his visits abroad, his observations and enthusiasms. The latter covered philosophy, religion, his reading material and his fellow artists. There are numerous extracts from his reading material, as well as his own musings and reflections. Reading these is indeed hard work but the notebooks provide an illuminating insight into the mind, outlook and working practices of an artist who was at the heart of the Celtic Revival. He had worked closely with Mackie at Ramsay Garden and Pitreavie Castle but there is only one tantalizing reference to 'Mackie's colour system' in notebook nine.[1] Lamentably, he provided no further elaboration. Those who heard first-hand what Mackie had to say were not always enlightened. His future patron and fellow Murrayfield resident, the accountant James Cowan, delighted in his company and would go to his Coltbridge Studio to hear him talk. He describes him as:

> a most interesting companion, with wonderful views of his own on the subject of colour and theories on the subject which were based on a well-thought out plan, but which, I'm afraid, afforded most of his fellow artists more amusement than instruction.[2]

Mackie was indeed ploughing a lonely furrow in the Edinburgh of his day, a fact acknowledged by his contemporaries in the Scottish Arts Club. They marvelled at his rejection of material advancement in pursuit of his ideal. The reaction of the RSA establishment was even more scathing. Cowan goes on to quote an

Academician and the comment is breathtaking in its nastiness and insularity of outlook. Cowan says that he asked this gentleman whether he understood Mackie's theories and received the response:

> To a certain extent. If the lady in the picture was walking to the right, she'd be in a blue dress. If on the other hand, she was walking to the left, she'd be in a red one.[3]

The remark reveals the ill-informed judgement of the critic, rather than showing any true understanding of the art of the avant-garde practitioner. When Mackie was later to find a ready pupil, in the person of Laura Johnson, the vacuity of that observation would be all too apparent.

Since we have no notebooks, we needs must look at the easel art of the period. Here we encounter the unhappy hand of history, since so little seems to have survived. The best known work is that owned by the City Art Centre, *There were three maidens pu'd a flower (by the bonnie banks o' Fordie.* (Pl.16). The painting is based on a Scottish ballad. Firmly rooted in the Celtic revival, it illustrates the gruesome tale in the ballad whose full name is *Babylon; or, the Bonnie Banks o' Fordie.* This featured in a little-known 1827 publication *William Motherwell's Minstrelsy Ancient and Modern.* This book and its contents might well have been drawn to Mackie's attention by his Kirkcudbright friend Hornel who possessed a copy, still to be found in the Broughton House library. It contains all the blood-soaked melodrama of the typical Scottish ballad, married to a moral outcome. The three maidens encounter 'a banisht man' who proposes marriage to each girl in turn, with the irresistible offer 'will ye be a rank robber's wife, or will ye die by my wee pen-knife?' The first two refuse and are laid to rest 'for to bear the red rose company'. The third shows more spirit and threatens that her brother in the wood will avenge her death. The robber is then told that the brother's name is Baby Lon. He realises too late what has happened: 'O sister, sister, what have I done!' He has killed his own flesh and blood. There can only be one suitable denouement: 'He's taken out his wee pen-knife, And he's twyned himself o' his ain sweet life.' The ballad thus combined virginal virtue, hidden identity, bloodletting and justified, self-inflicted retribution. It offered the painter an enticing tale but Mackie chose to let us see the three maidens before destiny intervened, on the point of 'pu'ing' a flower, so the Celtic romanticism was preserved intact.

This theme resulted in the small oil sketch now in the Hunterian (Pl. 9), a woodcut which featured in the Winter Edition of *The Evergreen* (1896) and the full scale painting which was bought by the Edinburgh City Art Centre in 1982. (Pl. 16) Thankfully, this was one Mackie that did not disappear into a private collection. It bears the distinctive Celtic M monogram and was exhibited in the 1897 RSA Exhibition, after which it appears to have sunk without trace for some time. There is no record of it being sold and *The Scots Pictorial* was critical of 'unconventional colour schemes worked out in a style bordering on the eccentric'. *The Scotsman* review was equally terse, as if the observer did not know what to make of it, merely calling it 'a decoratively treated group of three children in a landscape to which the title has been given *There were three maidens pu'd a flower* (Cat.186)'. Certainly damned with faint praise then, it can be seen now as one of the best examples of his work from this period and rewards close study. Its simple forms and bright colours are the direct product of his contact with the Nabis and Gauguin. The textures and patterns of the girls' pinafores, their positional relationship and the reflections in the winding brook in the background are all evidence of a highly crafted composition.

Paintings from this period are rare and I was overjoyed to locate another Mackie which could be dated since it carried that distinctive monogram. It is currently in Edinburgh and unfortunately there is nothing known about the provenance and there was no clue provided as to its title. The strong autumnal colouring, coupled with the monogram would also place it in the 1890s. It could well be *Oak in Autumn*, exhibited in the RSA in 1896 but we have no way of confirming that for certain. It did not sell at the time and was not mentioned in *The Scotsman* reviews. It was a delight to see what Mackie was achieving with colour, even on this small scale (the painting is oil on canvas and measures approx. 40 x 30 cm).

It is a truism, but Mackie was not alone as a painter in trying to wrestle with colour application and combination.[4] After all, we do not see the world in black and white or even shades of grey. Individual perception of colour combination has been proven to vary and optical contrasts of colour can create an intensity, brightness and shimmering effect. Was it the artist's illusion? Perhaps Mackie was seeking to rationalize what could not be contained within an exact system. A sixteenth-century Venetian painter, Paolo Pino, observed that 'colour is the true alchemy of painting'. Mackie's search for his own philosopher's stone was not to be totally without reward — but that lay in the future.

Fortunate to be born in the latter half of the nineteenth century, he benefited from the developments in chemistry of that era. Many new pigments were produced, with the added convenience of these ready-prepared oils being packaged in tubes. Large scale commercial manufacture meant that the artist now had easily available, relatively low cost and reliably tinted paints for his palette, without having to blend these for himself. It became feasible and affordable to paint out of doors for a length of time. *En plein air* had been born. Jean Renoir quoted his father on the importance of this revolution in art: 'Without paints in tubes, there would have been no Cézanne, no Monet, no Sisley or Pissarro, nothing of what the journalists were later to call Impressionism.' The artist's basic palette has changed little over the centuries: blue, green, red, yellow, white and black compose the essentials. Blue and green are crucial for the landscapist, while Turner made prolific use of chrome yellow (another nineteenth-century innovation). Viridian green, made from chromium oxide, was highly favoured by Cézanne, Renoir and Monet. The new reliable synthetic pigments were chosen for the intensity of their colour. The natural earth colours of ochre, sienna and umber could be used to mute the colour scheme while lead white had the added advantage of stability and preservation, if not health-giving for the artist. The other indispensable was red and it was the creation of red lake which provided a translucent pigment suitable for glazing. Mackie's finest works, often in the later years, all carry a signature flash of red. It has been said that art in the nineteenth century saw a veritable explosion of colour and that was largely due to the wide availability and relative cheapness of these new synthetic pigments.

Mackie and his Nabi friends were not the first to try and unlock the mystery of colour. Indeed, they staked their place in a long line of artistic theorists. In late fourteenth-century Italy *The Craftsman's Handbook* declared that the use of colour was 'the glory of the profession'. Leon Battista Alberti in his fifteenth-century treatise *On Painting* developed the theory of complementary colours, calling this 'a certain friendship of colour'. He also mentions the point at which grey is the outcome: 'complementaries are pairs of colours that cancel each other out when mixed, to produce white if they are coloured lights and grey if they are coloured paints.' It was possibly this borderline that preoccupied Mackie several centuries later. He might also have been aware of the writings of Michel-Eugène Chevreul of the Gobelin Factory, who had produced a seventy-two sectioned colour circle in 1867. It was thought that his work led artists to be more conscious in their deliberate use of juxtaposed complementary colour, in order to achieve a more powerful effect. We do not know if Mackie was aware of this writing but his French friends must have known of the theories and, intriguingly, Sérusier makes a reference to Gobelin tapestry in his letter to Mackie in 1894. Mackie had much to ponder and reflect on, but these were not years of monasticism. He might not be making much money from his pictures, in contrast to Hornel, and incomprehension greeted his ideas, but he was not hermetically isolated. Brotherhood was found in the company of his fellow artists, seated in the comfort of the leather armchairs and relishing the roaring fires of the Scottish Arts Club. Its motto, appropriately enough, was 'Brotherhood' and it was seen as very much a painters' club. It was a venue where lovers of art could meet practising artists and survey their works on its walls. (A minimum of twenty votes was needed for election to membership, a guide to an individual's standing with fellow Edinburgh artists.) The Rutland Square premises also housed a dining room and an excellent library, where fellow members would afford Mackie good company and like-minded conversation.

He also had the opportunity to play golf, alongside good friends such as Robert Nisbet, Robert Noble, W.S. MacGeorge and William Walls. The Scottish Artists' Golf Club was set up in 1891 and though there is a gap in the archives for the 1890s, we can garner a fairly accurate picture from the record extant from 1901 of what their activities would have been during the earlier period. A pattern had been set, with fortnightly matches played at local courses such as Mortonhall, Musselburgh and Murrayfield. The bunkers at Gullane proved too challenging for them and resulted in the abandonment of their score cards. The competition scores, the prizes won and the hospitality afforded are all noted down. The artists' golf season was in the months of November to April, when travelling and landscape painting out of doors might have been a perilous enterprise. Weather conditions were also noted, as 'high winds' or 'a slight covering of snow' did render the course at Murrayfield challenging. These regular 'friendlies' for members, with prizes such as golf balls, led on to what must have been the highlight of the season, in social, if not golfing terms. This was the annual match versus the Glasgow artists (which in later years, Edinburgh seem to win more often than not) and the day's enjoyment of all things golfing, including the nineteenth hole. A delightful picture is conveyed of jolly times had by all, 'The Glasgow Team entertained the Edinburgh Team royally ... with luncheon before the match ... and to dinner at the Glasgow Arts Club.' On another such occasion, there must have been much merriment when 'returning to Edinburgh by the last train the victors carried with them the Challenge Cup'. Mackie was a good club golfer who often won some of the prizes on offer. He would have been an excellent man to have on the team.

His other source of consolation during these years in the wilderness lay in his hopes for the advancement of modern art in Scotland. Much of his time would be devoted to this, supported by many of the friends whose names appear in the SAC notebooks. I kept encountering the same names: W.S. MacGeorge (now moved up from Kirkcudbright); R.B. Nisbet (best man at his wedding); William Walls (his brother-in-law but less proficient at golf); William Burn Murdoch (one of the Antwerp confrères and contributor to *The Evergreen*); Robert Noble (a friend from his time at the RSA Life School); Robert Hope (a fellow Lothian landscape painter) Robert Duddingston Herdman (his father was the first President of the SAC); James Cadenhead (another contributor to *The Evergreen*). These friends would provide comradeship throughout his career and the band of brothers would now come together in the 1890s to fly the flag for modern art in their homeland.

NOTES

1 Duncan, John op. cit., NLS ACC 6866, quoted by kind permission of the National Library of Scotland.
2 Cowan, John James, *From 1843-1932: Autobiography*, Edinburgh, 1933, p. 158.
3 Ibid.
3 Vid. Bomford, David and Roy, Ashok, *A Closer Look at Colour* (London: National Gallery, 2009). This guide and my own visit to the National Gallery exhibition on 'Making Colour' in June 2014 were most useful in understanding the evolution and use of coloured pigments by artists, as well as the historical context.

Seven

A letter to the Queen

In the library at the Gallery of Modern Art in Edinburgh a minute book can be found which relates the minutiae of all the activities of the Society of Scottish Artists. Mackie was present at its inception, fought its battles and nurtured its growth for nigh on three decades. That book provides us with a detailed insight into his work to promote modern art in Edinburgh and his support to the society. Another type of SSA record is also to be found safely housed in the same location.[1] Happily, some diligent SSA member of yesteryear chose to compile a scrapbook for the historical record. Against the odds this has survived, although its fragility demands careful handling. It is exciting to gaze through its eyes at this snapshot of very different artistic activities. The scrapbook is filled with menus, details on social events and a description of the annual banquet which preceded the private view of the SSA exhibition. More than one hundred guests joined to celebrate and enjoy the repast. It certainly made one's mouth water to peruse the menu for their official opening dinner, held at the Waterloo Hotel on Friday 22 April 1892, commencing at 7.30 pm: Soup, Fish, Entrées, Joints, Sweets, Sardines on Toast, Dessert, Ices. Edinburgh artists did not intend to starve in their garrets. On a more serious note, the scrapbook is prefaced by the aims of the new organization:

> You must educate, educate and again educate; and you must suggest purchase continuously; until you make the purchase and possession and understanding of pictures customary and fashionable in a middle class which is wholly indifferent to the fine arts.

There appears to be nothing novel in our own 'education, education, education' linked to economic motivation. While the SSA would later come to be honoured as one of the most forward-thinking and eminent of artists' organisations in Scotland, that was not guaranteed at the outset. The adventurous fledgling had to fight hard to survive and achieve its objectives of promoting young up and coming artists as well as fostering a taste for art. Expanding the membership base and ensuring a successful annual exhibition were the two key strategies pursued by its council. It was democratic in structure, with artists electing their own fellow artists both for membership and for committee posts. This was in marked contrast to what was felt to be the ingrained nepotism of the RSA. Honorary lay as well as professional membership categories widened access further and Patrick Geddes was admitted to the former on 31 December 1891. There was also no bar to women (termed ladies) being accepted, in May 1891 initially as honorary lay members, quickly followed in November of the same year by admission as full professional members 'on the same footing as gentlemen'. In that era of agitation for women's rights, such an emancipatory attitude has to be commended. (After all, they were used to the segregated entrances to the classes on the Mound: men entered from Princes Street, women used the back entrance.) Mackie proposed a number of women including Lydia Findlater, companion and friend to his sister Annie.[2]

Esmé Gordon, former Secretary to the RSA, penned his memories of these two ladies in his letters to Bill Mackie in Melbourne. Esmé was very fond of Annie, likening her to Dresden china but her lifelong friend Lydia was another matter. Described as 'horsey (with) voluminous skirts and cloche hats ... booming voice ... close-bobbed hair, ruddy complexion, tip-tilt nose and rolling gait'. It conjures quite a picture and a great contrast to her friend, younger sister to the artist himself. Charles had captured her demure demeanour in that early portrait of Annie, visiting his first RSA exhibits in 1880 (Pl. 15). However, Annie and Lydia were both competent watercolourists, exhibiting at the SSA right up to 1933, long after Mackie's death in 1920. Annie had also contributed her designs to *The Evergreen*, so it was not nepotism. This new society also wished to emphasize its Scottish identity since the London-centric art world often casually referred to Scottish artists such as Mackie, as English, assuming that would be acceptable. Then, as now, British was not synonymous with English in the eyes of any self-respecting Scot. There would be many dragons to slay in the battles that lay ahead. It was fitting that its logo of choice was a Scottish lion rampant, surmounted by the words 'A Fait Accompli'.

Ever in the vanguard, Mackie's presence was recorded at the inaugural meeting held on Monday 16 February 1891 and the other names listed read like a roll-call of his friends and associates: Blacklock, Nisbet, Noble, Walls, Burn Murdoch, MacGeorge. Unanimously chosen by his fellow-artists as convener, Robert Noble had to plan out the way ahead and the *modus operandi*. There was much to address and they prioritised deciding on the dates of their next meetings – three were held in February alone. They also resolved to make contact with 'kindred associations', including the Royal Glasgow Institute. Mackie had exhibited there from 1884 onwards and there were several strong personal links with the artists in the west of Scotland. The reply they received from the RGI provides a strong clue to the politics of artistic life in Scotland at the time and provides a pointer to possible troubles ahead. Referring to the SSA, the Glasgow artists in the RGI said that 'if this Society would start on antagonistic lines to the Royal Scottish Academy, they would support it'. It is a fairly blunt statement of the battle lines that had been drawn between enterprising Glasgow and stuffy Edinburgh. The artistic establishment in Edinburgh was referred to as 'the old gang'. It was not quite as forthright as Pittendrigh Macgillivray's 'damn the Scots Academy' but it underlines the prickly hostility to the RSA under the rule of President Fettes Douglas. By contrast, McTaggart would show his support for the new SSA in its future skirmishes with the art institutions in Edinburgh. His membership dated from 1899.

More tactfully, the new organization felt that the key to recognition would lie with a successful public launch at their first exhibition, so appropriate picture selection was vital. They wanted to promote young, original artists in Scotland but the works had to be of merit. Alongside this, they would also exhibit outstanding pieces of modern art, by artists living and dead. This twin aim would drive an agenda that, even prior to 1914, would see the arrival of Impressionist, Post-Impressionist and Futurist Art in Edinburgh. Friends, patrons, institutions and supporters would be approached for loans. Having been promised some exhibition space in the galleries on the Mound, the selecting and hanging committee proposed to visit artists' studios, in order to make their selection. Needless to say, Charles Mackie was one of the chosen visitors. They performed their task in groups of three and he was flanked by William Walls and W.S. MacGeorge. At an earlier meeting, they had built in a safety clause to guard against any resulting artistic outbursts in consequence: 'Any member who is considered to have become obnoxious to the Society may be expelled by the vote to be taken by ballot at the Annual General Meeting.' I could not find any evidence of this being invoked, so the selection must have been handled diplomatically. There were expulsions but these were justified on the grounds of non-payment of membership dues. As a preventive measure, they had already allowed for non-admission: 'one black ball in three shall exclude'. As a society created by artists, to benefit art and run by artists, they wanted to be sure that all members would be like-minded. Their policy seems to have been more focused on inclusion rather than exclusion. In 1910, when Cadell tendered his resignation, they asked him to reconsider and cancel. He did.

Various other practical arrangements were at the forefront of the discussions during those early months of February, March and April, with Mackie's name mentioned on more than one occasion. Making decisions on the venue, catering and administration all absorbed much of their time, since this was a venture into uncharted waters. The decision was taken to delay the launch of the inaugural full-scale exhibition till the next year 1892, since it was vital to ensure this first public foray was a success. All their artistic i's and t's had to be dotted and crossed before the new society was to be judged by the Edinburgh establishment. Key to that aim was the calibre of pictures chosen to promote the SSA and its aims. The aforementioned hanging and selecting committee members were officially congratulated on the 'very successful manner' in which they had performed their duties. Mackie's particular talent in this respect meant that he was to serve the SSA time and again on their selecting and hanging committees. The end of April 1892 saw the opening of their first exhibition and there must have been a collective sigh of relief, since it exceeded their expectations. Diplomacy and persuasion had secured some impressive loans. These included a Constable, a Joshua Reynolds and four paintings by John Singer Sargeant. The contributions of members flanked these already recognized masters of art. Two hundred and forty-two artists exhibited their works and there were 572 items on view. More than one hundred guests attended the preliminary banquet and the council recorded their own verdict of 'a great success as judged alike by the public, the press and the artistic profession'. There had been bumper sales and the resultant five per cent commission which went to the society was bolstered by the funds already accrued by membership fees. All in all, they concluded that by the beginning of July 1892 the financial position of the society was 'very satisfactory'.

There were no signs as yet of dark clouds forming on the horizon, in the form of covert intransigence and overt opposition from the RSA. The RSA president at the time of the birth of the SSA, William Fettes Douglas, was not noted for his accommodating temperament. A man of intransigent views, he had told female artists that they were better suited to matrimony, as well as antagonizing the leading Scottish artist of the day, William McTaggart. The latter went into a self-imposed ten-year exile from the RSA until welcomed back in 1902. Disagreement was thus the order of the day under the peppery rule of President Fettes Douglas until he died in office in 1891, to be succeeded by Sir George Reid. However, the legacy of his antagonistic attitude would outlast him until the RSA adopted a more diplomatic approach under different leadership.

Conversely, *The Scotsman* heaped praise on the new organization and its avowed aim of promoting the work of younger artists. The editor, Sir John Findlay, had shown himself a firm friend of the arts and a staunch advocate of artists. Its reviews contain a description of the colour scheme adopted by the hanging committee and Mackie's hand can be detected. Cherchez le gris? All the walls, except the central octagon, were hung with rough grey canvas, complemented overhead by a low-toned sage green valance. A maroon tint was present in the central octagon and the council was praised for the way the pictures had been hung. Pronouncing it an 'excellent artistic feast', the newspaper mentioned that John Singer Sargeant had loaned a number of pictures and the sculpture included the Rodin of *Victor Hugo*, lent by Glasgow Corporation. The feast included four paintings by Millet, three by Corot, three by Millais, two by Alma-Tadema, and a McTaggart. Three Mackie paintings are mentioned. *The Winnower* (Cat. 172) was judged to be 'of much merit'. The other two were landscapes (unnamed) praised for the contrast of rich evening (Cat. 47) with grey morning (Cat. 63).

Gratifyingly, the Edinburgh public must have shared this enthusiasm since they crowded the galleries to capacity at the private view. The artists must have been equally pleased with the financial outcome — £600 taken in one and half hours. Later in June the exhibition was opened to the public for free and this must have helped boost further sales. When the contents of the coffers were counted, the final total was £1,786 5/-. Prior to this there had also been a full report in the press on their banquet, where Professor Geddes proposed the toast to those who had loaned their pictures and the hosts excused themselves for such conviviality during their first year. They did feel that they had something to celebrate but they did not want to appear to be aping the customs of the RSA. *The Scotsman*'s final notice was a eulogy of their first chairman, Robert Noble, the newly elected ARSA and a paean of praise for his skill as an artist. He had said at the banquet that the SSA should be seen as 'a big brotherhood full of kindly sympathy to one another'.

Unfortunately, that kindly sympathy did not seem evident in the fraught relationship which developed with the RSA. In an article of May 1892, *The Scotsman* criticized the RSA for its 'dull level of respectability and convention'. Perhaps there was also a slight hint of the forthcoming rift contained in the complimentary verdict of *The Art Journal* review of the 1893 SSA Exhibition:

> the artistic success of the last Exhibition was very remarkable, and it is to be hoped that the Royal Scottish Academy will profit thereby in preparing for their own exhibition ... Anything, in fact, would be better than the lethargy into which Scottish art seems inclined to fall.

The Studio's verdict on the RSA Exhibition of the same year was equally scathing, reporting a 'predominance of bad work, bad hanging and bad decorations'. It was no surprise to observers that heated discussion between the Board of Manufactures, the RSA and the SSA subsequently ensued over the date and venue for the 1894 SSA exhibition. But the former two institutions held the trump card of control of access to the galleries on the Mound. Ill-feeling mounted and the upshot was that there was no SSA exhibition held in 1894. In consequence, *The Studio*'s review of the 1894 RSA exhibition must have carried additional sting: 'the general standard seems to continue as mediocre as ever'. Despite the healthy state of the membership roll, listing 121 professional artists and 358 non-professional members, the new society felt under threat. The committee members noted that the artistic old guard 'fatally cripples this flourishing Society in the attainment of its aims'.

The RSA then muddied the waters further by putting forward the principle that artists should have to choose between membership of the two organisations. To be a member of the SSA would automatically exclude the artist from the RSA. Feelings were running high and it was felt that the highest secular authority now had to be approached. On the 6 September, the SSA decided a letter had to be sent to the Queen in Council objecting in the strongest possible terms to the seventh clause in the proposed supplementary charter of the RSA, which would oblige artists to choose between the two. The SSA deemed this 'retrograde in character and detrimental to the interests of Art in Scotland'. The SSA also felt that the RSA and the Board of Manufactures were mounting a concerted campaign to strangle their rival at birth. Queen Victoria did not reply in person, but the Marquis of Huntly was not the president of the SSA for nothing. He had suggested that the missive be routed to the Queen via the then Secretary of State for Scotland, Sir George Otto Trevelyan. The SSA had its own champion in the artistic lists.

As is ever the case in Edinburgh, the letters page of *The Scotsman* show that the arguments were batted back and forth. At one point the RSA blamed railway construction for the problems, saying that the Waverley tunnelling works had affected the National Gallery and restricted the dates they felt able to offer the SSA for its exhibition. However, the weight of public opinion began to tell and outweigh the RSA grumblings. *The Art Journal* of 1896 endorsed the fillip that had been given to good art in Scotland by the SSA, saying that it had spurred on the RSA to greater efforts. Given its impressive membership, in terms of names and numbers, the SSA could command some clout.

The SSA was allowed to exhibit in the Mound Galleries in 1897, having cancelled or held the intervening exhibitions in what was considered unsuitable premises. 1898 saw refusal again, but they were successful in returning to their rightful venue in 1899 and 1900. During this unsettled period, when the SSA seemed to be fighting for its existence, they found support in the pages of *The Scots Pictorial.* Its July 1898 review did criticise some of the hanging, likening it to the chaos encountered at Waverley Station, but the overall verdict was encouraging, firmly on its side in the continuing skirmishes with the RSA. The SSA was a 'means of compelling the older body to set its house in order'. The lesson was reinforced the next year when *The Scots Pictorial* concluded that the SSA had provided 'a capital object lesson in how to make an exhibition attractive'.

1899 was also the year when his fellow artists recognized Charles Mackie, unanimously electing him vice-chairman, so that he became chairman of the SSA in 1900. At a time when he had been swimming against the tide of artistic convention, this was indicative of their support. They all knew they had to make up lost ground after the uncertainties of the latter years but the new millennium had started auspiciously for the SSA. It held its council meeting on the hallowed (and sometimes forbidden) ground of the RSA Galleries. Their new chairman can be seen in the official photograph, accompanying the two-page spread in the pages of the aforementioned *Scots Pictorial* (Fig. 7). He is seated, with the rest of his committee, in the RSA Gallery, with his parents' portrait behind him (Pl. 11). This review was lukewarm in its judgement overall, saying that that there were no outstanding works of art and that it was uninspired, if well hung. By contrast, the verdict of other sections of the press on the 1900 exhibition was very positive. *The Art Journal* commended the society for the healthy stimulus it had given to art in the east of Scotland and praised the decoration and hanging, features dear to Mackie's heart. The article mentioned all three Mackie works and illustrated *The Hill-Farm Pond* commenting on its 'good style in colour and handling'. The review in *The Studio* underlined the impact the exhibition had on viewers more accustomed to the offerings of the RSA:

> the most notable feature is the charming effect of the Galleries as a whole. It is somewhat difficult to believe that they are the same rooms as those in which the Royal Scottish Academy holds its annual shows. But a sufficiency, rather than a plethora of pictures, judicious hanging, suitable backgrounds, and arranging the sculptures tastefully, instead of dumping them down like Aunt Sallies at a fair, have worked wonders and the Society is to be congratulated on having made its exhibition a delightful place in which to linger.[3]

While the praise would have been welcomed by Mackie and his fellow council members, such barbs of comparison would not be forgotten by some in the RSA. Indeed, it had been a difficult road for the SSA from 1891-1900 and its survival had been far from a foregone conclusion. As chairman, Mackie now had to try and steer it into calmer waters. It would help that James Guthrie had become a member of the SSA in March 1900. He was subsequently elected president of the RSA in 1902 and worked hard at reconciliation. Both men helped to build the necessary bridges for peaceful coexistence.

In his new position at the head of the SSA, Mackie had many additional duties to perform. These included being a member of all committees and exercising the casting vote on any tied decisions. As vice-chairman he already had the experience of signing off any minutes if the chairman had been unable to attend. Consequently, he had been tied up with SSA business from March to July 1899, his presence evidenced by his signature on no fewer than eleven occasions. He had even imported his own colour scheme into picture selection. The minutes record that he 'explained his own scheme for balloting at the selection of pictures, when it was agreed that three counters be used, red white and blue'. There is no mention of grey or any further comment on its use. The adoption of this particular

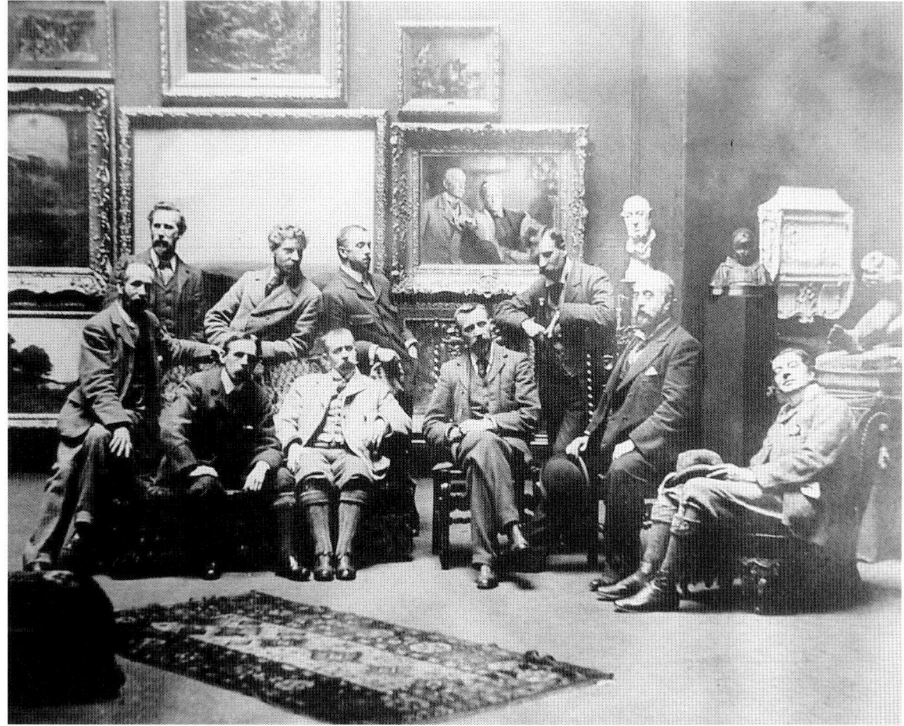

7 Council of the Society of Scottish Artists, 1900. This official photograph was taken at the Society's Annual Exhibition, held that year in the RSA Galleries on the Mound. Mackie's portrait of his parents Captain William Mackie and Mrs Mackie can be seen clearly in the background.
Front row: J. Riddell, Charles H. Mackie (chairman), J. Campbell Mitchell, T. Alison, Robert Christie (secretary), William Robson.
Back row: R. Duddingston Herdman, William Walls, Robert Burns (vice-chairman), Nasmyth Langlands.
Photograph courtesy of Bill Mackie

scheme seems to have died a death of its own accord. Mackie was called upon to make speeches, chair meetings and send off letters to ask for picture or sculpture loans. He also served with Robert Burns on the decorative committee, a responsibility that he had already exercised with aplomb. He was successful in securing a previously unexhibited McTaggart, as well as being promised a Manet and sculpture from London. For the travel involved in the latter negotiation, it was agreed that he deserved £5 for expenses. Since the public face of the SSA was crucial to its perception further afield, he also drew up the advertisements for the annual exhibition. The material pasted within the scrapbook shows he had a hand in the design of the SSA literature, since his distinctive lions rampant and thistle montage are well in evidence.

The Edinburgh expectation of other delights being on offer meant that he also had to oversee arrangements for many of the social gatherings which featured in their calendar. Delightful details and descriptions of these are contained in the SSA scrapbook.[4] (A contemporary wit in *The Scots Pictorial* commented in 1900 that the letters SSA did not stand for Sober Scots Association.) Mackie was known for his sociability and he attended many events in Edinburgh. Esmé Gordon related one occasion prior to Christmas when Mackie 'teased his well-oiled companion'.[5] They were walking back to Roseburn after an extremely successful Christmas revel at the College of Art, so this must have occurred after 1907. As they neared Murrayfield, they encountered the Edinburgh Christmas Carnival and Circus arriving in town. There were caravans, zebras, elephants and all that one might expect to see in such a procession. 'Charlie, do you see anything? After a look, the reply was "No".' His companion must have concluded that he had imbibed more than he had thought! Anecdotes like these bring home his humour and humanity.

As chairman he would sometimes need to exercise such qualities. In the formal minutes, there is an intriguing reference to ongoing RSA dirty tricks, in the form of a press leak from W.G. Stevenson RSA, who had given information illicitly, ahead of the agreed timing for the press release. It allowed the *Dispatch* to beat the *Evening News*. The chairman was asked to write to the gentleman concerned 'giving him an opportunity to deny having anything to do with the matter'. At a later committee meeting the chairman read out the letter of apology he had received, so the gentleman must have been guilty as charged. Dealing with any correspondence of import, like the press issue noted above, was Mackie's personal responsibility. It was also noted that the outcome of his loan requests had been impressive. The report on the 1900 exhibition noted that among the 295 works of art, he had secured two Sargeants, a Manet, some McTaggarts and some English sculpture. Manet had always been a favourite of Mackie's after those heady days in Paris in the 1890s. This Manet, *Jeune fille au fichu*, given a central place in one of the galleries, aroused particular interest as not everyone could travel to see such works abroad. *The Art Journal* pronounced that 'the extremely clever manipulation of the paint has decidedly made it a thing of artistic beauty'. The society's original emphasis was being borne out by its practice. Warm words praised Mackie's enterprise in the matter. The vote of thanks was 'most heartily given'.

As with everything he undertook, Mackie had worked hard during his year of office as chairman of the SSA. Committee meetings can be tedious and were certainly time-consuming for an artist without external means of support. In addition to the major task of organizing the exhibitions, there had been a conscious effort to promote a range of social activities. The minutes record the detailed discussion, planning and arrangements which underpinned the wide variety on offer from the SSA. Typical of their era, these included smoking concerts, conversazione, with music and refreshments, afternoon tea in the galleries and fancy-dress balls. Mackie had steered the SSA through another busy and turbulent year. He would feel well pleased that the general verdict on its health was 'flourishing'.

However, old issues surfaced once again when the SSA was refused access to the Mound Gallery for its next exhibition and had to use the unsatisfactory French Gallery in 1901. These had been bruising battles with the Edinburgh artistic establishment and Mackie did use his retiring address to excoriate their attitude as 'dog in the manger', lamenting the lack of civic recognition of art in Scotland's capital city. He made a plea to the wealthy burghers of Edinburgh to give the society a permanent gallery. Their hands stayed firmly in their pockets. His plea went unanswered but the SSA went from strength to strength in the remaining years of Mackie's life. It retained its innovative approach, exhibiting two Picasso paintings in 1913; *Cubist picture* and *Femme tenante une coupe* sold for £140 and £200 respectively. It had widened its contacts in the pre-World War I period and Mackie's works had acted as ambassadors for Scottish art in this regard. Through the auspices of the SSA, his works were among those sent to exhibitions abroad, including the Munich Glass Palace in 1902 and 1907. In the 1902 Munich exhibition, thirty members of the SSA exhibited more than fifty paintings. The correspondence cites a whole range of other cities and countries where the SSA tried (and often succeeded) in winning access for its members to the wall space vital for artistic promotion. These included Leeds, Birmingham, Liverpool, Wolverhampton, Vienna, Dusseldorf, Dresden, Berlin, Hanover and Amsterdam. True to its democratic spirit, the members voted on the most eligible candidates, whose works would be selected to represent the society. The paintings of Mackie were always on show in these years.

Nonetheless, the two decades before the death of Queen Victoria on 22 January 1901, had seen mixed fortunes for Mackie. Having earlier achieved success and recognition, his determination to 'cherchez le gris' had led to a downturn in his fortunes. It would have been hard not to have been downcast. The promotion of modern art and the young artist were issues dear to his heart.

Fighting those battles shoulder to shoulder with his comrades in the SSA had been exhausting, but they finally emerged triumphant. Despite the slings and arrows, he had evidently valued his time in office. In April 1902, William Robson, in his capacity as Chairman of the SSA, had written to Mackie to congratulate him officially on his election as an Associate of the RSA (Fig. 8). His time had come, after the earlier disappointments.

Proposed in March 1902 by his friend Robert Noble and seconded by two other Edinburgh worthies, J. Campell Mitchell and W. Birnie Rhind, the official distinction of ARSA was recognised in the press of the day. An earnest young man in checked jacket was shown in *The Scots Pictorial*, alongside his friend Robert Burns. While excoriating the RSA for its neglect of painters outside Edinburgh, it accorded Mackie a positive tribute:

> He has done a geat deal of work in decorative and applied art, and has devoted some time to etching. He is an eloquent theorist and altogether a progressive influence in the art world.

All this would have been known to his fellow-artists in the SSA and to their chairman. Mackie's courteous reply underlines the deep affection he still felt for the organization he had served so loyally. Having thanked the society for their congratulatory letter, he goes on,

> But I may say that no honour can ever be done to me which could equal in pleasure that of having been entrusted with the helm of your Society.

Perhaps he could also feel justifiably proud of his own contribution to its success.

Despite these early travails, the SSA had imbedded itself into the artistic life of Edinburgh, secured its place in the social calendar of the summer months and built up a healthy bank balance. Its exhibitions had garnered much praise for their content and the manner of their display, breaking new ground. Loans had brought the works of French and English artists to the attention of the Edinburgh public. Their galleries had not been overcrowded — a criticism that had been levelled at the hanging in the RSA exhibitions. The tendency to pack in as many pictures as possible on the walls had prompted a wry comment in the Glasgow press. 'Edinburgh folks like to get value for their shilling ... In Edinburgh they measure the artistic value of their exhibitions by the wall space.'[6] Mindful of this danger, particular care had been taken with the display of sculpture. As a newcomer to the Edinburgh art scene, the SSA had not seen itself shackled to outworn convention and had walked determinedly down its own path.

The Scots Pictorial, moving from lukewarm reception to enthusiastic endorsement, maintained that the society's exhibitions 'were in artistic effect the best to

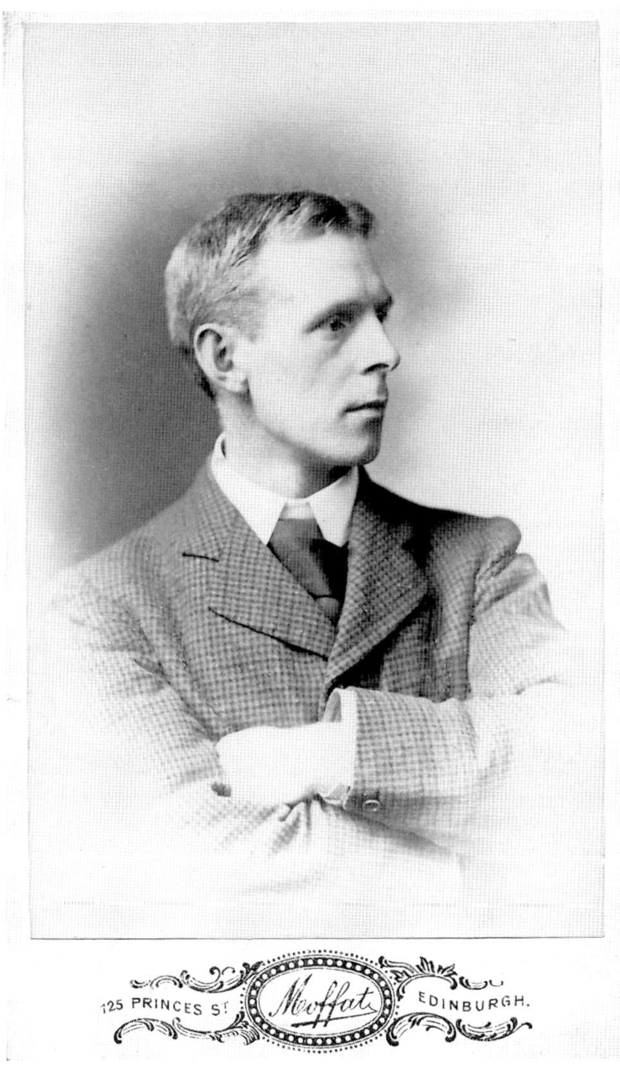

8 Photographic portrait of Charles H. Mackie on becoming ARSA.
This was the picture that was reproduced in *The Scots Pictorial* April 1902.
Photograph courtesy of Bill Mackie

be seen anywhere either at home or abroad'. This was praise indeed and though that paper later changed the emphasis of its reporting to concentrate on the wearing of pretty gowns and dainty hats, its 1902 verdict was a fair reflection on its achievement. It had more than fulfilled its original mission. It was seen by contemporaries as a society of artists, for artists and run by artists. The exhibitions had been lauded as templates that other institutions should copy and they had opened eyes and purses in support of modern art. The society reflected its members' vision for the future of art in Scotland and their desire to rouse it from the lethargy and torpor which they felt had engulfed it at the hands of the RSA. The SSA had been more than a necessary stimulus. It had survived, flourished and now provided a platform for the promotion of modern art and originality, which was its central tenet. No wonder Mackie felt those years were some of the most meaningful for him, as man and artist. Like the society he had helped to found, the efforts had not been in vain.

NOTES

1 Society of Scottish Artists archive, Scottish National Gallery of Modern Art, GMA A/57/51.
2 Annie Mackie was elected a professional member in 1905; Lydia Findlater in 1910.
3 *The Studio*, 1900, Vol. 19, pp. 269-70.
4 GMA A/57/5/1.
5 Gordon–Mackie correspondence, courtesy of Christopher Gordon and Bill Mackie.
6 *Quiz*, 7 February 1895.

Eight

A windmill of the imagination

Moving away from the city in the summer months, many artists found the countryside and coast a welcome invigoration. Mackie was no exception. A new seaside colony of artists beckoned him in the late 1890s. Not as distant as France, it made for easier travelling with a two-year-old boy in tow and offered new vistas of landscape waiting to be painted. Spiritual succour, fresh inspiration and new friendships awaited him on the coast and moors of Yorkshire. There he was to find a special harmony between the places he painted and the people he met. Before the turn of the century he had already begun to explore the area round Whitby in north Yorkshire, which was also a most paintable place. The expansion of the railway system made such travel much easier, with the Whitby line opening in 1875 and subsequently extended to Staithes in 1883. Runswick and Staithes would both provide him with a seascape which shared many features with the East Neuk of his youth. The views now appear exactly the same as recorded in his paintings, even if the fisherfolk have long gone and holiday cottages now predominate. The headlands and agricultural settings offered new themes for his canvas and he adapted these using his imagination. Leeds Art Gallery own a beautiful oil painting from this period, entitled *The Windmill* (Pl. 18) which was purchased in 1904, having been shown under that title earlier in 1900 at the RSA (cat. 33). It now hangs in Leeds City Chambers, in the room used for wedding services.

The artist's file held by the gallery contained its own unexpected treasure – a previously unknown letter written by Mackie, answering the query from the purchasing committee regarding the location of said windmill, since he had not given it a name. They might well have thought that they recognized it, given the similarity of the backdrop to Boulby headland. There is a well-known landmark in the area, Ugthorpe Mill, which might have provided the germ of an idea and it has been painted by many artists. However, the letter provides the artist's own confirmation that his painting was more than a realistic portrayal:

entirely a composition being no particular windmill nor at any particular place.

This is what I would like a windmill to look like in a country I would hope to find some day.'[1]

It was a windmill of the artist's imagination. The letter also provides an insight into his character and his courtesy towards his purchasers. He thanks George Birkett, the committee chairman, for 'speaking so kindly of my work'. He then confirms that he can provide a 'hallmark' by outlining his career to that point. The most enlightening comment is on his early years: 'I am artistically entirely self-educated though I attended art schools to my undoing.' He then goes on to confirm his pedigree, by mentioning that he first exhibited at the RSA as a sixteen year old, then regularly thereafter including at the RA and international exhibitions all over Europe. Mackie's memory must have played him false, as he was eighteen when he first exhibited at the RSA in 1880. He does list what he earlier referred to as 'misleading encumbrances of a painter's career': Chairman of Society of Scottish Artists 1900-01, elected as ARSA and RSW 1902. These encumbrances would help provide the hallmarks valued by any purchasing committee, a fact of which he would have been well aware. This letter, clearly dated 20 June 1904 is a good guide to the light in which he viewed his own artistic journey to date.

In Yorkshire, he found other sights for his pen as well as his paintbrush, executing works in pen and ink, as well as watercolour and oil. This wild, beautiful coast was matched by stunning skies and this synthesis produced an evocative atmosphere for a painter like Mackie. He definitely visited Whitby for there is a fine pen-and-ink drawing of its old harbour bridge, with sailing ship passing through, dated and signed 1900. The boat depicted was a Yorkshire yawl, designed for herring fishing and already doomed to extinction with the advent of steam trawlers and Scottish competition. *The Harbour Bridge, Whitby* was reproduced in *The Studio* in 1901. In the RSA exhibition of that year he exhibited *Whitby Bridge* (cat. 314), the first firmly identifiable Yorkshire subject, as *The Windmill* of the previous year was not yet publicly claimed as such.

In fact, the Mackie family had taken up residence further inland from Whitby, renting a room in the Redman farmhouse at Roxby, right on the edge of the moor. The only spare bedroom was shared by the Mackies and their young son, as well as doubling as the artist's workplace. Mr Redman was the stonemason on the Roxby Estate and his wife was the physical mainstay on the farm. She kept her pig and its pigsty spotless, and would weep for its passing when the time for bacon arrived. Ploughing and reaping posed no challenge to her, since she was of sound physique apart from the need for dentures. She appears to have been a jolly, homely woman who would have made her artist-lodgers welcome. This would be the place where the Mackies always stayed during their years in Yorkshire. Their simple, happy domesticity impressed the young Laura

Johnson. She stayed there one winter after the Mackies had stopped coming. After her marriage to Harold Knight in June 1903, the young couple also lived at the Bowman farm next door. She remembered that Bob, the friendly brown and white sheep-dog, would scrounge scraps from the visitors after his day's labour was over. Her time there was later tinged with grief in April 1906, when she and Harold were asked to visit Mrs Redman as her husband had just passed away. Laura loved the countryside of coast and moor, inspiration for her painting and for that of her new-found teacher, Charles Mackie.

These moors lie above Staithes and the seven mile walk there and back, with artistic accoutrements, would have kept Mackie fit. The hill down into Staithes is as steep and taxing now as it was in Mackie's day. The sound of raucous seagulls still fills the air as it would have done then, though the staithe (wooden quay) is long gone and the fishermen's cottages have become the ubiquitous holiday homes. The high cliffs at nearby Runswick overlook a broad sweep of bay, which can be reached by an equally steep road from Hinderwell. It was a scene that must have gladdened the painter's eyes, as he breasted the top of the hill. *Moonlight on the Bay* would capture that vision in a haunting and romantic watercolour (Pl. 20). Close friendships, mutual support, encouragement and cooperation were made possible by the geographical proximity of Staithes and Runswick. Artists had long been drawn to the area, attracted by the people as much as their surroundings. The life of the fisherfolk was one of hard, unremitting toil, interlaced with the uncertainty of life at sea. They kept aloof from most strangers but the painters seemed as poor as them and they were accepted on their own terms. Their fishing boats (known as cobles), simple cottages and distinctive dress, including the women's bonnets, are all shown in the pictures painted by the members of the Staithes Group.

This is the term used to describe those who painted at Staithes and Runswick in the years 1894-1909 approximately. This was deemed to be the period of most intense activity, though the membership of the group was fluid, numbering up to thirty-four individuals at any one time. A long list of eminent artists would qualify for the title, including Rowland Henry Hill, Frederick W. Jackson, Henry Silkstone Hopwood, Robert and Isa Jobling, Joseph Bagshawe, Lionel Townsend Crawshaw, Ernest Dade, Mark Senior, Fred Mayor, Harold Knight and Laura Johnson, who would later become Dame Laura Knight. These are some of the names that recur in *The Whitby Gazette* and other contemporary accounts. It was described as a very loose collection of artists, with very mixed backgrounds but who were drawn to this corner of Yorkshire with its artistic colony and lively outdoor life. The group might have been short-lived but many would go on to influence the course of British art. In an article written well after the demise of the Staithes Art Club, *The Whitby Gazette*, dated 30 July 1926, concluded that:

> There is no doubt that this group, which were at that time regarded as extreme

Modernists, have had a great influence on British Art.

Much earlier, back in 1887, the Yorkshire Union of Artists had been formed and their annual exhibitions had already offered a platform for sales. In 1901, the Staithes Group decided to go further and augment this by staging their own exhibition in the Fisherman's Institute in the village itself. The only account of the proceedings is to be found in the secret diary of a local girl, Enid Lucy Pease Robinson.[2] She recorded the date as Monday 26 August and she described the events of that day, paying particular attention to the weather. As it happened, the timing proved unfortunate since the weather was distinctly unkind – a cold, dull morning developed into a violent storm, with gale force winds in the after-noon and evening. She noted that there was no definite opening ceremony and apparently, nothing happened before 4pm, when a few people wandered in and, one hopes, bought some paintings. The accounts showed a paltry profit of 15/2d. *The Whitby Gazette* made minimal mention of the proceedings. On 13 Septem-ber, under the heading *The Picture Exhibition at Staithes*, it noted that: 'Several of the artists ... have got up a very interesting little exhibition of their work in the upper room of the Fisherman's Insititute in Staithes, ostensibly in aid of the funds of the Institute.' It could not have been judged a success. Thereafter, there was a definite attempt to be better organized and put everything on a more professional basis. Since Mackie was listed as a member of the Staithes Art Club at this point, the committee elected to improve the organization of the exhibition could call on his experience from the SSA. After all, he had been at the forefront of the picture selection, hanging, publicity and promotion for their highly success-ful first exhibition in 1892 and had only just relinquished his chairmanship. He had an established reputation as an artist and promoter of modern art. His French connections and contacts would have underlined his familiarity with the new ideas and techniques. He no doubt shared this knowledge with his Staithes colleagues, among whom he would make good friends. He proved similarly gener-ous with his time and advice on the colour palette, as Laura Johnson would later find out. All this pointed to his willingness to support the new venture and his paintings would figure in their catalogues in future exhibitions.

Mindful of their initial experience, the date for the second exhibition in 1902 was moved back to 1 August, when the weather might be kinder. Only accredited paid-up members were allowed to exhibit, being limited to four framed medium-sized paintings and four mounted sketches. The committee absolved themselves of all responsibility for the paintings but ensured that the Fisherman's Institute would benefit. The 2d entrance fee was directed to its coffers. The published catalogue of forty-one paintings included three Mackies. Now acknowledged as an ARSA, he could command the most expensive prices for his art. *Moonlight on the Bay* was priced at £60, *The Hill, Runswick* cost twelve guineas and *The Pool below the Bridge* was ten guineas. The most expensive picture had also been exhibited at the RSA and RSW in 1902, winning praise from *The Scotsman* on both occasions, as 'a work of much ability' with 'fine rendering of an evening effect.' (Pl. 20; this recently changed hands for over £6,000. Perhaps Mackie's fine watercolour is finally receiving the recognition it deserves.) He did not send any pictures to the third annual exhibition, with *The Whitby Gazette* commenting 'we miss from the walls the work of Mr. Charles Mackie A.R.S.A.'

His travels abroad, particularly in Spain, would account for his absence. He would, in fact, exhibit some work from Spain in the fourth annual exhibition in 1904, which went on to Hull after Staithes. *On the Tagus at Toledo* was his most expensive picture, priced at £12; *A Roadside Study* was £6; and *A Nor' Easter* and *Sundown at Runswick Bay* were £8 each. His fellow Staithes artist, Lionel Crawshaw, also exhibited some oil sketches from Toledo at this exhibition. According to Anne Mackie, they had travelled together to Spain. Their professional friendship also endured, since Crawshaw exhibited at the SSA in 1905, 1908 and 1910. An unusual venue for a Doncaster-based painter, concentrating on Whitby scenes, Mackie's friendship must have provided the Edinburgh connection.

A rich collection of paintings had resulted from their Spanish sojourn. Mackie's watercolours were bought *en masse* by an American dealer Frederick C. Torrey, who planned to stage an exhibition in San Francisco. Their correspondence is held by the Victoria & Albert Museum and there was warmth in the words exchanged. However, the timing proved unfortunate since the San Francisco earthquake of 18 April 1906 resulted in a massive fire which destroyed much of the city and Mackie's watercolours went up in flames. It was thought that nothing had survived but I possess a Spanish watercolour which bears an uncanny resemblance to the Tagus at Toledo. I cannot give any provenance or proof but would like to think it might have been that Staithes exhibit.

This fourth Staithes exhibition was a much larger affair, with a total of eighty-eight paintings. Thereafter, the remaining exhibitions of the Staithes Art Club were incorporated into the annual autumn exhibition of the YUA. August was a month that clashed with other exhibitions and the growth of the venture meant that there was increasing difficulty in finding a suitable location. It seems ironic, after that disastrous first exhibition, that it had become a victim of its own success, choosing to end its separate existence in 1907. The venue for the fifth, sixth and seventh (last) exhibition of the Staithes Art Club was Whitby, and Mackie appears to have made his final contribution in 1905. On this occasion, *The Whitby Gazette* was profuse in its praise for what it judged 'A Choice Exhibition'. It commented on the aims and methods of the key artists, saying, 'They each try to give the broad truths of nature, ignoring almost entirely anything which would detract from the first impression'. Much praise was lavished on Mackie's *Étaples* and his other submissions. 'We now arrive at a group of watercolours, and find Mr Mackie at his best in *Whitby*, a drawing well seen, full of colour, and rich in every sense.' The conclusion was that this was 'the best little show we have seen in Whitby'. As well as the two paintings mentioned in the review above, Mackie also exhibited *Stokesay Castle,* pricing it at twelve guineas, *Bait-Gatherers* for ten guineas and *Runswick* for seven guineas. Little of his art remains in the area, with the Pannett Art Gallery possessing only one small watercolour of *Whitby Market.*

These artists painted *en plein air* in often challenging climatic conditions, since this was the North Sea, not the Mediterranean. There is a first-hand description of the discomfort this entailed. Rowland H. Hill was interviewed by *The Yorkshire Evening News* in August 1939 and provided some interesting reminiscences from his time in Staithes and Runswick:

> Our ... canvases would be tethered by large stones and we would sit painting away
> in a cold wind with as many clothes on as it was possible to wear. Charles Mackie
> I remember brought something like a chestnut seller's stove and took it on the
> beach with him. He used it for warming his hands and drying his watercolours
> when there was a lot of moisture about.

In the summer, Hill remembered each painter would have a big parasol to shelter under. Mackie's early mentor, William McTaggart used to take his own canvases out on to the beach and tether them with ropes and stones. This master of Scottish seascapes also advocated facing the storm as well as the sunshine and Mackie did paint the angry North Sea as well as calmer waters.

His Staithes colleague Fred Jackson was also a firm believer in the desirability of painting out of doors, whatever the weather. In the 1905 catalogue he said they tried to 'represent their honest interpretation of nature.' The emphasis was on the artist's veracity. Jackson's hands, ears and nostrils paid the price for such exposure, since he persisted with *en plein air* painting even when he visited Russia. Mackie and he were firm friends, Fred the driving force behind the Staithes Art Club and Charles the respected Scottish practitioner. Both had been muralists and supported the Arts and Crafts movement. Their travels abroad might have overlapped, since France and Italy were common sources of inspiration. Both were inveterate travellers and set up summer studios in Normandy, Mackie near Étaples and Jackson at Montreuil-sur-Mer. The locations are not far apart and they surely would have kept up their strong friendship. Venice was visited by both men but Jackson had been there before Mackie's later travels, though they did overlap in 1909. It does not stretch credibility to think that Jackson would have talked about all he had seen and the fertile scenes that city offered a painter. In addition, Jackson was a founder member of the New English Art Club and friend of Walter Sickert, who would later express admiration for Mackie's work. Temperamentally they were compatible, as Jackson was noted for his reticence and unpretentiousness; the latter also characteristic of Charles Mackie who gifted his painting *Woodland in Autumn* to 'my friend Jackson' in

1900.[3] Both men were known for their qualities of kindness, patience and gentleness, particularly in finding time to tutor the younger artists.

The sight of an artist, paintbrush in hand, was commonplace at Staithes and the local people paid them no heed. However, the artists had to respect the Sabbatarianism of the fishing community and one unnamed individual who broke the taboo was pelted with fish heads. The artists' equipment could be left safely, without fear of theft or vandalism. If it was fine weather, Rowland Hill recalled that much lay about — umbrella, pole easels, paint box, brushes, paints etc. It would all remain there, undisturbed, until the artist returned to his easel in the morning. There was also much conviviality in the colony and his memories were of concerts, tableaux and sports. Unsurprisingly, the tableaux had very picturesque settings but the dresses and the scenery were more makeshift. The concerts were very successful and their favourite song was *There is a Tavern in the Town*, which came to be regarded as the National Anthem of Runswick. Perhaps it was this behaviour that led *The Whitby Gazette* to describe the group as a colony of artists who 'Bohemianise'. Rowland Hill offered a belated apology: 'I'm afraid we were a somewhat hilarious and sociable crowd, prone to fits of exuberance.'

Much of the socializing took place in Fred Jackson's home in Hinderwell. He had a large wooden studio behind the house suitable for parties. Laura Knight recalled the cosy warmth of Ivy Cottage, with the crumpets and homemade plum bread provided by their host on Sunday afternoons. The camaraderie even resulted in one elopement in 1902, when Hannah Hoyland and William Frederick Mayor ran off to wed. The artists organized the first ever sports day at Runswick and there was 'some grand fun racing on the sands'. There were organised cricket matches, billed as *Artists v. Whitby Visitors*, and one would like to imagine Mackie joining in with all his usual enthusiasm. Knight remembered that she had initially met him at one of the wild hockey matches played at Hinderwell; she and Harold visited the happy Mackie ménage at the Redman farm shortly afterwards. All this healthy activity and socialising would have appealed to the Mackies, now accompanied by their young son Donald. In many ways, it was a welcome breath of fresh air after Edinburgh.

Staithes would give Mackie time to reflect on his art and the practical application of his colour theories. Any teacher will confirm that mastery of one's subject is not gained purely by study alone; it is vital to impart the facts and interpretation to a student. Only by teaching is one's subject absorbed, refined and understood fully. It is the essential discipline imposed by the need for clarity of explanation, example and application. The teacher has to ensure understanding and be able to answer questions, as well as justify any critique offered. For Mackie, this period where he taught regularly, to a student eager to learn, was as valuable to him as it was to Laura Knight. He not only had to clarify his own ideas but also present them in a way that was intelligible to this young artist. I would argue that this process not only benefited the student but was also crucial for him. It allowed him to move forward with his own art, replacing perceived distortion with fluidity, muting his colours and widening his experimentation in other media. It would be the period after Staithes that would see his finest art but the groundwork was laid in those weekly lessons given to his young protégée.

Normally Mackie's movements are notoriously difficult to pin down but Knight's two autobiographies furnish detailed descriptions of the lessons, her homework and Mackie's technique. He was generous with his time and his encouragement at a point when she felt that she was losing her way. This reflects his instinctive generosity of spirit, to help a fellow artist who was struggling and to give up hours that could have been spent at his own easel. According to Knight, he had the nickname 'Charcoal' Mackie as he used this medium to criticise the pictures of his brother artists. So, no doubt, he applied his charcoal to her studies as well. She had the habit of sketching with anything available, whether it was pen, pencil, chalk or charcoal and these on-the-spot drawings provided material for the finished work. Appropriately, she entitled one of her autobiographies *The Magic of a Line*. She had been experimenting with her style and with unusual combinations of colour. Mackie was well-known as a colour theorist who was abreast of Continental developments and the Paris art scene. Her stamina and devotion to her craft attracted his sympathetic interest. This resulted in the weekly lessons which she described in detail in her second autobiography, *Oil Paint and Grease Paint*. He would walk down from the moor and spend every Wednesday afternoon with her. She was given the task of preparing abstract diagrams for him, focusing on the effect of one colour on another. She was then asked to extend the technique by balancing a pale spread of one colour with one concentration of colour. It was his system and she described it as 'coldly intellectual' but it evidently had a profound and positive effect. She goes on to describe in detail how he taught her to lay out her palette and to restrict her range of colours, so that a better effect would be achieved. She supplies a detailed description of his colour system:

> He told me, too, how to lay out my palette — white on the left — then through the rainbow range-yellow-orange-scarlet-red-crimson-purple-blue-black-green. I still make use of his plan. Another tip he gave me was to use as few colours as possible, earth pigments for preference — now and again to omit one of the primaries, blue, yellow or red, and see how near it was possible to get to it by the play of a dominant note of its opponent colour, so that the spectator's eye, tiring of its strength should find the non-existent colour in a neutral grey — a possible illusion that holds greater beauty than gaudy paint, and a most fascinating game to play.

He taught her about the beauty of colour — it was not just the paint squeezed out of a tube. Here was a teacher who had spent many years in his quest to 'cherchez le gris' and she was now benefiting from all that he had learned and internalised. She was conscious of 'an immense improvement' in her work as a result of his lessons and their joint efforts. When they had first met he had also given her another piece of advice that she took to heart. Many years later she remembered the very first thing he had told her: 'Stop trying to fake pictures – go out and paint what you see.' He wanted her to paint simply and directly and face up to her difficulties. One canvas attracted his criticism. He told her that her depiction of a cliff edge looked like wool, not the reality. Any fall on her cliff would have been harmless. One of his earliest works was *Peeling Potatoes*. Laura also observed and painted this activity, applying his teaching. It exists in pencil and watercolour, a homely scene which captures the simplicity of this domestic task. Sadly, Mackie's version has not been traced.

Laura Knight benefited a great deal from the criticism, the hard work and the encouragement of the more experienced artist who urged her to think for herself and develop her own style. Truly, she had learned a valuable lesson which she took to heart:

> Mackie had shown me that there were no short-cuts to making a work of art, and that other people's manners when imitated only turned to empty mannerisms.

This was a lesson he had learned for himself over the past difficult years. Her praise was fulsome and sincere as she appreciated the time and trouble he had taken. She judged him a 'marvellous teacher' and paid him the supreme compliment:

> I never take up a brush to-day without giving thanks to Charles H. Mackie.

In the light of her later achievements and distinguished career, British art is also in the debt of Charles Mackie.

These contacts in Staithes were extended further by his election to the council of the Yorkshire Union of Artists. Though the YUA was designed to be a successful vehicle for the promotion of the work of Yorkshire artists, its rule book did allow for exceptions. Neither Mackie nor his friend Hornel could claim a Yorkshire birthright but they were recognized as being 'of high status in the art world'. This gained them admission to the YUA exhibitions and allowed them to send in submissions from Scotland. Hornel was a vice-president and elected member of council in 1908 and is recorded as sending in his work from Kirkcudbright from 1906 to 1912. Mackie preceded him, as he was a vice-president from 1907 and elected member of council in 1908 and 1912. Based at his Coltbridge Studio, he exhibited from 1906 to 1909 from Edinburgh. It is worth noting that Mackie and Hornel were the only two from Scotland who were elected council members. The YUA in its heyday before World War I was regarded as the largest and most successful provincial art society in the country

Unfortunately, their records are patchy and hard to locate, so it is impossible to ascertain what the two well-kent Scotsmen exhibited or sold. However, exhibitions in Leeds and Bradford would have opened up new markets in cities renowned for their public philanthropy and industrial wealth. Mackie's time in Yorkshire had meant more than another outlet for his paintings and commercial success. He had made good friends, found new subjects for his canvas and benefited from his time as a teacher. The Staithes interlude did provide personal vindication for him as an artist, allowing him to move forward with renewed confidence in his abilities and his vision. The breathing-space provided by the Yorkshire air had revived both the man and the painter.

NOTES

1 Artist's file, courtesy of Leeds City Art Gallery, quoted by kind permission of Bill Mackie.
2 Hart, James, *The Secret Staithes Diary of Enid Lucy Pease Robinson*, (Harrogate: Historical Publishing, 2010).
3 This painting is thought to be a possible first study for a later woodblock print, *Wild Hyacinths* (Pl. 26).

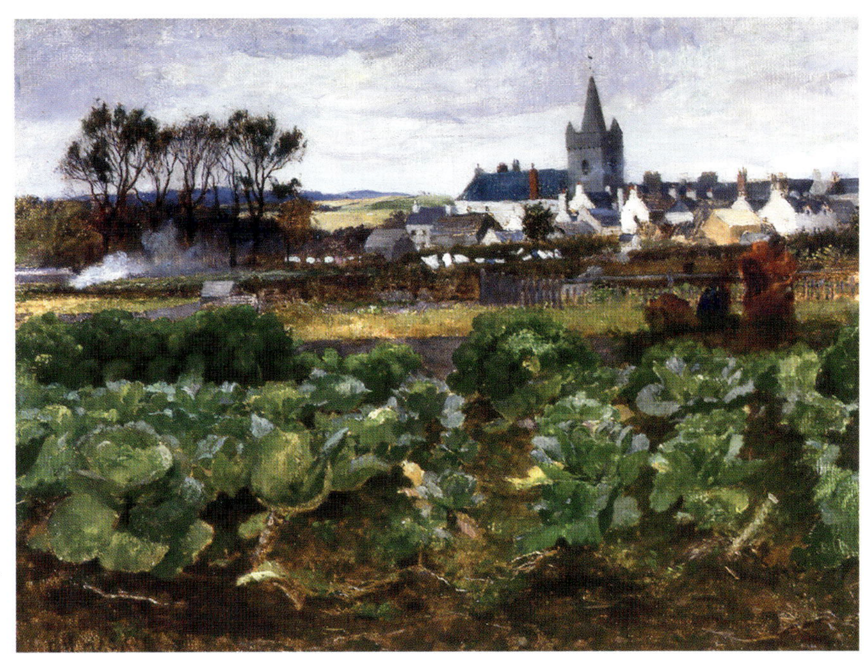

pl. 1 ***The Crofts, Kirkcudbright***
*c.*1884/5 | oil on canvas | 25 x 36 cm

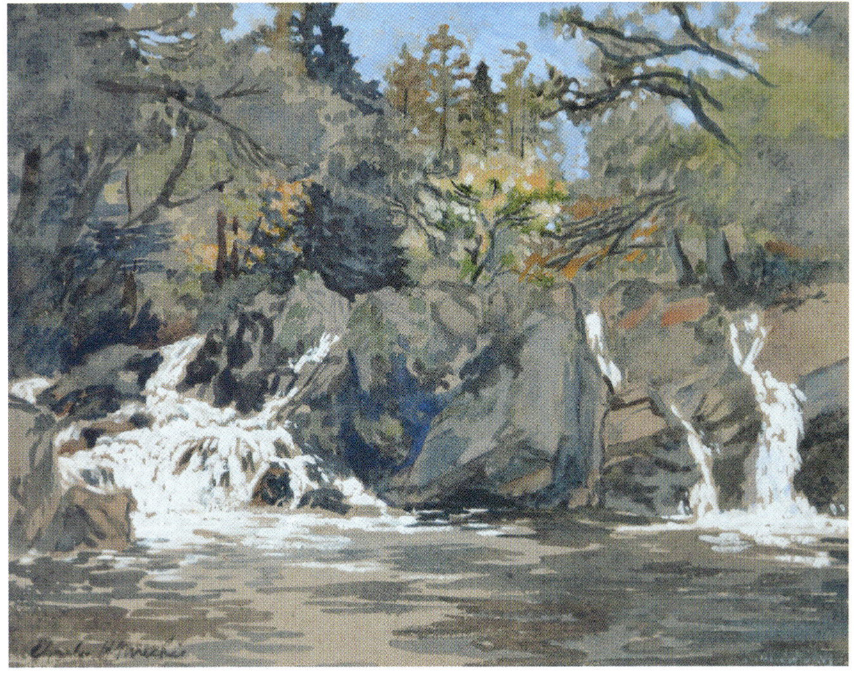

pl. 2 ***The Pool of Ness***
*c.*1894 | watercolour on paper | 28 x 33 cm

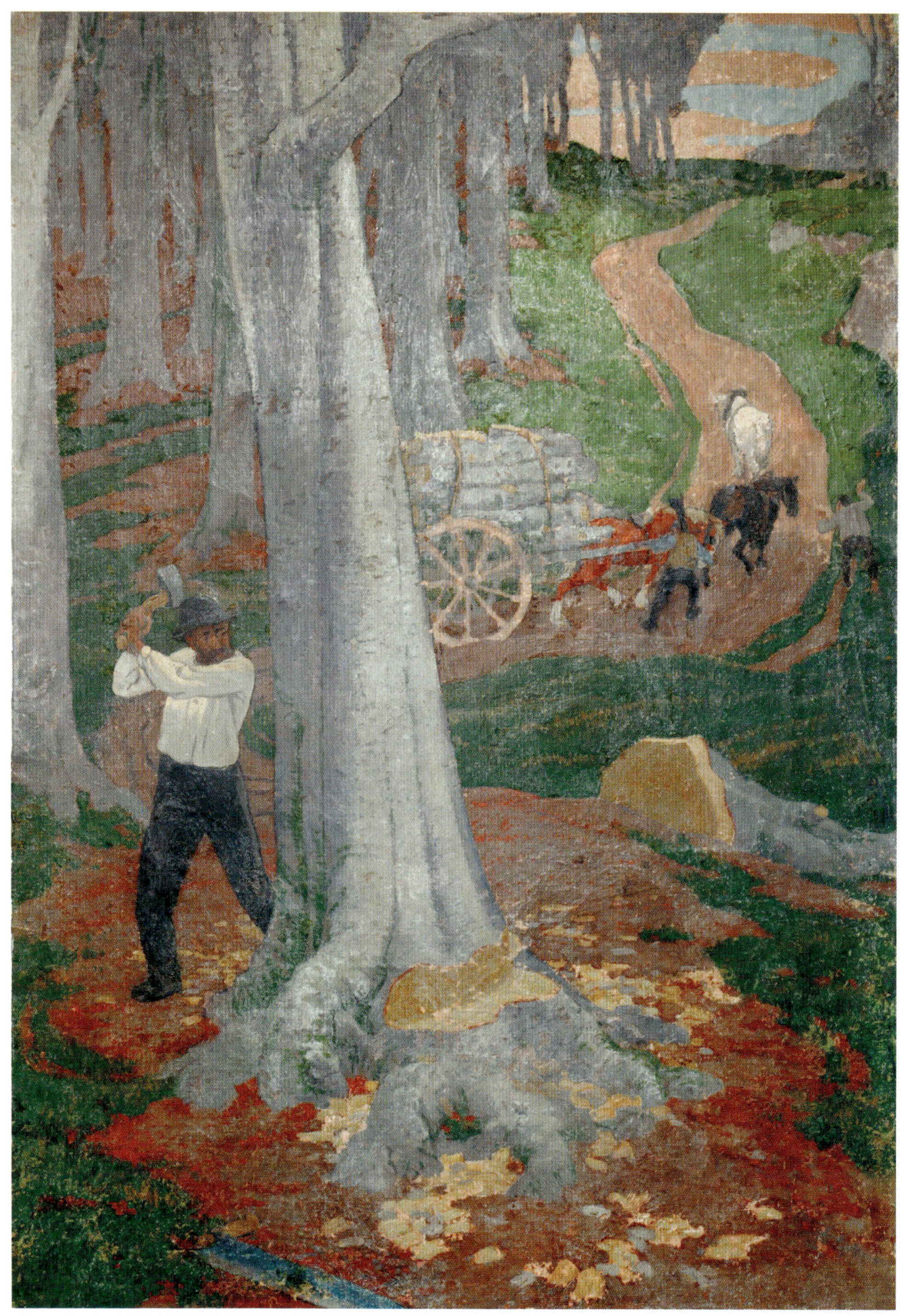

pl. 3 *Felling Trees in a Beech Wood*
c.1894 | mural: oil on canvas | 143 x 107 cm
© NATIONAL TRUST FOR SCOTLAND, RAMSAY GARDEN

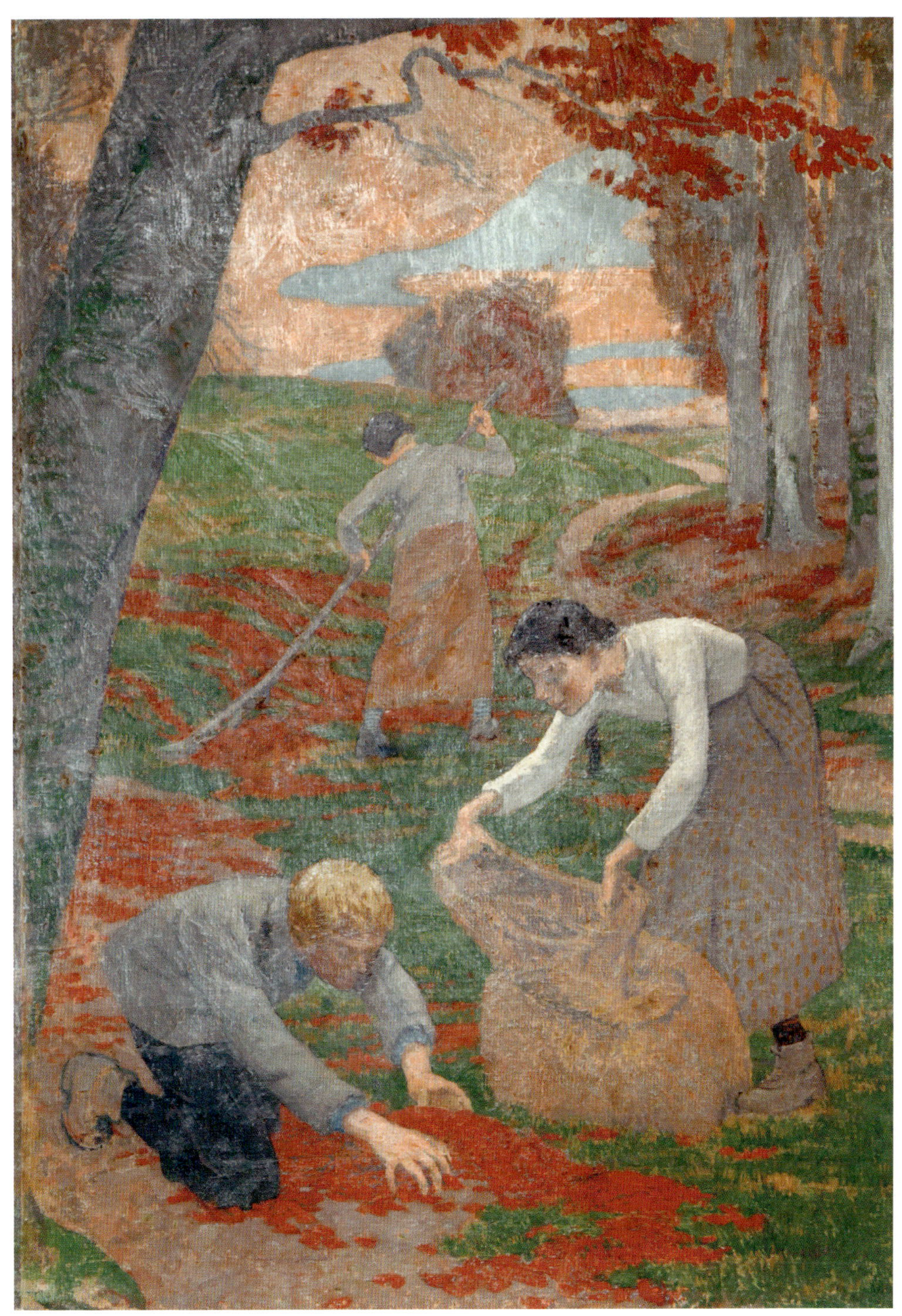

pl. 4 *Gathering Winter Leaves*
c.1894 | mural: oil on canvas | 143 x 107 cm
© NATIONAL TRUST FOR SCOTLAND, RAMSAY GARDEN

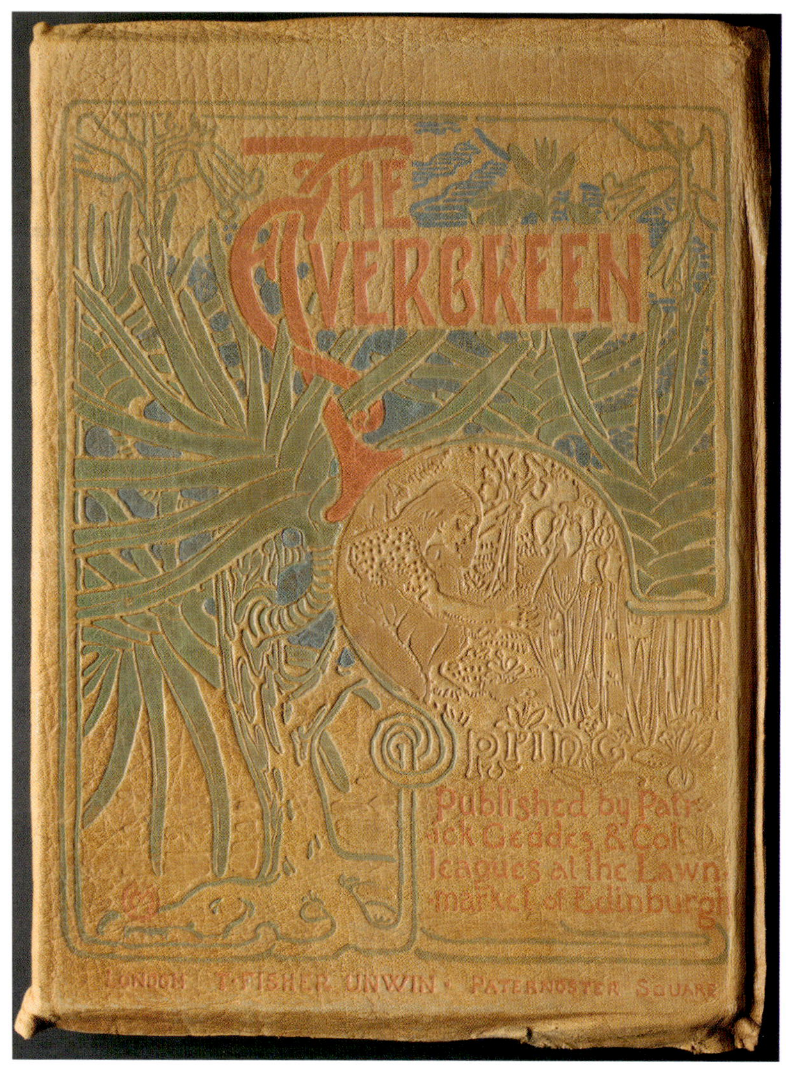

pl. 5 *The Evergreen*
April 1895 | blind stamped on leather | 25.4 x 18.8 cm
COURTESY PERTH MUSEUM AND ART GALLERY, PERTH AND KINROSS COUNCIL

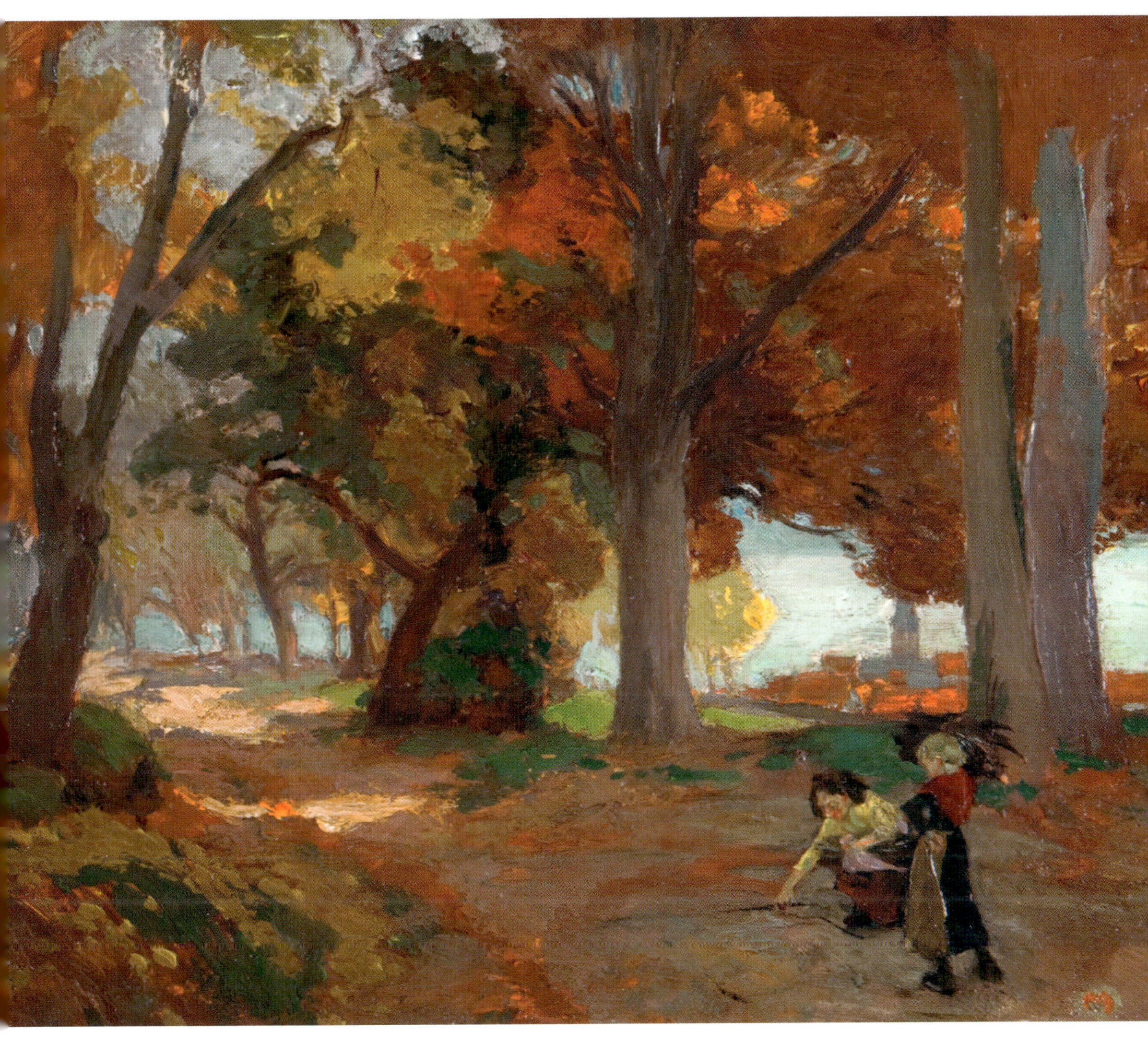

pl.6 *The Faggot Gatherers*
*c.*1894 | oil on board | 30.2 x 39.7 cm
© THE HUNTERIAN, UNIVERSITY OF GLASGOW 2015

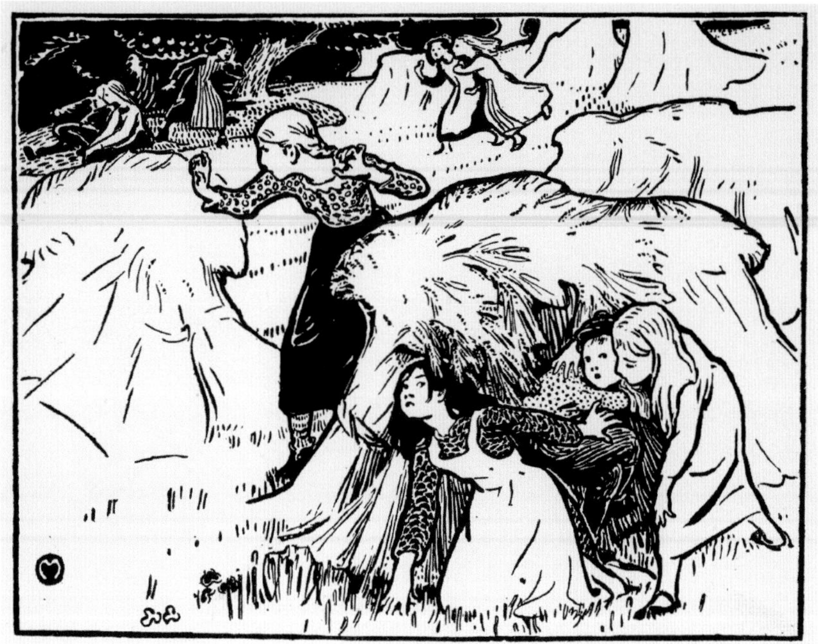

pl. 7 *Hide and Seek*
woodblock print on paper | 17.5 x 23.5 cm
COURTESY PERTH MUSEUM AND ART GALLERY, PERTH AND KINROSS COUNCIL

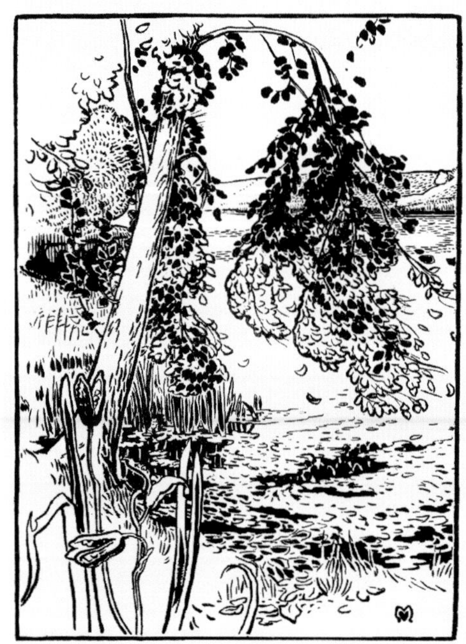

pl. 8 *Lyart Leaves*
woodblock print on paper | 18.1 x 13.3 cm
COURTESY PERTH MUSEUM AND ART GALLERY, PERTH AND KINROSS COUNCIL

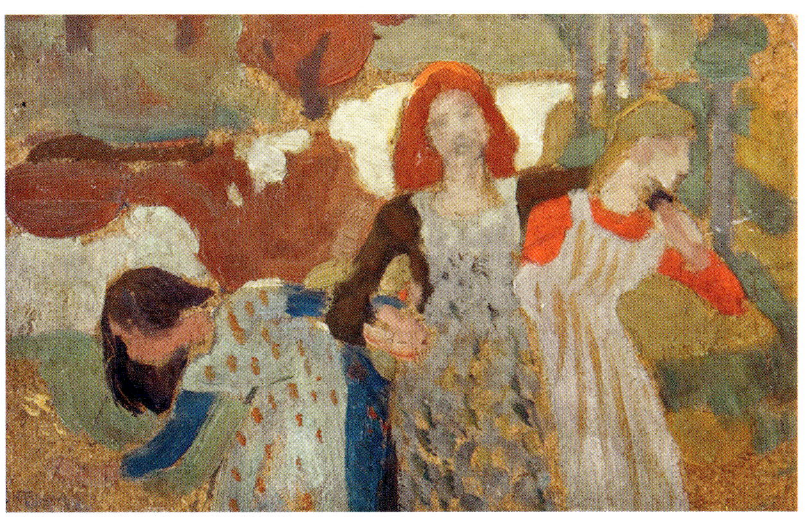

pl.9 ***The Bonnie Banks o' Fordie***
*c.*1894 | oil on card | 14.9 x 24 cm
© THE HUNTERIAN, UNIVERSITY OF GLASGOW 2015

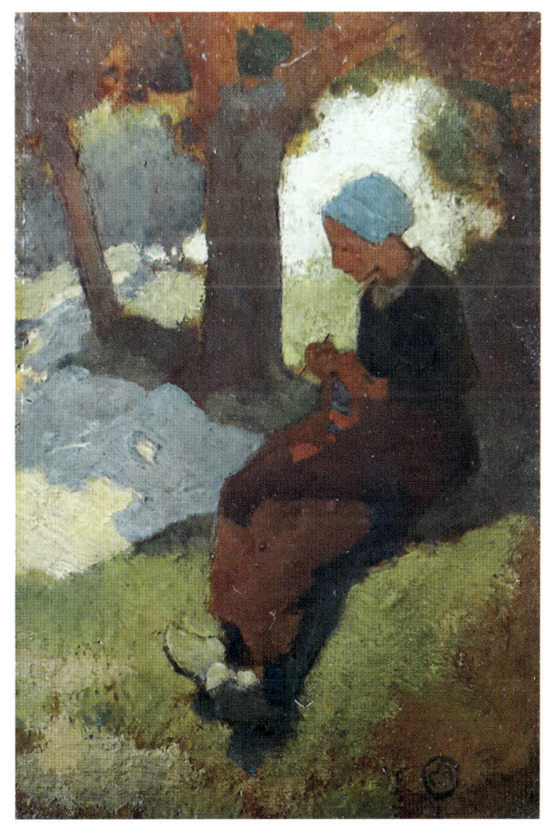

pl.10 ***Breton Girl Crocheting***
*c.*1892 | oil on wood | 26 x 20 cm
PRIVATE COLLECTION

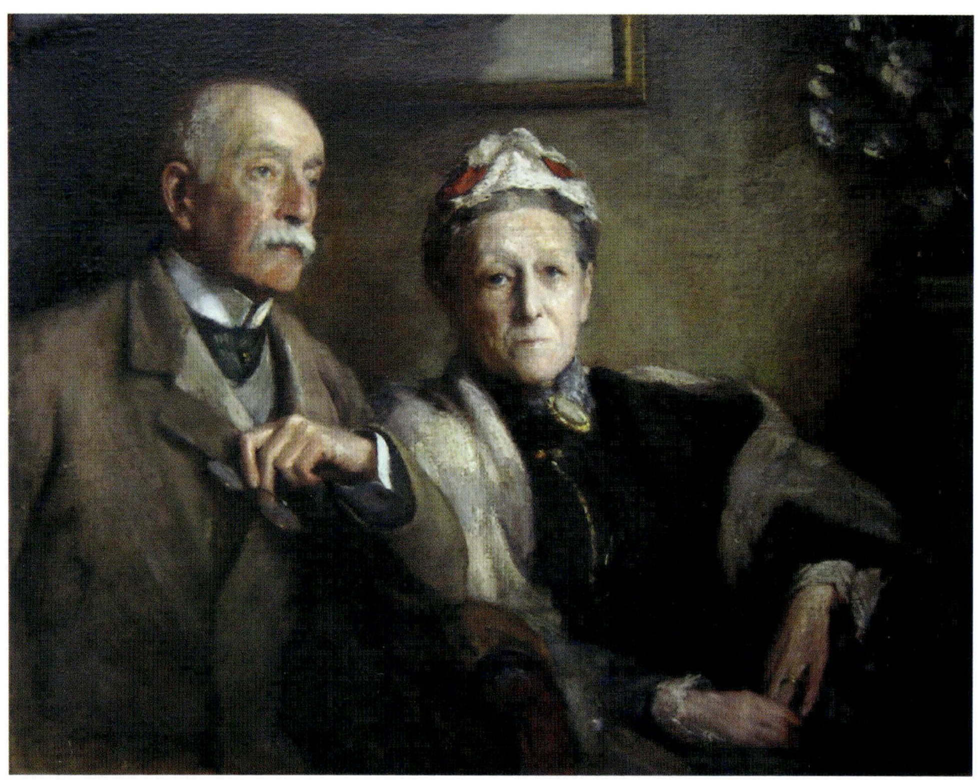

pl.11 ***Captain William Mackie and Mrs Mackie***
1900 | oil on canvas | 60 x 90 cm
PRIVATE COLLECTION | PHOTOGRAPH COURTESY BILL MACKIE

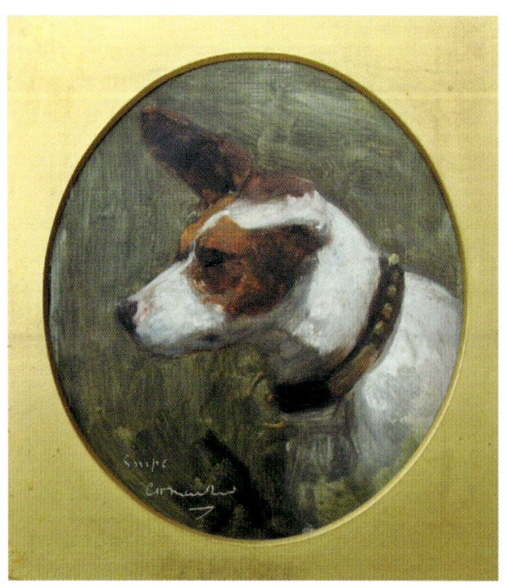

pl.12 ***Snipe***
undated | oil on board | 20 x 18.5 cm
PRIVATE COLLECTION | PHOTOGRAPH COURTESY BILL MACKIE

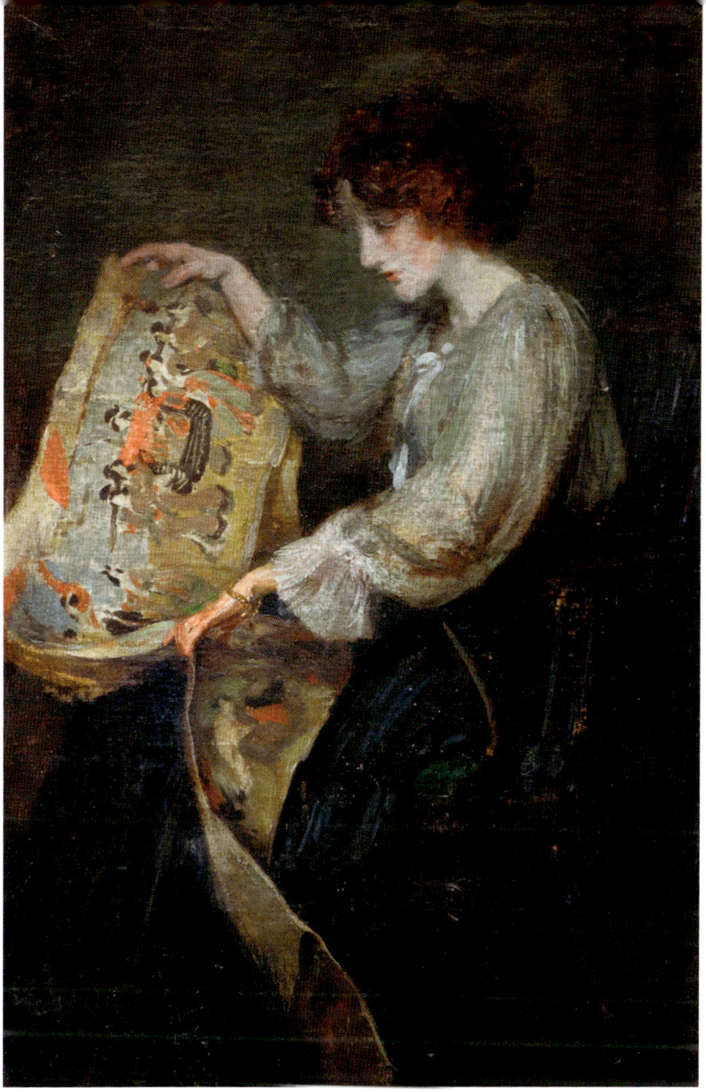

pl. 13 *A Japanese Album*
1904 | oil on canvas | 70.9 x 47.9 cm

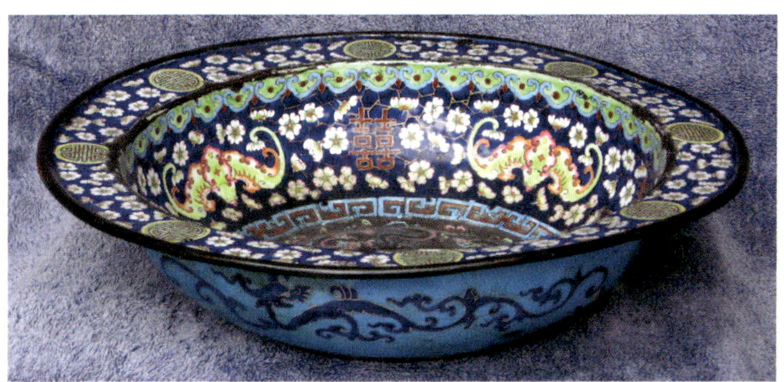

pl. 14 unknown craftsman | Cloisonné bowl | Chinese provenance

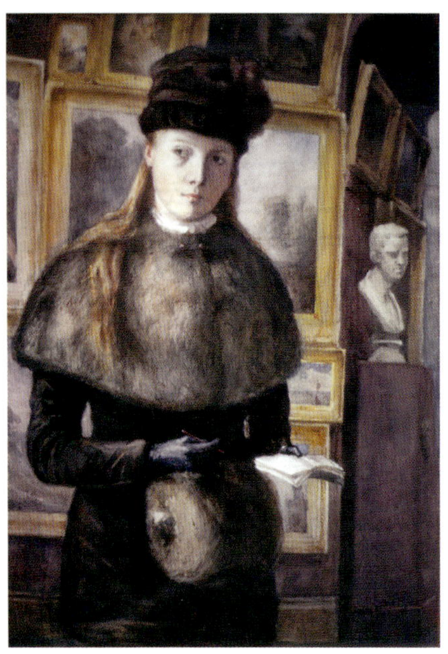

pl.15 *Annie Mackie*
1880 | oil on canvas | 41 x 28 cm
PRIVATE COLLECTION | PHOTOGRAPH COURTESY BILL MACKIE

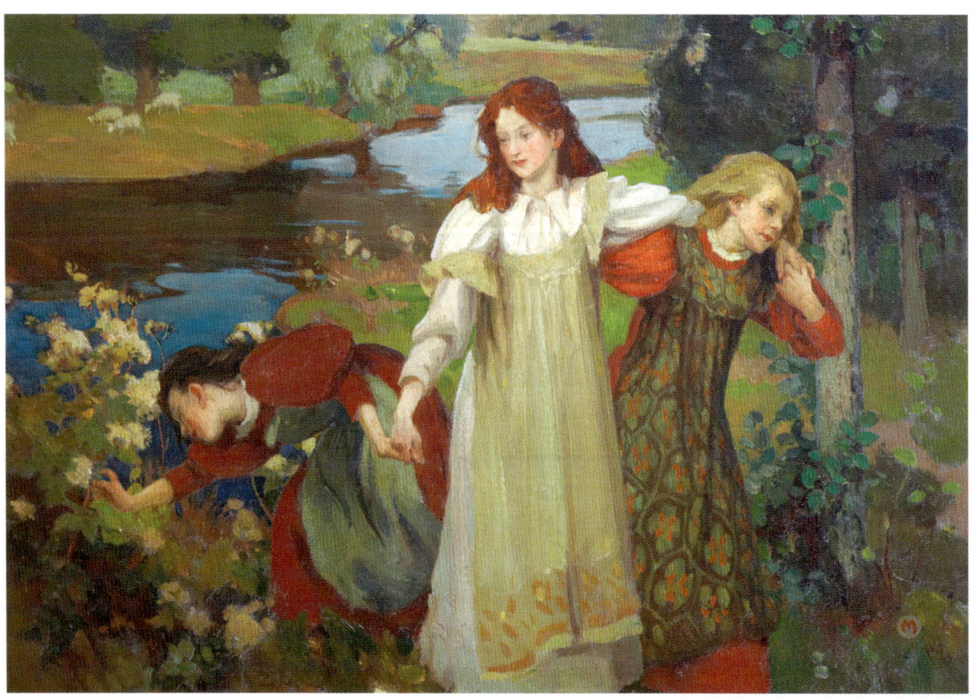

pl.16 *There were three maidens pu'd a flower (by the bonnie banks o' Fordie)*
*c.*1897 | oil on canvas | 62 x 91 cm
COURTESY CITY ART CENTRE, EDINBURGH MUSEUMS AND GALLERIES

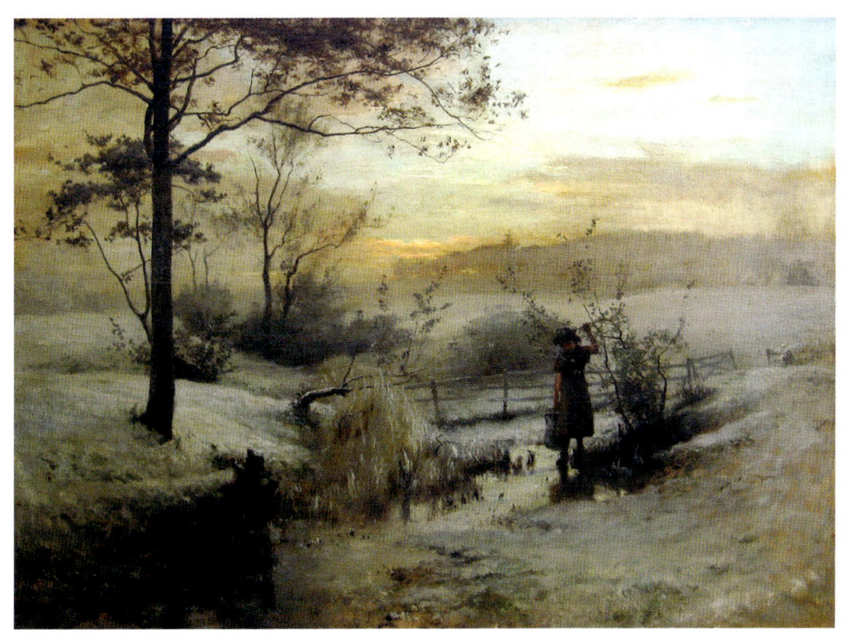

pl. 17 ***An Early Frost at Sunrise***
1888 | oil on canvas | 56 x 76 cm

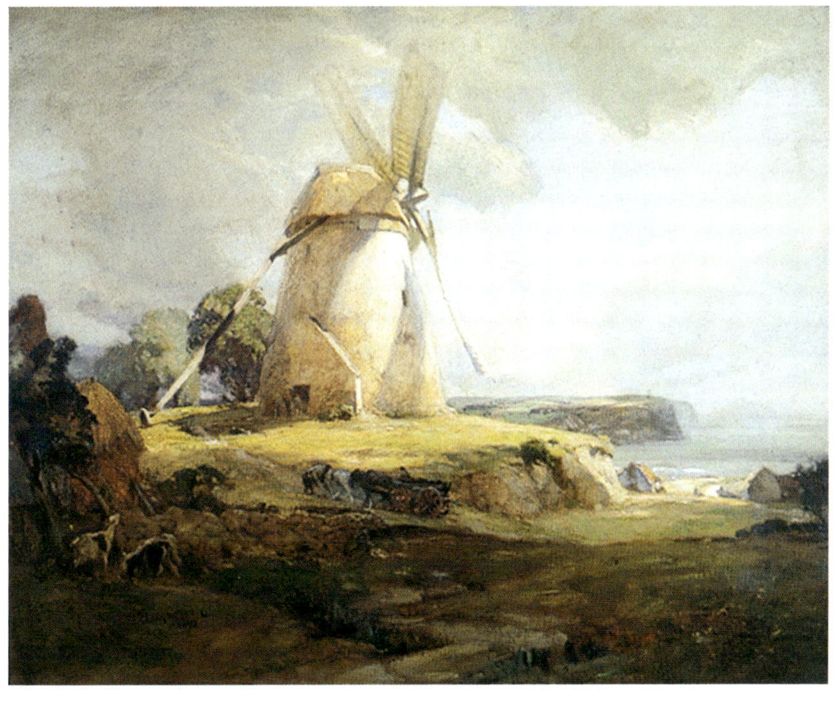

pl. 18 ***The Windmill***
1899 | oil on canvas | 114 x 142 cm

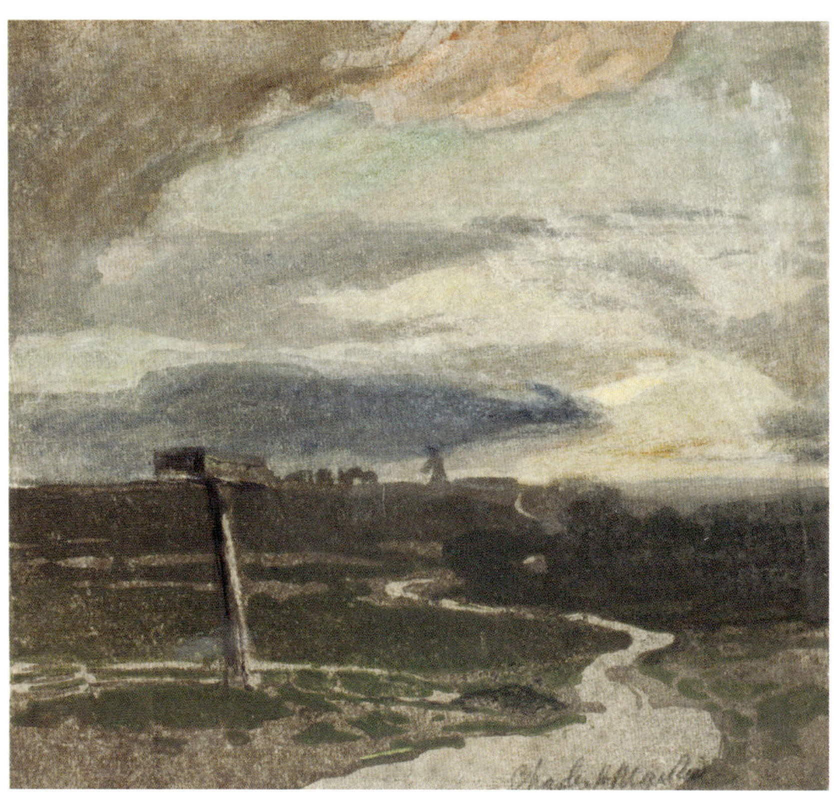

pl.19 *The Finger Post*
coloured woodblock print on paper | 19.8 x 21.5 cm

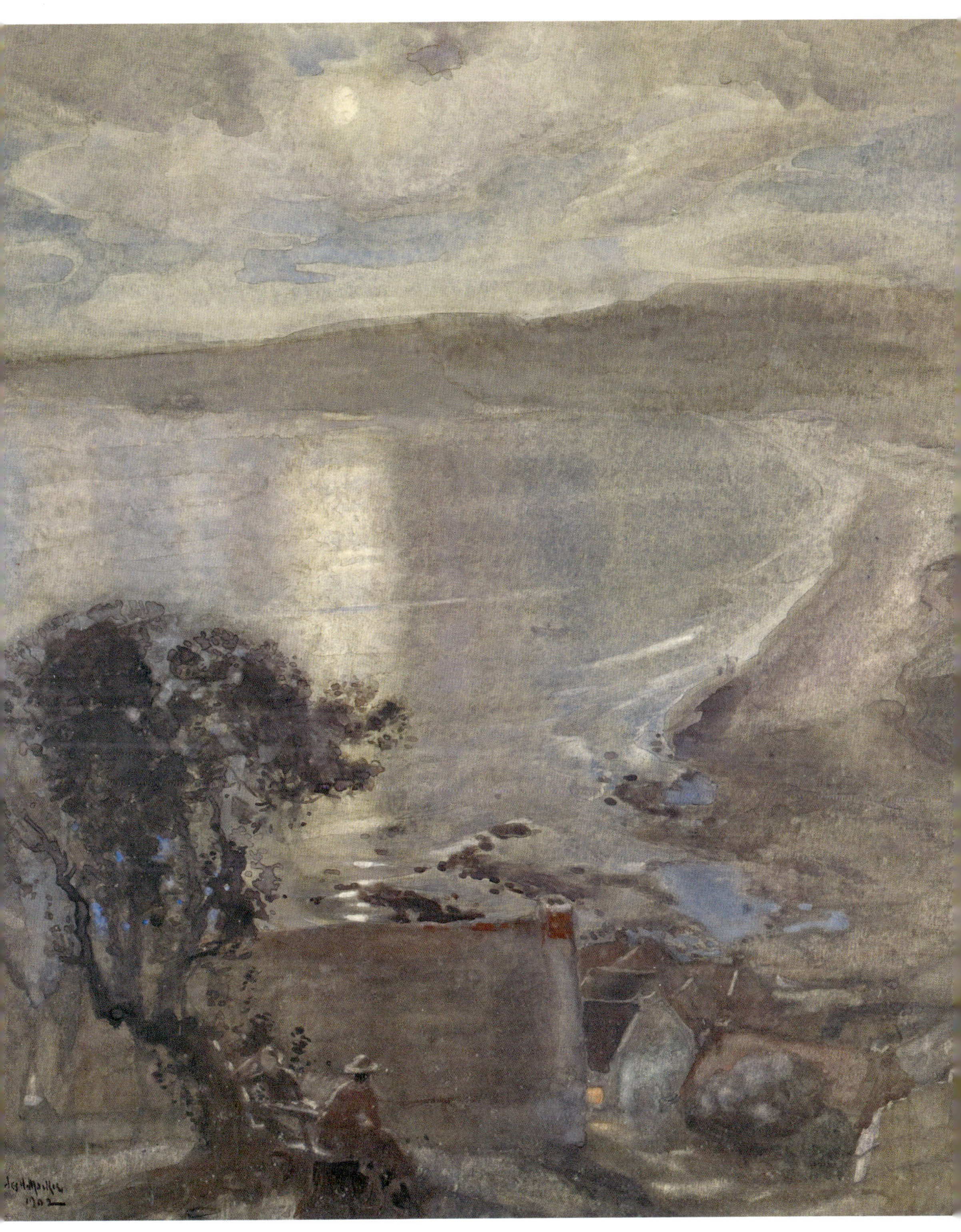

pl.20 *Moonlight on the Bay*
1902 | watercolour on paper | 63 x 56 cm
PRIVATE COLLECTION | PHOTOGRAPH COURTESY THE FINE ART SOCIETY, EDINBURGH

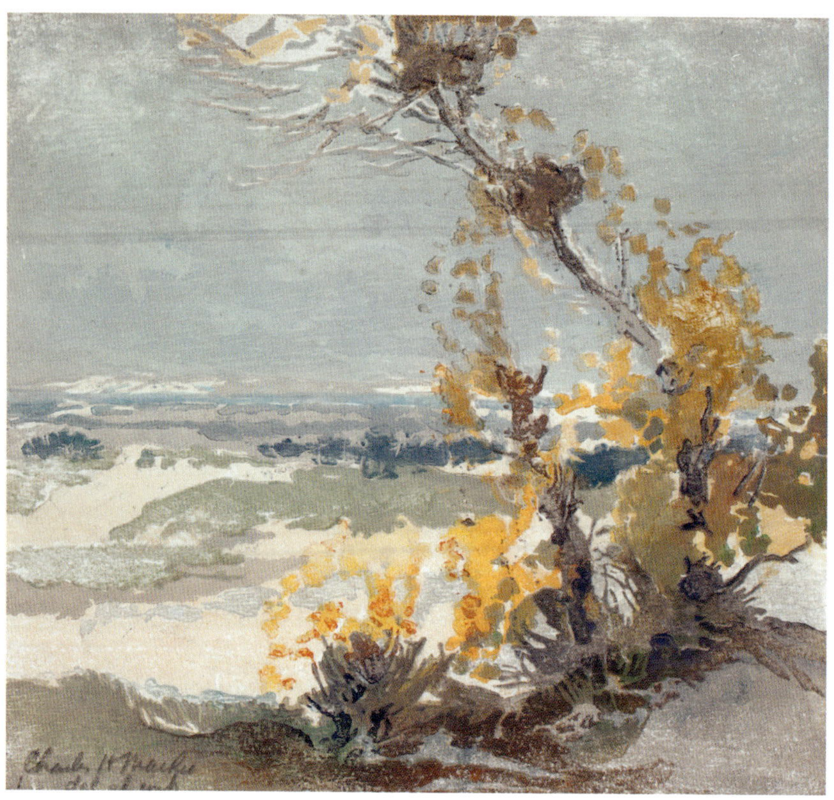

pl. 21 *Picardy Poplars*

1902 | coloured woodblock print on paper | 22.4 x 24.3 cm

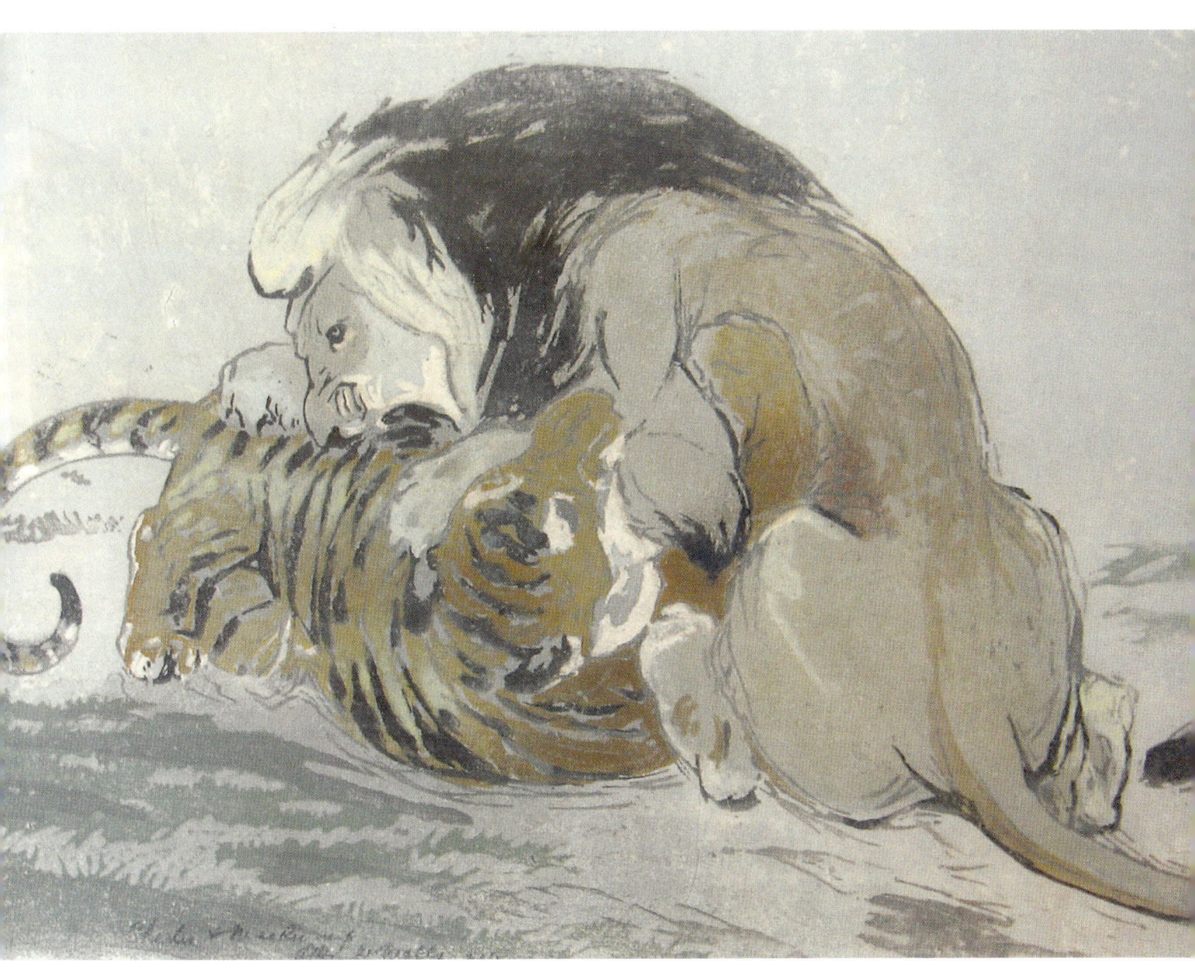

pl.22 *The Combat*
1902 | coloured woodblock print on paper | 42 x 59 cm

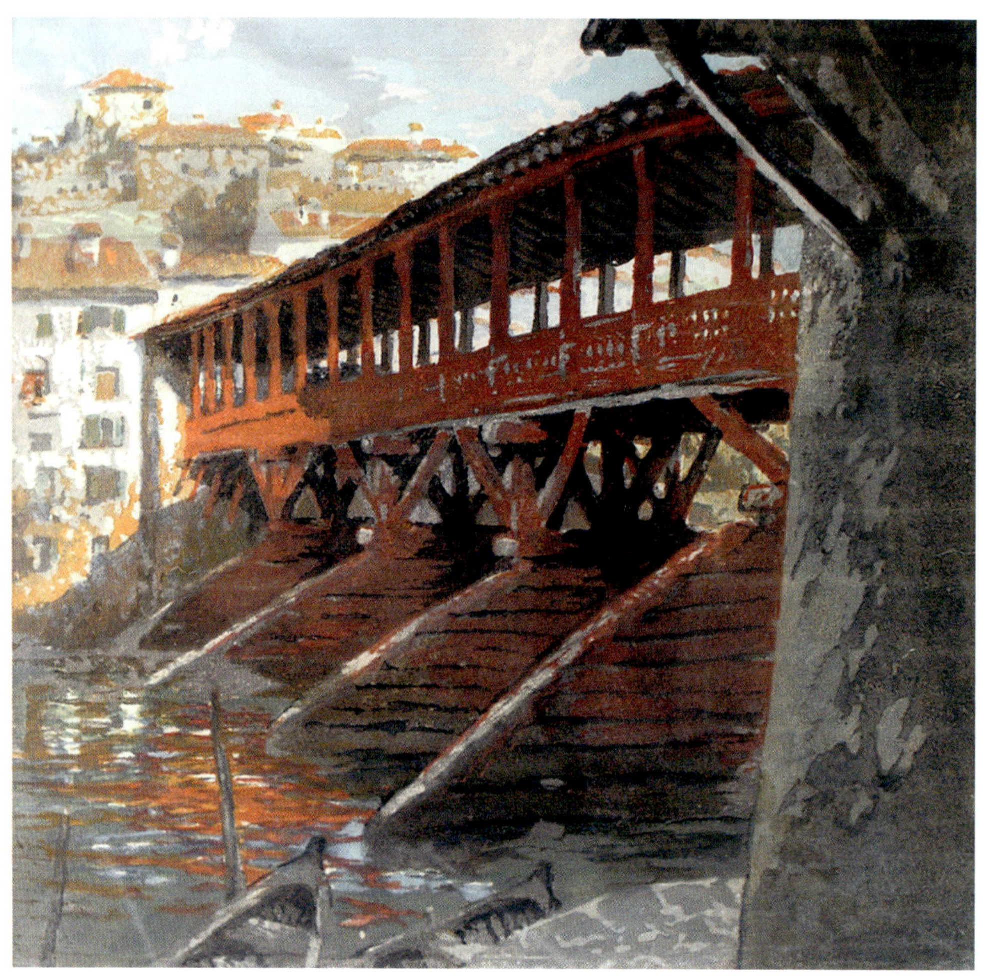

pl. 23 *The Red Bridge at Bassano*
1911/12 | coloured woodblock print on paper | 49 x 52 cm
PRIVATE COLLECTION | PHOTOGRAPH COURTESY BILL MACKIE

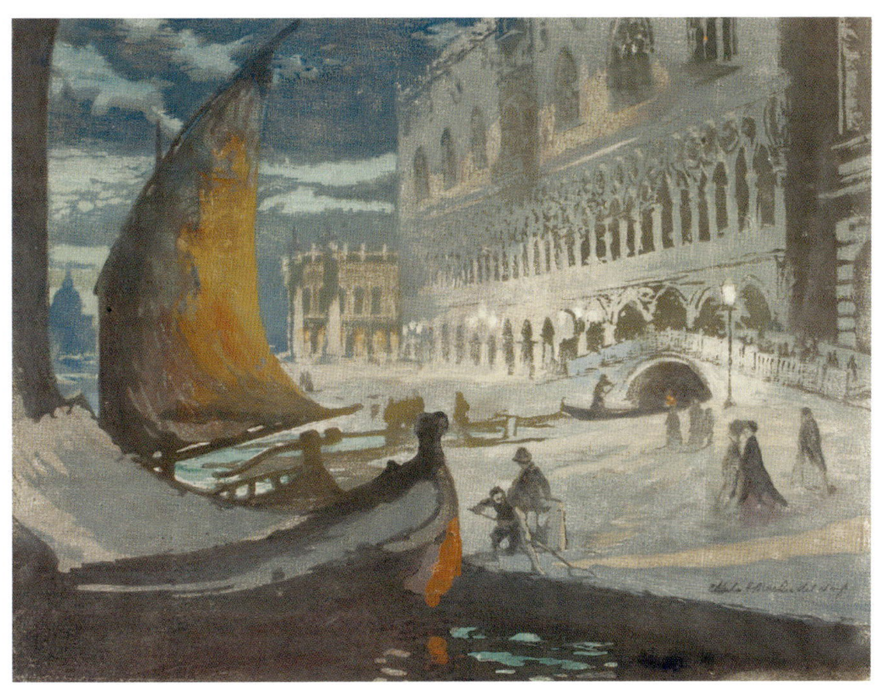

pl. 24 *The Doge's Palace, Venice*
coloured woodblock print on paper | 43.1 x 55.3 cm

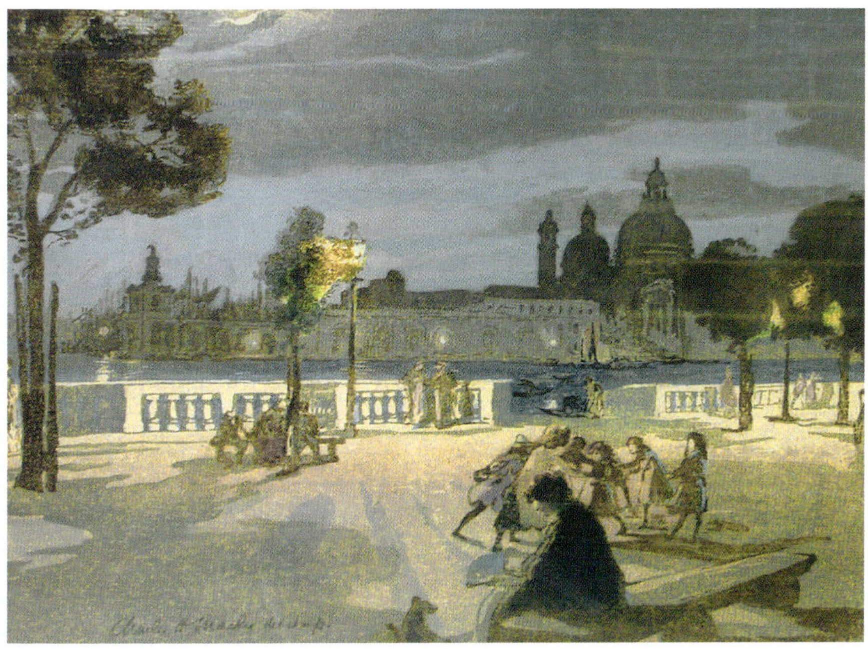

pl. 25 *The Palace Gardens, Venice*
coloured woodblock print on paper | 40 x 55 cm

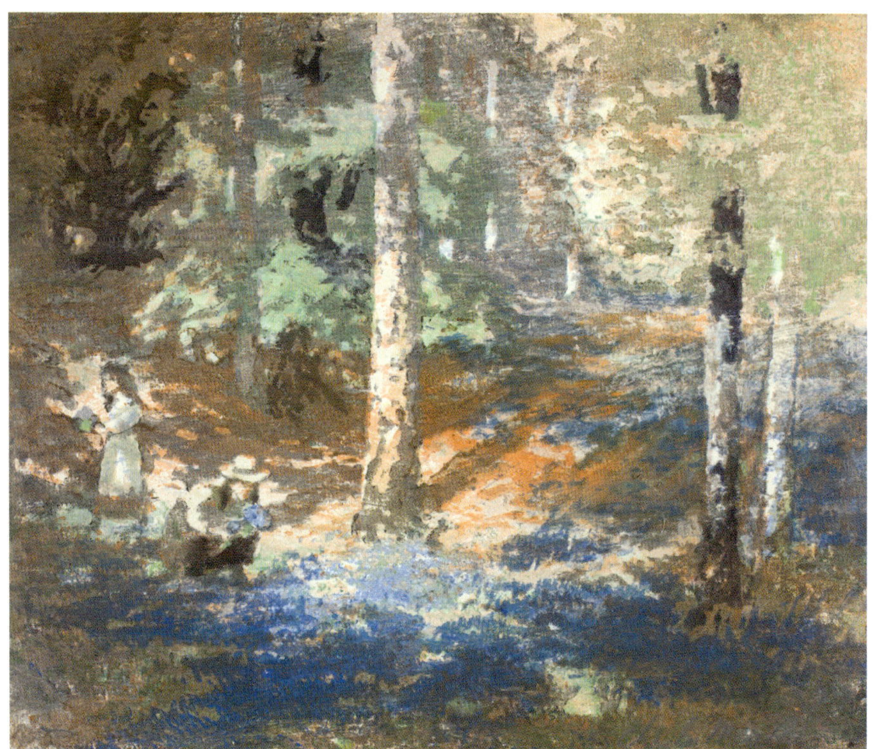

pl. 26 *Wild Hyacinths*
coloured woodblock print on paper | 22.1 x 26.4 cm
COURTESY PERTH MUSEUM AND ART GALLERY, PERTH AND KINROSS COUNCIL

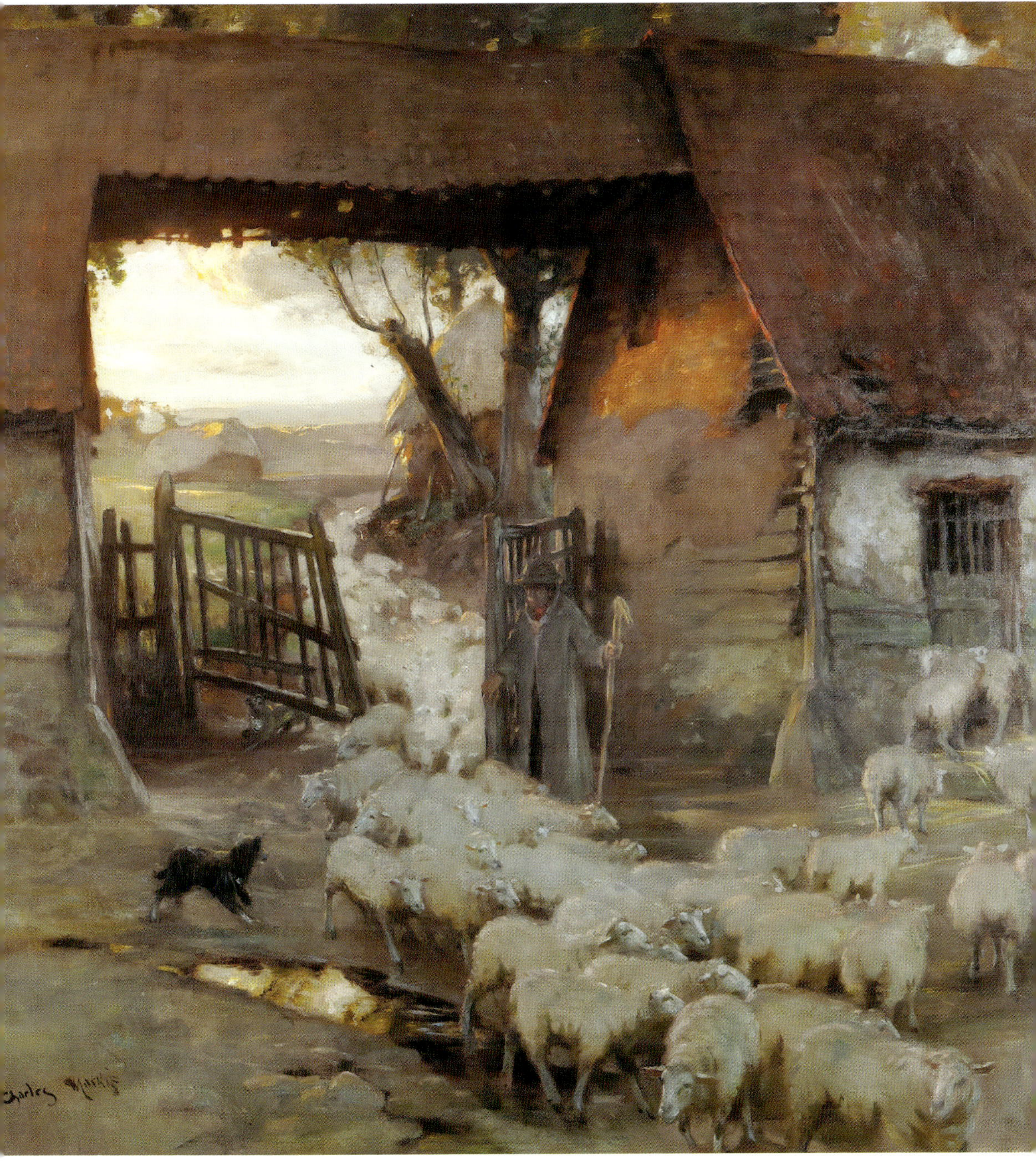

pl. 27 *The Return of the Flock to the Fold*
1907 | oil on canvas | 152.5 x 152.5 cm
PRIVATE COLLECTION | PHOTOGRAPH COURTESY LYON AND TURNBULL, EDINBURGH

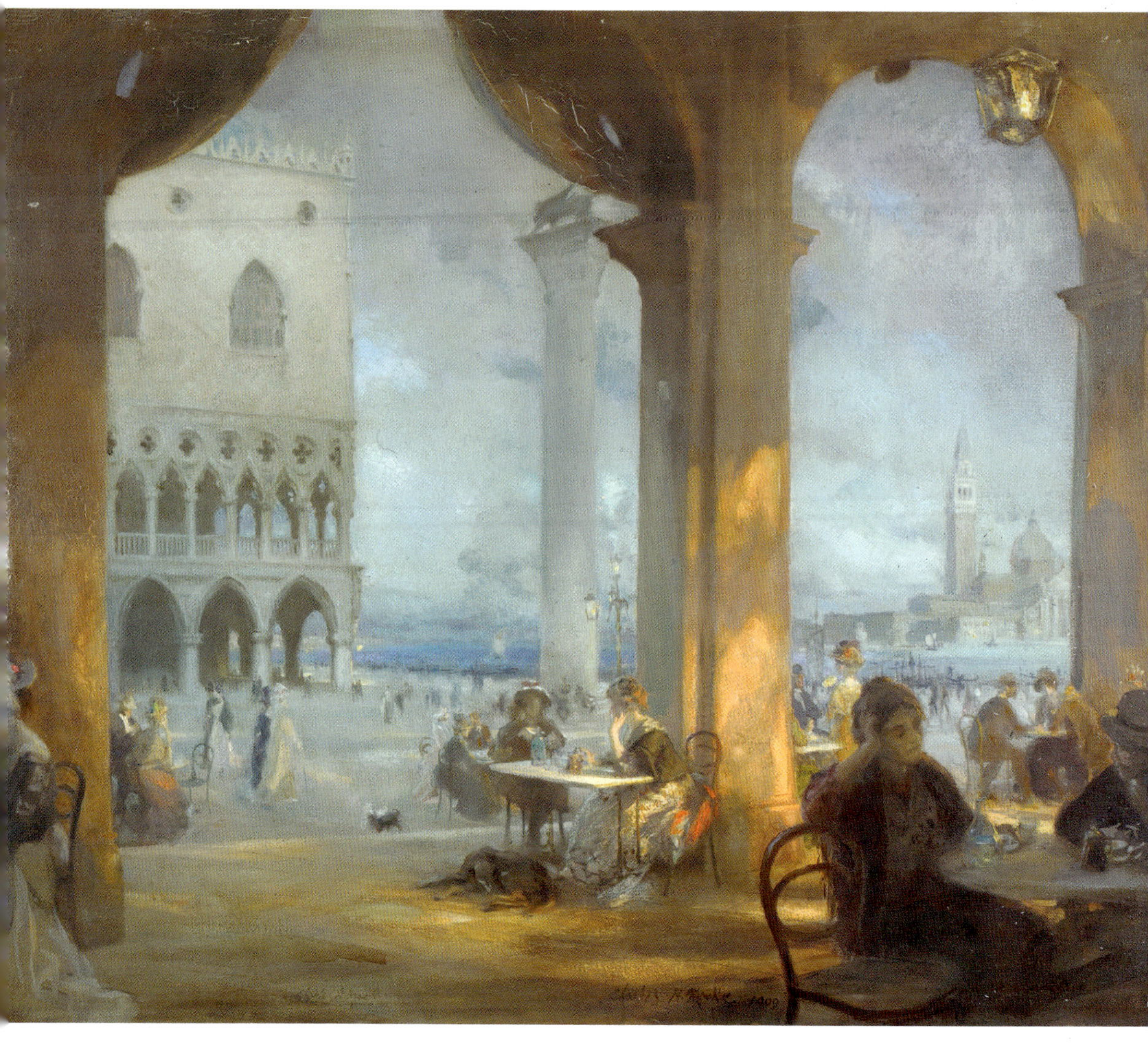

pl. 28 *La Piazzetta, Venice*
1909 | oil on canvas | 100.7 x 125.7 cm
COURTESY CITY ART CENTRE, EDINBURGH MUSEUMS AND GALLERIES

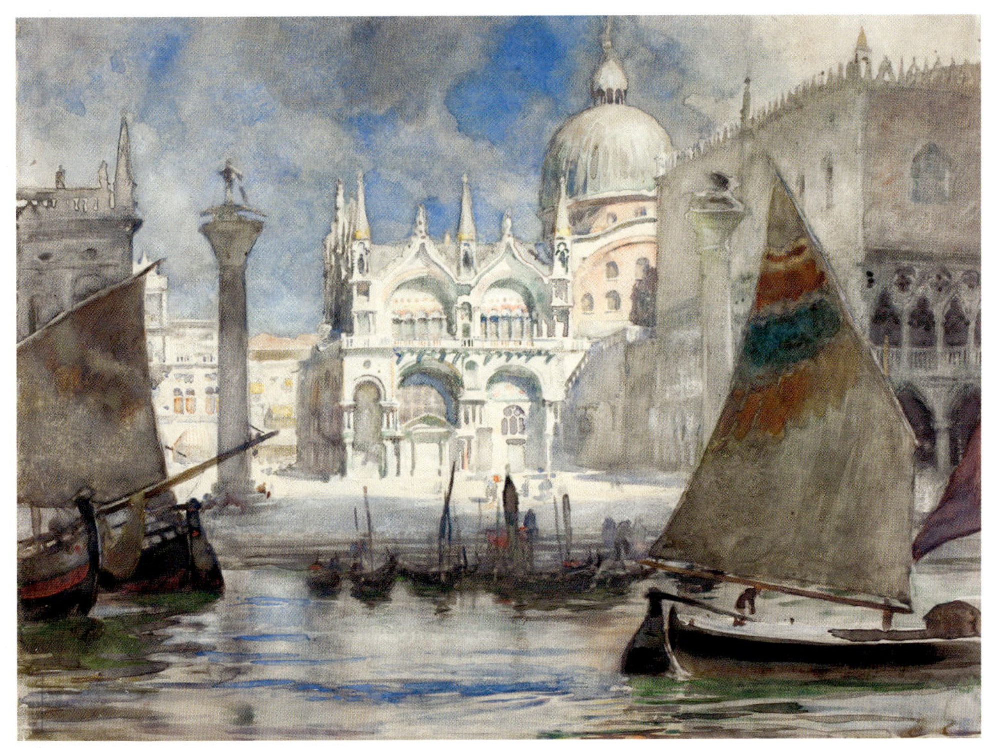

pl. 29 *St. Mark's, Venice*
undated | watercolour on paper | 41.6 x 56.5 cm

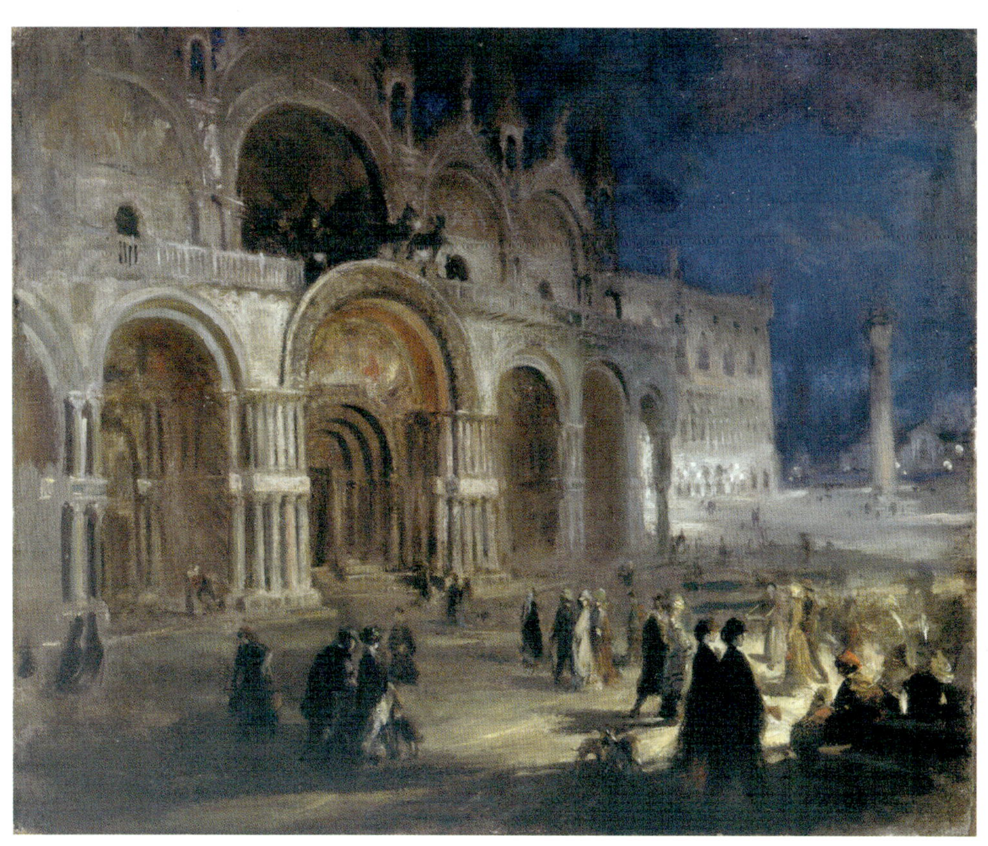

pl. 30 *St. Mark's by Moonlight*
1910/11 | oil on canvas | 65.4 x 78.8 cm
COURTESY ABERDEEN ART GALLERY AND MUSEUMS COLLECTIONS
BEQUEATHED IN 1915 BY MRS MARY MILNE IN MEMORY OF GEORGE COOPER

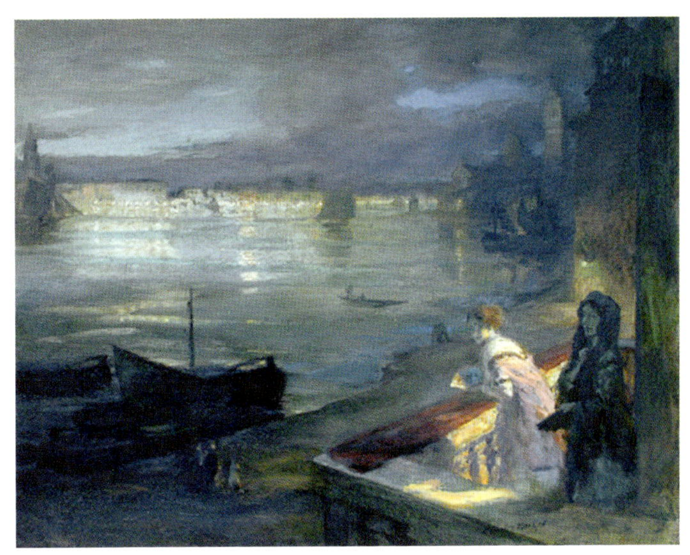

pl. 31 *Evening in Venice*
1909/10 | oil on canvas | 63 x 78 cm

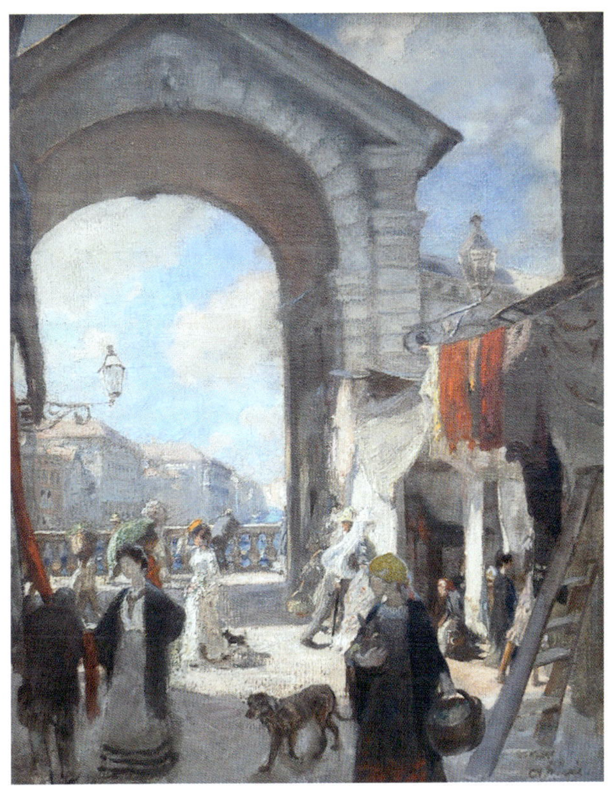

pl. 32 *Arch on the Rialto Bridge, Venice*
c.1910 | oil on canvas | 93 x 73 cm

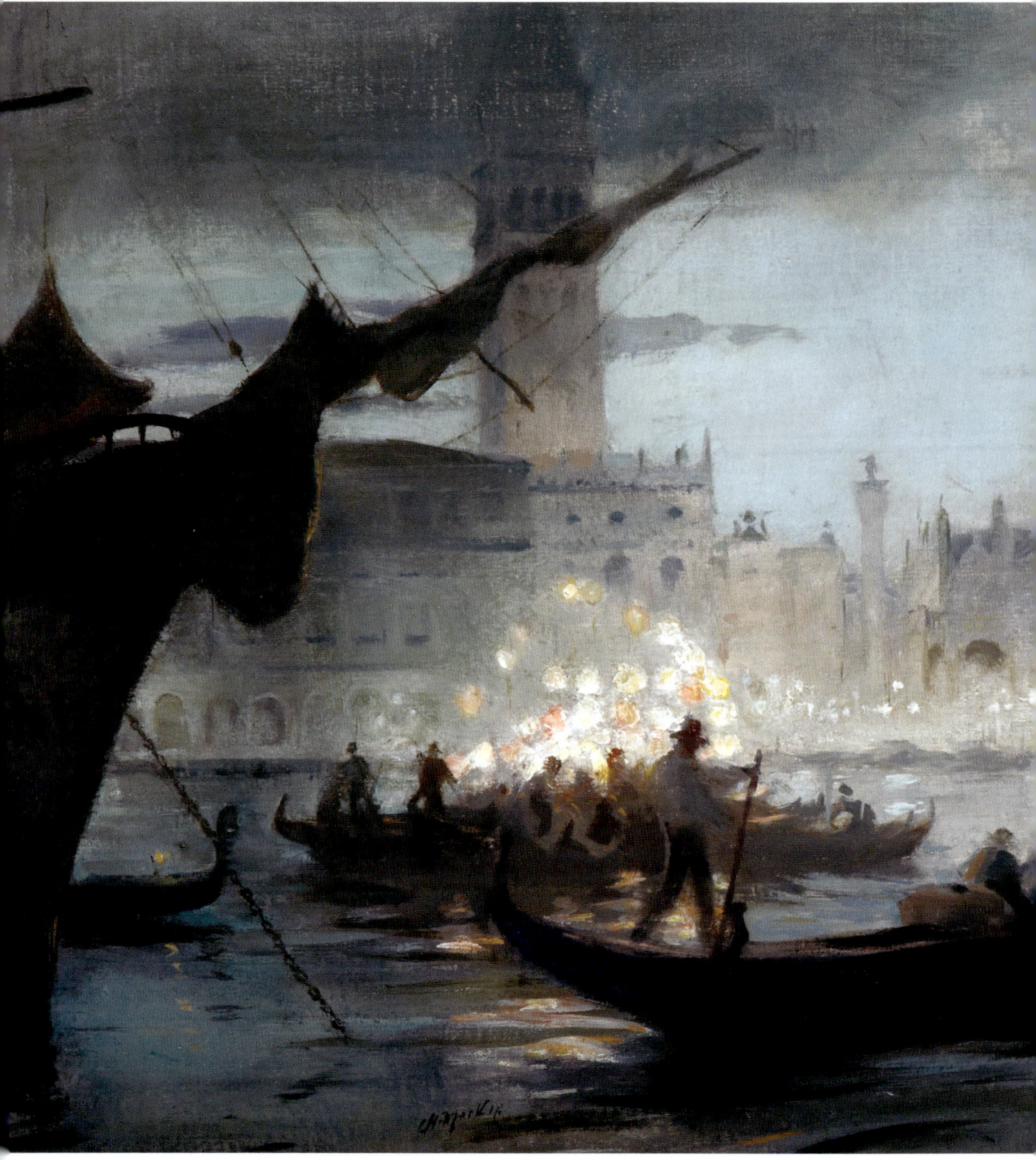

pl. 33 *La Musica Veneziana*
1909 | oil on canvas | 53.3 x 101.6 cm
COURTESY CITY ART CENTRE, EDINBURGH MUSEUMS AND GALLERIES

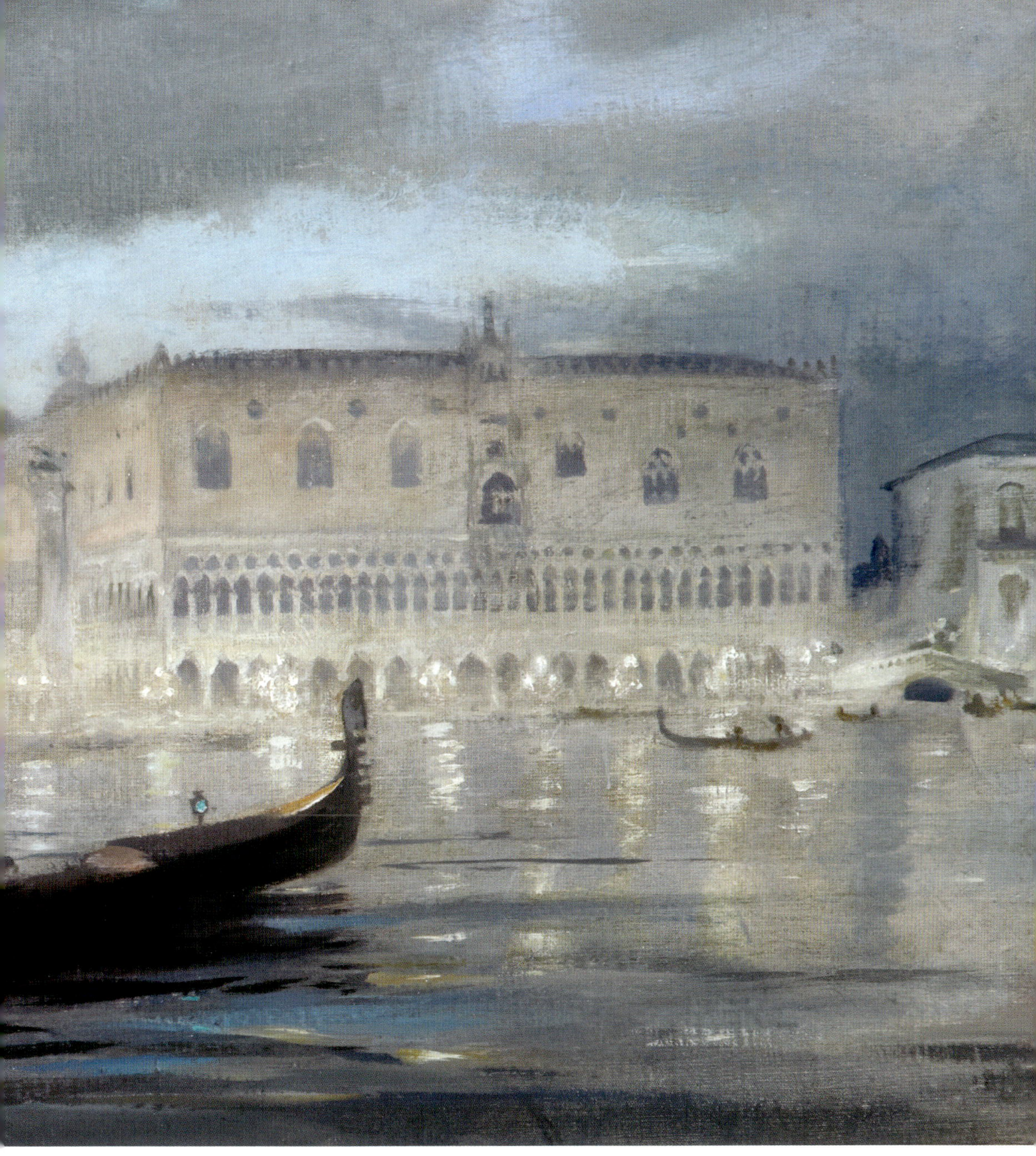

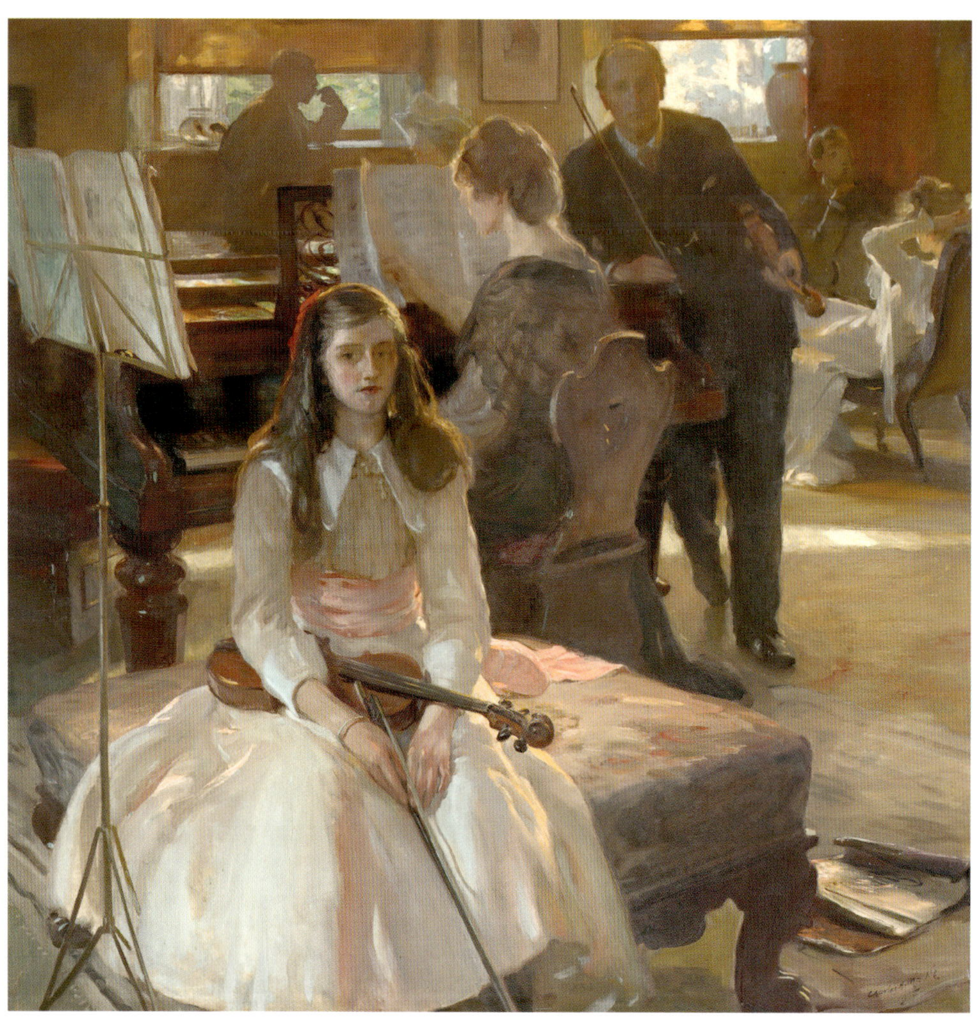

pl. 34 *Musical Moments*
1905 | oil on canvas | 152.5 x 153 cm
NATIONAL GALLERY OF VICTORIA, MELBOURNE (FELTON BEQUEST, 1906, 265-2)

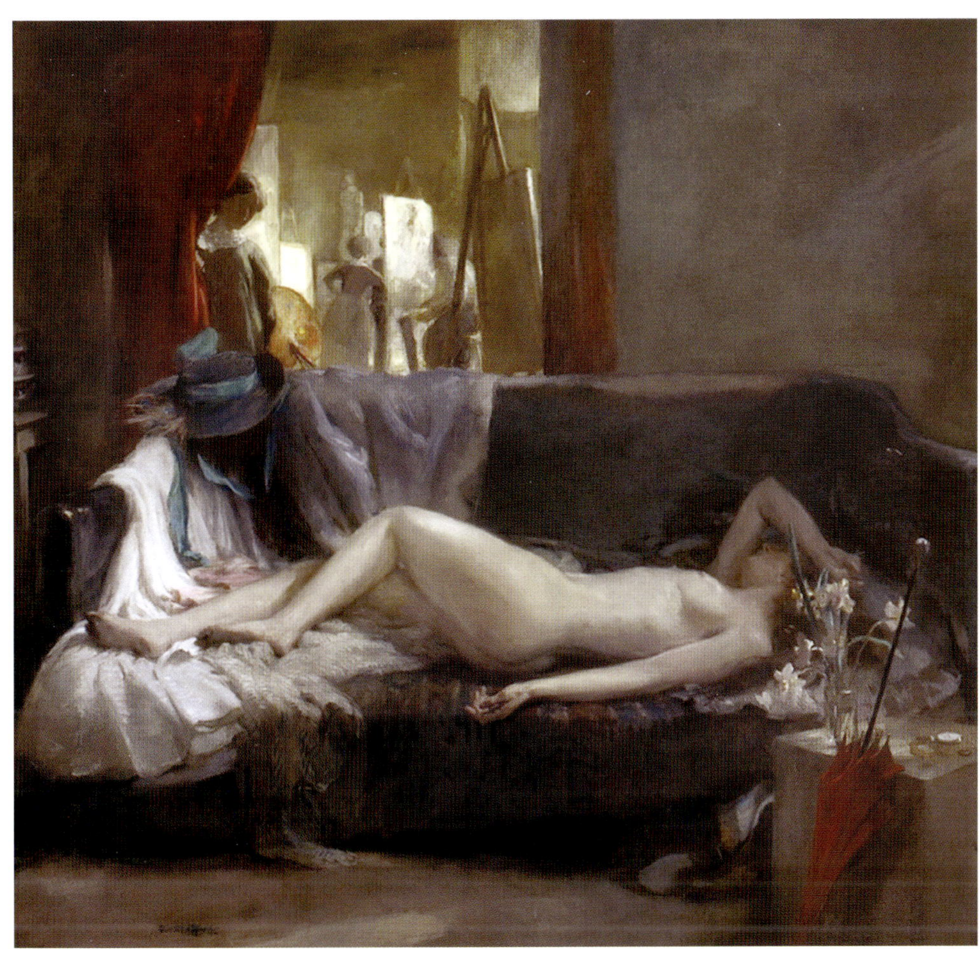

pl.35 *Artis Ancilla*
c.1910 | oil on canvas | 142.2 x 152.4 cm
PRIVATE COLLECTION | PHOTOGRAPH COURTESY PATRICK BOURNE & CO., LONDON

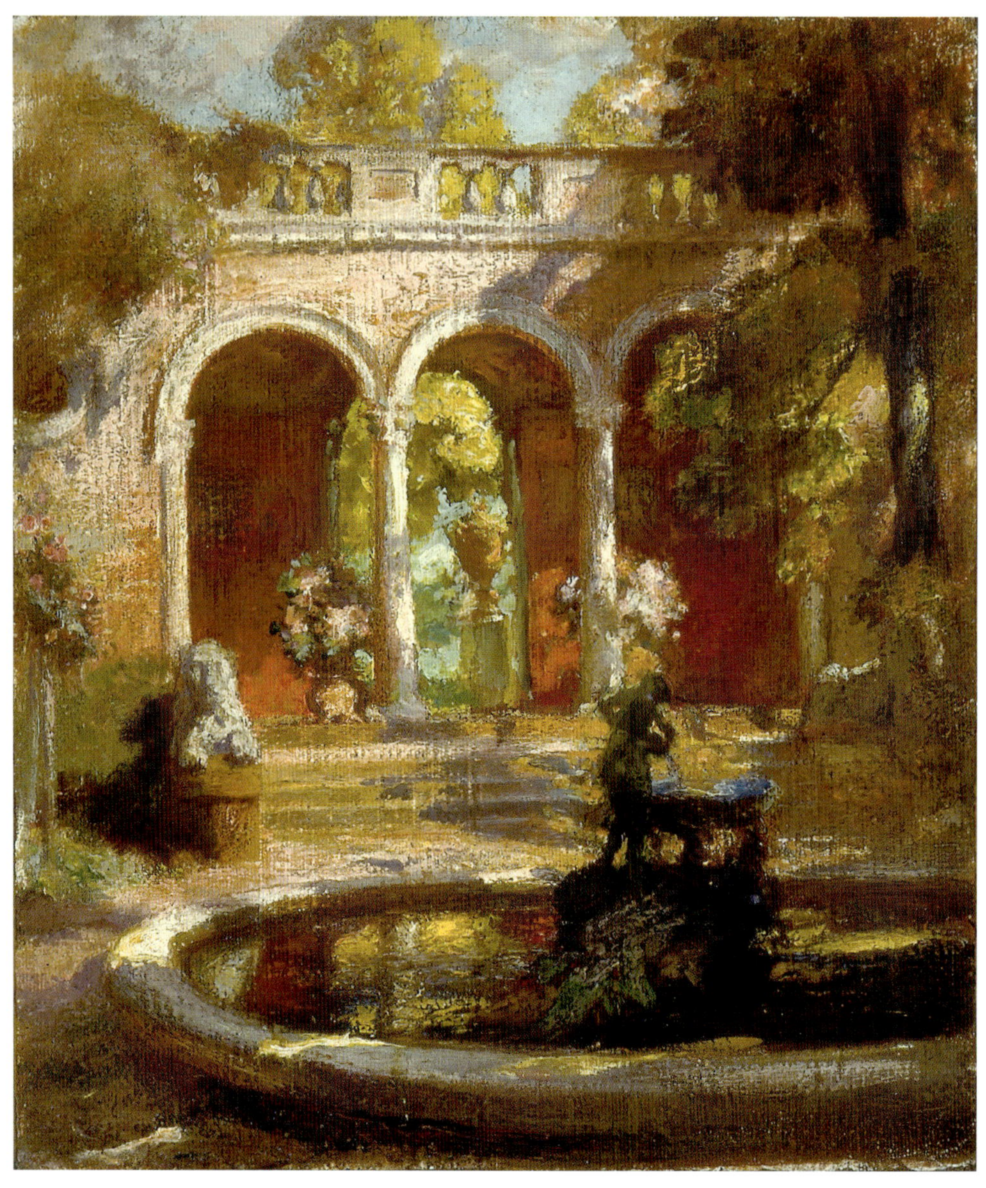

pl. 36 *In the Borghese Gardens*
1913/14 | oil on canvas | 61 x 53.3 cm
COURTESY CITY ART CENTRE, EDINBURGH MUSEUMS AND GALLERIES

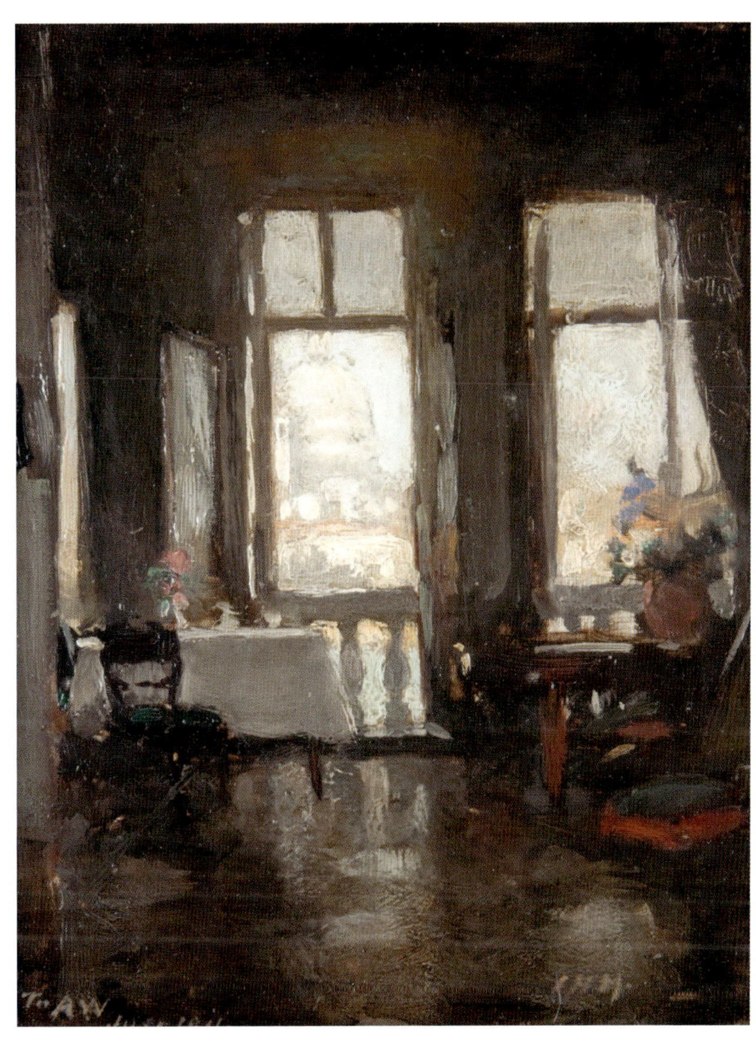

pl. 37 ***An Interior, Venice***
1914 | oil on mahogany panel | 27.1 x 22.2 cm
© THE HUNTERIAN, UNIVERSITY OF GLASGOW 2015

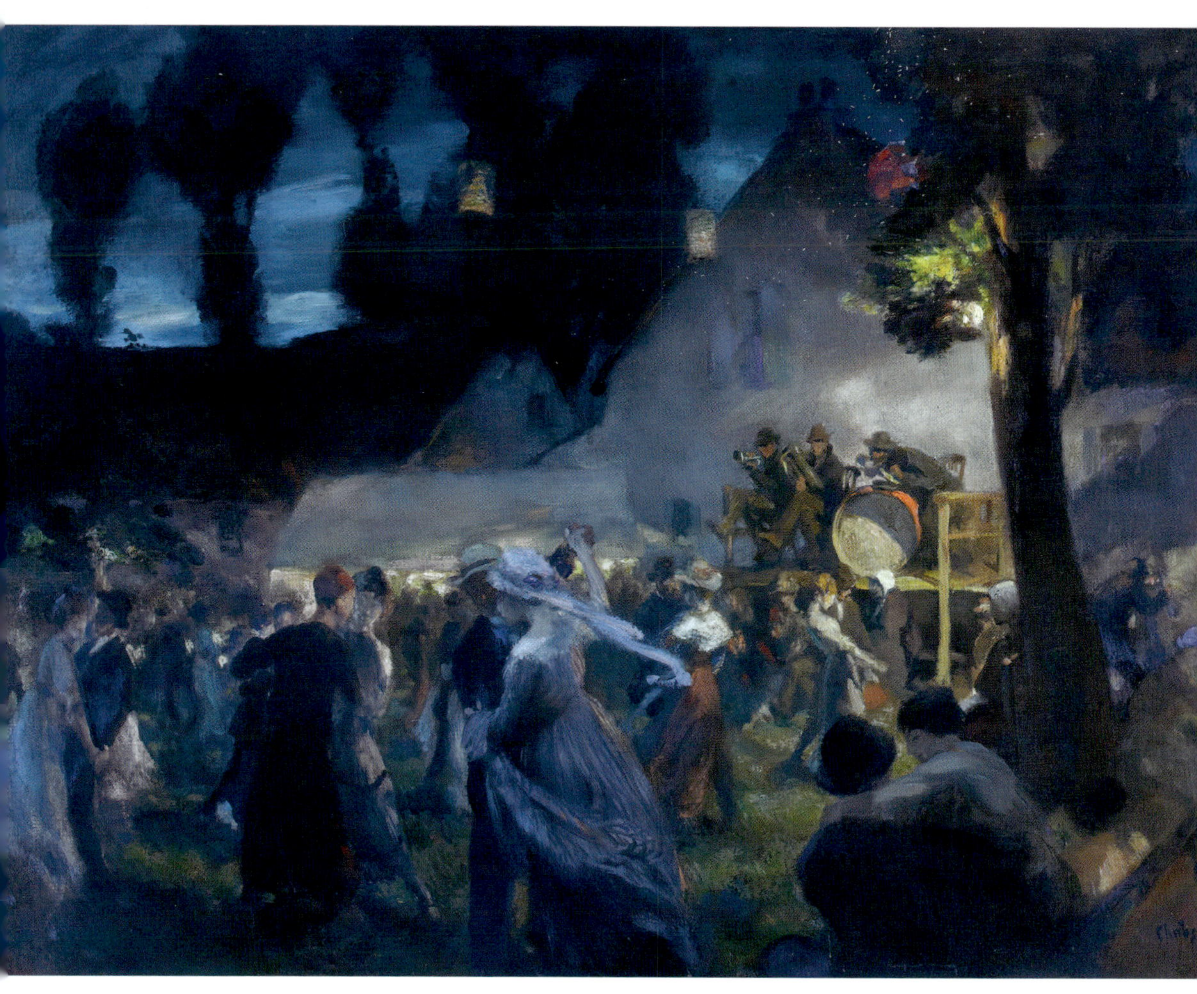

pl. 38 *La Ducasse (La Danse du Village)*
1914/17 | oil on canvas | 81 x 111.3 cm
COURTESY THE ROYAL SCOTTISH ACADEMY OF ART AND ARCHITECTURE

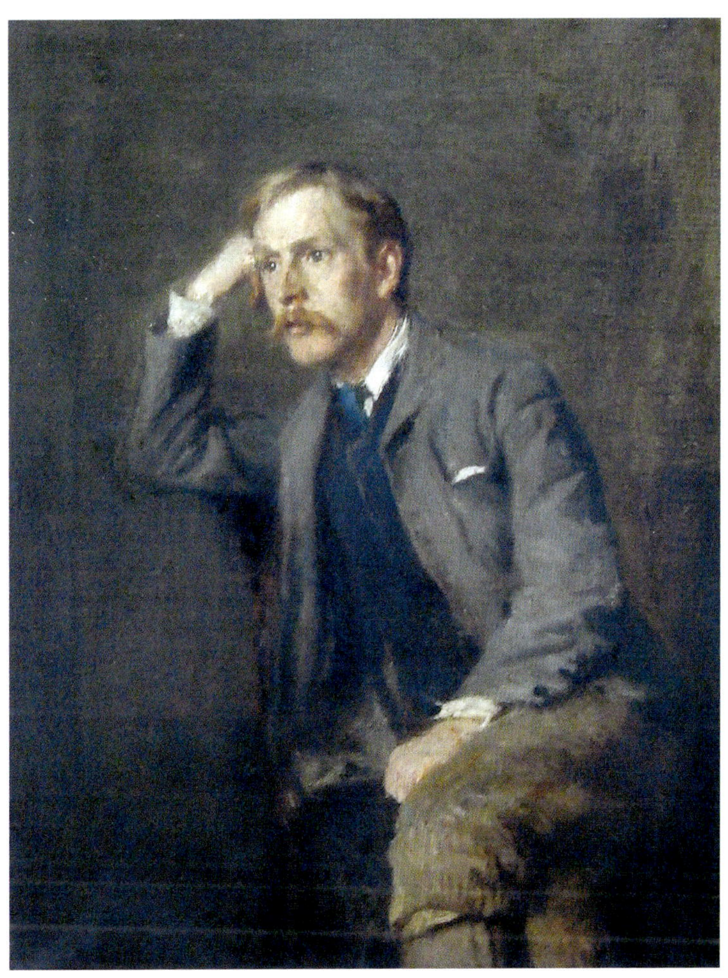

pl. 39 **Sir J. Lawton Wingate** PRSA
Portrait of Charles H. Mackie RSA RSW
c.1900 | oil on canvas | 32 x 24.5 cm
PRIVATE COLLECTION | PHOTOGRAPH COURTESY BILL MACKIE

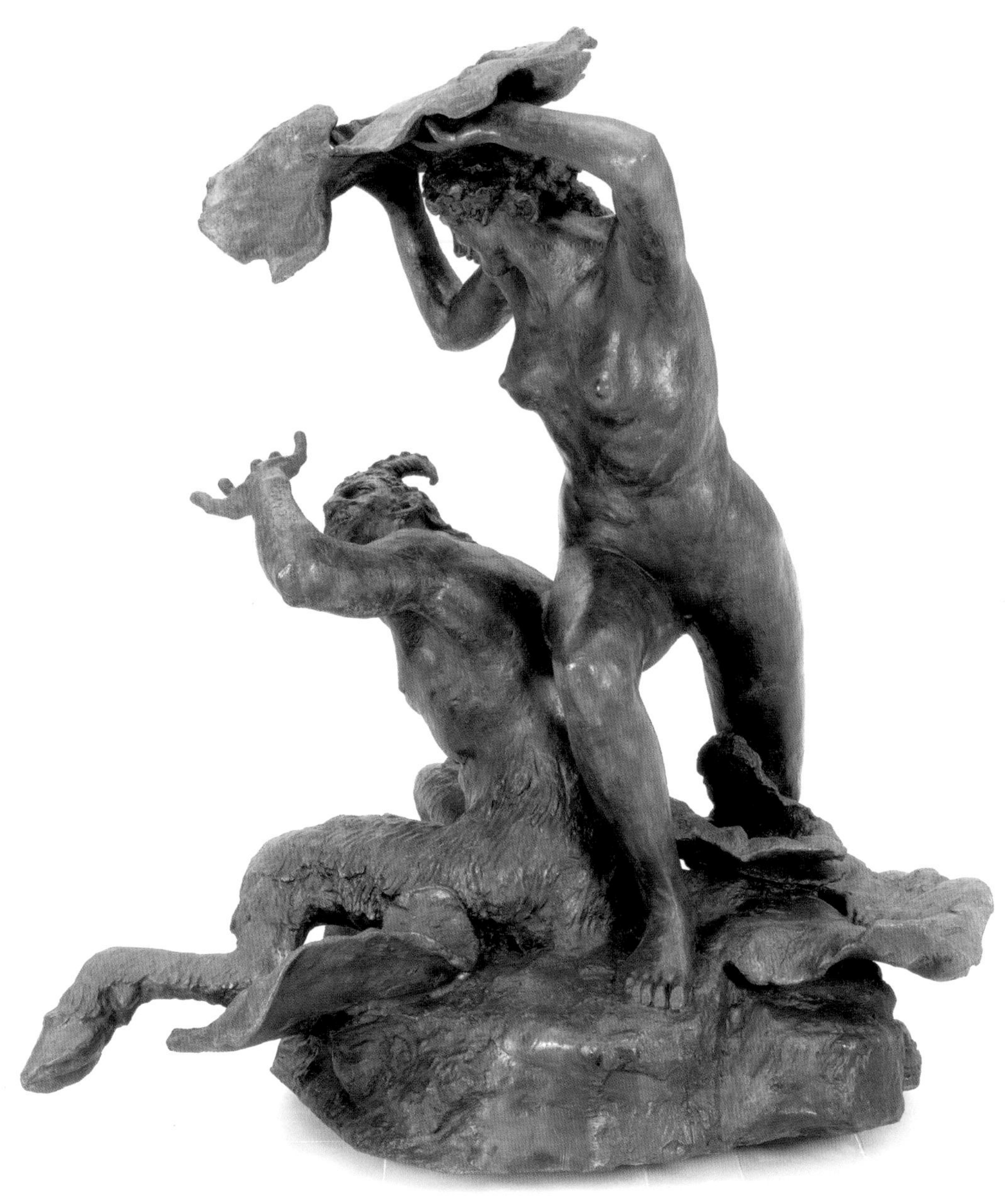

pl. 40 *Nymph and Faun*
1914 | lead sculpture | 180 x 168 x 123.5 cm (life size)
© NATIONAL MUSEUMS SCOTLAND

Nine
Water, wood and Walter

On yet another visit to a gallery basement, occasionally down on my knees or climbing up a ladder, I did not anticipate that I was to come upon one of Charles Mackie's finest creations. Perth is home to the stunning original watercolour of the *Red Bridge of Bassano*, bequeathed to its Museum and Art Gallery by the artist's son, Donald. The exquisite tones and sharpness of depiction were to make it the most reproduced and accessible of his woodblock prints (Pl. 23), but to see the pristine original was to gaze on it through the artist's eyes. Mackie's watercolours would provide him with the source for his prints and the end result would elicit praise from no less an artist than Walter Sickert. That connection would, unfortunately, not be made until 1914, ultimately swept aside by the war, leaving only unanswered questions.

Mackie's admiration for Turner long pre-dated this later link to a London artist. Ever the experimentalist, Turner painted equally in oil and watercolour; a double dexterity that Mackie was also able to master. Watercolours provided a different challenge, since they were less malleable than oils and mistakes were not so easily corrected. Following the sweep of Turner's brush, Mackie's watercolour painting similarly strove for a romantic effect. The portability of the medium appealed, since much ground had sometimes to be covered on foot before paint could be applied to canvas. Many innovations in equipment, materials and moist watercolours in the nineteenth century aided the outdoor artist.[1] For a committed traveller like Mackie, recording these journeys was made easier as a result. There could be an immediate, direct response to the scene or place he encountered, whether in the heat of Spain or the chill of the Yorkshire coast. However, a deft hand was needed given the added challenge of the paint drying quickly in hot climes.

While Mackie was an impressive draughtsman, the watercolour paintings evidence more focus on the overall sensory impact. He was to prove himself particularly adept at capturing light, such as moonlight or the modern effect of artificial illumination. They do show mastery of detail on occasion but it was not his intent to take an artistic photograph. Instead, Mackie sought to convey more in terms of atmosphere, radiance and feeling. Ephemeral moments would be frozen in time through the combined skill of eye and brush. The lighter texture of the watercolour medium would prove ideal for the achievement of such transience. The resulting impression was achieved through the artist's conscious choice of timing, lighting effect and the angle of its impact. Mackie's mastery of watercolour technique testifies to his originality and skill in this field, as well as his determination to hone his craft as an artist.

In his reading he might well have encountered Ruskin's eulogy to watercolour, in its ability to capture subtleties of light, shade and nuances of colour. Ruskin considered it the best means of recording the visual world. It was also a very democratic artistic medium, appealing to amateur as well as professional. Mackie's sister Annie was a gifted amateur watercolourist. Both painted what they encountered on their journeys at home and abroad, and both exhibited regularly at the RSW.

This new venue for exhibiting watercolours in Scotland had opened up for artists in June 1875. The Glasgow birth of what would become the Royal Scottish Society of Painters in Watercolour was in response to the perceived lack of watercolour representation and exhibition in the north. However, the water-colourist in Scotland was well served by the vivid colours of the landscape, whether it be purple heather, azure blue lochs, snow-covered mountains, yellow gorse or white sands. In its unspoiled hinterland, the artist could gaze out over vast areas, populated often only by cheviot sheep. His hands might well be cold but he would be breathing the fresh air of Caledonia. The tradition of water-colour painting was long established south of the border and the Royal Watercolour Society, established in England in 1804, provided an institutional model to follow. Despite setting out fifty-four rules of governance for the new RSW, the founder members in Glasgow were optimistic. Exhibitions, with the associated sales, could only enhance its status, not only in the second city of empire but throughout Scotland and further afield. Royal patronage and endorsement came in 1888 but Mackie, according to their records, does not appear to have exhibited until 1893; his contributions were irregular, although it is worth noting that an 1896 exhibit *The Incoming Tide* would later provide the basis for another woodblock print.

To be elected to the status of RSW and carry the letters after his name, the artist needed the support of two-thirds of the membership, having sent in two drawings for inspection. It was by no means an automatic process – Cadell was rejected twice in the early 1900s. Mackie's election was secured on 26 February 1902 and he would exhibit a total of fifty-two works at the RSW. The one diploma work to survive is *The Ypres Tower, Rye*, currently languishing in the lower reaches of the McManus Gallery in Dundee. When the RSW exhibition was held in Edinburgh in 1909, *The Studio* credited his pictures with 'the certainty of artistic insight'. Mackie also appears to have served on the council from 1909 to 1911, another testimony to his high standing in the eyes of fellow artists. Unfortunately, the RSW minutes for this period no longer exist so it is not possible to gauge the scale of his participation.

Mackie's watercolour paintings covered the breadth of his travels — Whitby, Runswick, Rye, Madrid, Picardy, northern Italy, Rome and Venice. In the catalogue for 1912, *The Red Bridge of Bassano* is cat. 200 and priced at £50. Also known as *Ponte degli Alpini*, the current structure is a modern replacement for the one Mackie painted, since the original fell victim to the ravages of war. However, to walk across it and explore the countryside round Bassano del Grappa is yet another ghostly journey tracing the artist's footsteps.[2] The Italian sun still casts its glow over the small town, though Mackie's ears would not have been assailed by the sound of Vespas and motor cars. It must have been an idyllic spot in 1911. The outbreak of the World War I curtailed these travels, limiting him to north Wales and his native Scotland, with illness later having its own impact after 1917. *The Scotsman* noted in its review of the 1918 RSW exhibition in March that the show was 'certainly the poorer' because he was unrepresented. Loans to the RSW meant that he figured in their catalogues up until 1927 and his surviving watercolours still occasionally emerge from hibernation on to the art market.

Mackie would use several of his watercolours as the basis for an experimental venture in woodblock printing. His prints of the Tay and illustrations for *The Evergreen* in the 1890s had already shown an impressive skill in design and execution. Pushing the boundaries further, he achieved distinction, recognition and uniqueness in both method and end product. There are ten identified woodblock productions, all apparently based on original watercolours, though I have not tracked down the original for *The Finger Post* (Pl. 19). For two of Mackie's themes he was in debt to his brother-in-law William Walls, a celebrated animal painter. The latter had even built his house near Edinburgh Zoo, to be close to his subjects. *The Combat* (Pl. 22) depicts a lion and tiger so engaged and was based on the large oil painting which Walls had just completed. A sketch was duly produced by Walls and Mackie showed his gratitude and appreciation in his return gift. He paid for a life membership of the Zoo for William's son, Hamish. The letter of thanks that he sent to 'My dear Willie' reveals yet again the kindness and solicitude inherent in his character.[3] Having intimated the news of the gift to his nephew, he then adds:

> This is in no way an acknowledgement of kindness to me personally but as recog-
> nising to the full that wonderful public spirit that you invariably show and which
> makes one so proud of you. I know fully that our being kin made it more difficult
> for you and it is perhaps the greatest part of a great honour that you found cause

> enough to surmount that obstacle. In speaking of 'you' I include your wife and I
> hope that the form of recognition will please her too.

One can imagine the whole family feeling a warm glow on receipt of the letter
and gift. A private collection in Edinburgh now contains the original chalk
drawing made by Walls, which enabled Mackie to trace it for his woodblock
stencil; juxtaposed on the wall is the print he made; and a later print which was
made by Anne Mackie. 'After William Walls' is the acknowledgement made on
The Donkey, his other animal print, also in this private collection. It is simple,
touching and effective.

However, Mackie's most favoured sources of inspiration lay in the landscape
of the countries he visited, in particular France and Italy. *The Return of the Flock*
and *Picardy Poplars* (Pl. 21) can be traced to France; Italy could claim *The Red
Bridge at Bassano*, with Venice providing two: *The Ducal Palace* (Pl. 24) and *The
Palace Gardens* (Pl. 25), the latter being purchased by Sickert. The precise locations
for *The Incoming Tide*, *The Finger Post* (Pl. 19) and *Wild Hyacinths* (Pl. 26) have
not been identified, though Galloway is a good candidate for the latter — particularly in the light of Hornel's choice of a similar title for his 1890 oil, *Among the
Wild Hyacinths*. This was deemed 'an impressionist picture' by *The Scotsman* and
was exhibited in the Grosvenor Gallery in London in May of that year. The reviews
all emphasised the vivid colour of the scene and Mackie must have seen it. Indeed,
he might well have walked in that wood with his friend Hornel.

What can be verified is Mackie's method and the approximate timeframe of
his woodblock printing. His black and white prints for *The Evergreen* were
described in Chapter 3, but there was no experimentation with colour at that
point in the mid-1890s, except in the leather cover. In her journal his widow
said that while in Paris they had made a point of buying Japanese woodblock
colour prints. The presence of these in his home would have afforded constant
inspiration. Mackie's passion for this form of art never left him, and he is on
record in February 1901 visiting Glasgow to obtain more examples to add to
his collection. Accompanying Peploe, Mackie visited Alexander Reid's gallery
and exchanged one of his own watercolours for six Japanese prints.[4] The
technique adopted by the Japanese masters such as Hokusai and Hiroshige
involved the primary use of a key block, creating the outline. The colour shapes
were then overprinted within this frame. The forms were simple, the main
composition was off centre and they tended to have large, flat fields of colour.
All this would influence but not determine Mackie's own design.

The 1894 visit to Gauguin might well have shown him the woodcuts on
display in the Rue Vercingétorix studio, since they had not sold well at the Paris
dealer Durand-Ruel's the previous November. He had kept them on permanent
view, possibly in the hope of further sales, after the disappointing reaction to his
first solo show. Though print-making had a long and noble tradition, the

technique stood in need of revival, something which Gauguin helped to pioneer. His experiments, such as *NOA, NOA* would have struck Mackie forcefully as an aggressive attack on the wood, more akin to sculpture that conventional techniques in the medium. Gauguin's final image was not polished but reflected the passion of his personality.

The Nabis had also promoted the print and poster with enthusiasm, as a way of bringing art closer to the people, since their relative cheapness and availability would bring art within the reach of all. Additional impetus would have been provided by Mackie's diligent research on Hornel's behalf for the 1895 lecture on Japan. All these contacts would surely have deepened his interest in the potential of the print medium. Surviving illustrations confirm that he was already a more than competent draughtsman in pen and ink. *The Harbour Bridge*, was praised in *The Studio* in 1901 for its 'extraordinary effectiveness'. A number of etchings and pen-and-ink drawings had also been produced by that time. *Ye Olde Palette* is the earliest example, albeit a private gift to a friend in 1883. An etching of his father-in-law, Provost Walls of Dunfermline had been exhibited in the SSA Exhibition of 1893, so he was certainly *au fait* with the conventional zincography, using metal plates to produce a finely detailed image.

Seeds had been sown and a commission in 1900 to supply the illustrations (and cover) for the book *Greeks and Persians* led to further rumination on technique and process. The author was the Mackies' friend Elizabeth Pagan, a later secretary of the Arts and Crafts Club in Edinburgh, so her choice of illustrator was more than just fortuitous. The cover records Mackie as 'Inventor' and hints at his trial techniques, which did succeed. Reviewing in *The Studio*, the critic enthused:

> The main interest of the prints lies in the technically excellent results obtained ...
> the work is impressed from blocks cut by the artist himself, the said blocks being
> of materials other than wood. The effects achieved are quite unique.[5]

There is also a tantalizing reference to a 'new method of hand printing ... some remarkable examples of polychromatic work'. They were described in a later review as 'Mr Mackie's block-print caprices in the manner of Greek vases'; he continued to exhibit them up to 1914.[6] Perhaps Mackie's pride in the initial results had led to that gift of the book itself to Hornel, as mentioned in Chapter 1. The real leap forward was to come when he moved away from metal plates and worked with woodblocks. Printmaking held considerable allure for the professional artist. By their very nature, prints were multiple in number, so they could ensure a steadier income than one-off expensive oil paintings. This is one area where we know in detail how Mackie executed his work, since we have access to his own description of his *modus operandi*. This can be found in an article by Malcolm Salaman in *The Studio*.[7] Having praised his 'interesting individuality', Salaman stated that the wood of choice was oak, with colours being an emulsion, containing a minute quantity of oil. What was considered most impressive was his independent approach to the act of creation and his dispensing with the usual black key block. This was the point at which the reviewer let the artist speak for himself in detail:

> I am so profoundly impressed with the inability of the Western artist to rival the Eastern colour-printer in the use of suggestion of tone along with a key block, that I have discarded the key block entirely, and I rely for my effects on colour-shapes carefully juxtaposed. I use seven or eight oak blocks for each print, and do not limit myself as to the number of times I may lay the print on each block. Briefly, I might describe it as an emotional use of the printing-press, different from painting only in block shapes being used instead of brush marks.

This was not a process that had emerged overnight and his remarks revealed his determination to achieve a painterly outcome. Imagination, deft use of colour and careful manipulation would all ultimately produce a distinctive picture. Mind and matter had to be combined in a way that certainly must have appealed to the rational side of his nature as an artist. This is clearly explained at the end of the extract, confirming that this journey had been a long one:

> One thing that has particularly struck me in this work, in which I have been experimenting for about fifteen years, is the capital exercise it affords of the picture-making faculty, since one sees one's picture grow to completion in such a logical way. No more perfect exercise, in fact, could be devised for educating the logical side of an artist, for one has to plan the whole result from the beginning, when one chooses one's forces and sequences of the block colour-shapes, while throughout the printing one has to be constantly on the alert as in brush-painting, perhaps even more so, as any error in tone is irremediable.

The stakes were high with such an inbuilt risk of error and yet his persistence would pay dividends. *The Red Bridge of Bassano* proved that the combination of artist's eye, technical skill and patience could produce a masterpiece. Comparing the original watercolour composition with the final print, one can detect deliberate alterations, simplification and intensification of colour. Clarity of image and visual impact were thus both attained in the final vision he had for his print.

All of Mackie's original woodblocks were destroyed (possibly when the widow and son moved to Blairgowrie in 1946) but the British Museum owns some of his proofs. The two sets of *Picardy Poplars* were presented to the British Museum by Anne Mackie in the early 1920s. These progress and trial proofs are incomplete but, by laying them out in line, it is possible to see how Mackie built up to his final picture. The method was to start with the drawing of the horizon line across the middle. Colour was introduced by applying the palest of the wash colours, such as pink; different colours would then be applied at each stage, building up to the darker colours such as dark brown or the deep blue of the sky. There is special emphasis on the texture of the sky and definition of detail in the trees by the final stages. Mrs Mackie confirmed my instinctive observations in an undated (possibly 1947, due to its reference to the Edinburgh Festival which began that year) letter written to Australia. Talking of the blocks, she says:

> a different one [was used] for each colour ... the 1st was painted a pale colour all over to give the lights – then each colour on its own block – then different greys to tone any bright colours that needed toning to make a harmonious whole.

The importance of grey tonality had evidently never been forgotten by the friend of Paul Sérusier. The subtle tonal harmonies he achieved are also reminiscent of other French artists such as Bonnard or Vuillard. Colour carried emotional and psychological significance for artist and observer.

An article in *Scribner's Magazine* in February 1914, on the subject of 'Contemporary Engraving on Wood' confirmed that very beautiful results were achieved by Mackie in both colour and tone. The writer made a link to the effect achieved by the watercolourist using washes, but Mackie's end result was deemed to be better in terms of texture and depth. It was due in part to his use of quality wood, whose grain had bettered the result. Given the praise, one has to forgive the American critic William Walton for saying that Mackie was 'one of the most successful of the color-block engravers in England'.[8]

The climb to this pinnacle had been challenging and certain materials had been tried and rejected along the way. After his death, Anne later produced some prints, no doubt to ease her financial worries. Having observed his way of working, she felt sufficiently confident to employ the woodblocks and copy his technique. In his final illness, he might well have explained to her the method of applying the colour and producing the prints. Some of his blocks were definitely used by her in the 1930s, as more Mackie prints came onto the market at that point. This deliberate dilution of the limited edition did not meet with the approval of Annie Mackie, Charles's sister. It appeared to be an illicit undermining of his memory, albeit to aid the family finances. The information provided by the widow and their son Donald does, however, give us an insight into the process, from those who had seen it first-hand. They supply important details not given by the artist himself in the magazine interview.

Initially, they said that he had used thick cork linoleum for his blocks. However, this was found to degrade too quickly, losing the sharpness of outlines under continued pressure. *The Incoming Tide* was one of his earliest prints and was produced in this way. Japanese fine-grained oak became his preferred material for the blocks and specially ordered Japanese vellum for the actual print. As stated earlier, an original watercolour was usually the inspiration for the same-sized print or, in the case of *The Combat*, an oil painting, which then needed a chalk sketch. The outline would then be traced and transferred to celluloid, which furnished the stencil for cutting the blocks. His son Donald compared this to creating a jigsaw puzzle, with each block having the parts cut away that were not to be painted at that stage. Ten was the norm for the number of blocks created. The influence of Japan was also evident in the nature of the paint used. It was an 'emulsion' of Mackie's own devising, mixing a very small amount of oil with the watercolour pigment. According to Donald, sometimes the ingredients included oil of lavender but other oils were very expensive. Ground lapis lazuli was chosen to provide the striking colour for the *Wild Hyacinths* (Pl. 26). Deemed to be the most prized and thereby the most expensive of pigments, the contemporary cost of £10 an ounce was a major investment for any artist. Each block would be coloured by hand, using a brush or a roller, to arrive at the right impression. Some twenty or thirty such impressions were needed for each print, so it was labour intensive. Approximately forty to fifty numbered prints were possible, though not all would carry his signature with 'del. et imp'. The smallest of errors could ruin the print and a whole day's work would have been wasted. It says much about Mackie's firmness of purpose and resolve, working in such a medium of high risk and hard graft. Each is an individual work of art and Mackie's uniqueness in this field was recognized by a wide range of his contemporaries. It had been a conscious move from painter to *peintre-graveur* (painter-printmaker).

However, membership of the Society of Graver-Printers in Colour was not open to Mackie since he did not cut all the blocks himself. As an act of generosity he had rescued a promising artist from the slums and employed him in this task. It was to prove a controversial choice. Hugh Munro (1873-1928) would later go on to become the art critic of *The Glasgow Herald*. However, this mantle of respectability arrived after earlier notoriety. Scandal was occasioned by his marriage in 1916 to the niece of the Earl of Minto, Mabel Victoria Elliott. The judgement of society was that the social gulf was too wide, despite both parties being of mature years, since she was thirty-one and he forty-four. After Munro's death, she remarried the next year. Her second husband was one of Mackie's old confrères, W.S. MacGeorge. This probably accounts for her Mackie bequests to Perth Museum and Art Gallery on her death in 1960. They include an unusual small lithograph by Munro entitled *The Bridge of Sighs*. It is technically proficient but with none of the colour skill of the master. Mackie himself had never reproduced his prize-winning oil painting on the same subject as a print.

However, the SGPIC did invite Mackie to exhibit with them, since they deemed his methodology unique. His very unorthodox approach had produced a highly individual, impressionistic type of print which had attracted attention. In 1910 at their first exhibition, the prints chosen were *The Finger Post*, *The Return of the Flock*, and *The Palace Gardens, Venice*. In 1911, only one was exhibited — *The*

Ducal Palace, Venice. In 1912, he returned to an earlier composition, *The Incoming Tide*. Two of the original illustrations from *Greeks and Persians* provided *Xerxes and the Hellespont* and *Themistocles and the Delphic Oracle* for the 1914 exhibition. In addition, his work won him entry to the Louvre, where he exhibited under the auspices of the Société de la Gravure sur Bois originale anglaise. A veritable cornucopia was presented for the eyes of Parisians in this 1912 show, including six works from Mackie: *Le Palais Ducal à Venise*; *Le Jardin du Palais, Venise*; *La Marée montante*; *Le Retour du Troupeau*; *Peupliers de Picardie*; and *Le Poteau indicateur*. It was a sign of his standing in this field that he figured in the Goupil Catalogues for 1910, 1911 and 1912. Included in the 1910 entries were *Return of the Flock*, selling at 160 francs (equivalent to six guineas at the time), and *Picardy Poplars*, selling for 105 francs (four guineas). Both were limited to fifty signed copies. Handwritten comments by his son provided more detail on these, since he identified the flock's farm entrance as being near Lefaux, sketched as the basis for the larger oil of the same name. The poplars were located on the outskirts of Étaples. Mackie's location in the catalogue also had symbolic significance, in more ways than one. The entries were next to Lucien Pissarro, whose woodcuts in the 1890s had certainly impressed Mackie and influenced his style. His prints figured in a number of exhibitions at home as well, including the Liverpool Autumn Exhibitions of 1916 and 1919. The Walker Art Gallery bought *The Public Gardens, Venice* in 1911 for eight guineas and Perth Museum and Art Gallery acquired the other prints by bequest.

Salaman's article referred to above also contained a colour illustration of *The Palace Gardens, Venice* (Pl. 25). This 'sumptuous pictorial print' was noted as the property of Sickert, an artist who was well-acquainted with Venice himself. Anne Mackie made a later biro addition to her original journal which explained the connection. Apparently, Sickert had actually written to Mackie to tell him how much he admired his prints and requested Mackie's permission to write an article for his magazine. The widow's reference is vague and it might have been a request to use Mackie's prints as illustrations. Sickert was interested in the practical techniques of the craft and Mackie's approach stood out as groundbreaking. Both shared a facility for delicate draughtsmanship and an appreciation of careful colour composition. Although she does not provide a name, the magazine might well have been *The New Age*, a weekly publication, to which Sickert was a regular contributor. At the end of 1913, busily engaged in editing an article called *Modern Drawings* he planned to include his own drawings, as well as those of other artists. A complete set of prints was apparently sent to Sickert but his last contribution to the magazine was in June 1914 and no further trace of them has been found. The correspondence between the two artists was disrupted by the outbreak of war in August 1914. When hostilities commenced, Sickert had found himself in Dieppe and never resumed contact with Mackie. The widow never found out whether the article was ever written or whether the exigencies of war had put paid to the publication of the magazine itself. In 1915, the Carfax Gallery in London did publish a set of Sickert prints, including some Venetian scenes, but they terminated his contract in 1918. Sickert directed his energies in the intervening years to helping the war effort by painting Belgian themes.

It is an ironic footnote that this admirer of Mackie's prints found himself in Edinburgh three years after the death of his Scottish contemporary. Invited to give a lecture at the Edinburgh College of Art in January 1923, Sickert's hosts were the SSA. No doubt he discussed printmaking at some stage, since the Principal of Edinburgh College of Art, Frank Morley Fletcher, had published a handbook on the Japanese style of woodcutting and colour printing in September 1916. Since Morley Fletcher was later judged to be one of the most instrumental advocates of the potential of colour woodblock printing, he surely knew of Mackie's pioneering and influential work in the field.

Sickert aside, we are fortunate to possess a fair number of surviving prints from the hands of Mackie. The Venetian scenes are remarkable for their atmosphere, haunting and evocative. Those years of experimentation had borne fruit, built on the firm foundation of his skill as a watercolourist. What he produced was not paralleled by any of his peers. His prints have a quality of luminosity all of their own. Sinuous outlines interplay with shadow and fluidity of colour. Although planned in detail, the final result is impressive for its deceptive fragility and apparent spontaneity. Mastery of technique and painterly vision had been blended with both control and freedom of expression. What we see is singular, idiosyncratic and impressive. Venice was to provide the painting-ground where he would prove that he was both a colourist and an impressionist of distinction.

NOTES

1 Moist watercolours were developed by the English firm Winsor & Newton in the 1830s; they rapidly replaced the dry cakes of colour, as they were more flexible. Portable paintboxes and backpacks were also widely advertised, in response to the demands of the outdoor 'worker-painter'.
2 The original bridge was designed by Andrea Palladio in 1569. When Mackie visited, the town was known as Bassano Veneto and was renamed Bassano del Grappa after World War I, in tribute to the many battles and huge loss of life in the area. There are still many ossuaries dating back to the fierce fighting which took place round Monte Grappa.
3 Walls–Mackie family correspondence, courtesy of Bill Mackie.
4 The visit is mentioned by Frances Fowle in *Van Gogh's Twin: the Scottish Art Dealer Alexander Reid 1854-1928*, (Edinburgh: National Galleries of Scotland, 2010), p. 118.
6 *The Studio*, 1914, vol. 62, p. 65.
7 *The Studio*, 1913, vol. 58, pp. 295-96.
8 *Scribner's Magazine*, Vol. 55, Jan-June 1914, pp. 271-72.

Ten

La Serenissima

The charms of Venice have lured many an artist to paint its stones and people. There is still a magic to be found in the piazzas and canals, where light and colour are the ever-changing backdrop to the majestic buildings. Familiar as he was with the Venetian artist Carpaccio,[1] many of whose works were to be found gracing the walls of the Accademia, Mackie yet found his own way to interpret the well-known scenes when he viewed them himself. In the years before World War I, the Mackie family spent much time in both Italy and France. Venice would provide the coda to these continental travels and to his journey as an impressionist.

Before finally reaching the hallowed cities of Rome and Venice, he honed his craft further in the fields, fairs and farmyards of France. As ardent Francophiles, he and Anne had already spent many summers in Normandy and Picardy. The inspiration for his woodblock print *Picardy Poplars* (Pl. 21) was drawn from its countryside. The exact location of his base near Étaples has not been found but it was known to fellow Scottish artists of the time. In Guy Peploe's book on his grandfather, he mentions an abortive visit by Samuel Peploe in 1907. He and his brother had cycled over there and identified it as a village about eight miles distant from Paris-Plage, but did not give the name. Unfortunately, the artist himself was not at home, having gone away for the day to Boulogne. Mrs Mackie did not even invite them in, so they repaired to the village estaminet and then went home. Peploe put this all down to a case of Edinburgh shyness but others might not have been so generous, since the round trip amounted to at least sixteen miles on bicycle.[2]

Mackie did exhibit an oil entitled *Étaples* at Staithes in 1905, so it was a destination of choice even then. The town itself is located on the River Canche, just behind the more glamorous resort of Le Touquet-Paris-Plage. The review in *The Whitby Gazette* eulogized it as 'a very Whistlerian impression of a well-known French fishing-place. One would like to linger over this work and study the drawing of the sand in the foreground, and the pools of water, which are certainly very masterly in their painting'. Thus, the choice of location might not have been entirely accidental, since friends from these Staithes days could also be found only eight miles distant from Étaples, at Montreuil-sur-Mer. Both Frederick Jackson and Henry Silkstone Hopwood were denizens of the area and both had already travelled extensively in France and Italy, including stays in Venice. (Hopwood made his final home in Edinburgh, dying there in 1916.) These friends also all shared an admiration for the works of Millet and Corot, with their sensitive depictions of nature. The paintings Hopwood and Jackson produced mirror many of the themes tackled by Mackie. One example is *The Last Load*, a large oil exhibited at the RA by Jackson in 1897 and now in the Pannett Art Gallery in Whitby. Mackie produced a watercolour of the same name for the RSW exhibition in 1907 and an oil also bearing the same name is currently in a private collection. A similar, though not identical scene, *The Hay Cart*, can be found in the basement in Perth Museum and Art Gallery.

At this point in his career, it has to be Mackie's art that provides the guide to his life, since he wrote no account. Anne's journal also tells us very little, 'the pastoral life of France caught his imagination.' There would also have been the fresh impetus provided by viewing paintings such as *The Sheepfold, Moonlight*, painted by Millet and shown in the Durand-Ruel Grafton Gallery Impressionist Exhibition in London in 1905. Millet had been drawn to the peasant life in and around the village of Barbizon — hence, the Barbizon School. Mackie would have been well-acquainted with their output. This painting by Millet showed Mackie the painterly potential of these humble (and widely available) animal models. Attracted to the theme before, in early Scottish studies such as *Shepherd bearing a Wounded Ewe* (1886), *The Shepherdess* (1887), *Round the Old Ash Tree* (1890) and *Folding Sheep at Gloaming* (1892), he had achieved major public success by having the latter exhibited at the Royal Academy in London in 1893.

In the more benign environment of France, he returned to this earlier theme to paint *The Return of the Flock to the Fold* (Pl. 27). His son confirmed the location as Lefaux, in the Pas de Calais regions, near Étaples. Signed and dated 1905, it was exhibited at the RSA exhibition of 1907. So pleased was the painter with the outcome that it also supplied the model for one of his woodblock prints of this period. A print which Malcolm Salaman selected as 'my own favourite ... a pastoral scene of engaging originality'.[3] Andrew Carnegie, the industrial magnate of Dunfermline origin, bought both the oil painting and the woodblock print from the artist. For many years they graced Dunfermline Library. Unfortunately, the Carnegie Trust sold the painting at auction in 2014 so it is no longer in public hands. In its day, it was hailed as 'the picture of the year' and other tributes lauded it as 'a fine piece of painting'. The installation of incandescent light in the RSA Galleries the previous year no doubt made it and its fellow exhibits all the more attractive. Since it is no longer accessible to public view, the detailed description provided by *The Scotsman* gives a good insight into its impact when it appeared in the RSA exhibition:

> In the Great Room ... is a large landscape by Mr Charles Mackie which will greatly
> enhance his reputation. It is called The Return of the Flock to the Fold and consti-
> tutes a picture of pastoral life of much charm. It is well-composed. Through a
> lofty arch, in a line of old barns, a flock of sheep press into a farmyard, set in soft
> shadow. An old shepherd in a blue smock holds open a rickety gate, a dog on the
> watch is on the other side, and beyond is a delightful glimpse of a hilly country
> on which fall the warm rays of the setting sun. The sheep are well-studied, and
> with the buildings and landscape, are painted with a dexterous brush.

The flock were also painted returning at midday, in an oil currently in Perth
Museum and Art Gallery, and at a swing gate, as well as safely in the sheep-fold.
This was subject-matter which appealed to that dexterous brush. The other
attraction in France lay in the delightful old towns such as Parthenay, captured
in a small oil also to be found in Perth. That idyllic first pilgrimage had opened
the young couple's eyes to their charms. Now the more mature painter, Mackie
could tackle these townscapes, showing that his talents were not limited to
farmyard animals. One casualty of time, a hasty decision and the dampness of
the Scottish climate was a distinctively different study. Alternatively titled *Ride
to Nowhere* or *Merry-Go-Round*, it had been painted in the fairground at
Étaples. Exhibited at the RSA in 1905, *The Scotsman* had praised it for being
'full of movement and colour'. When the widow was packing up their possessions
in 1946, the unsold painting had deteriorated in condition, having been lodged
next to an outdoor wall. Anne Mackie offered it to the National Gallery of
Scotland, and the director, Stanley Cursiter declined. His explanation:

> large areas of the paint are scaling off ... you may think it would be undesirable
> to present to a permanent collection a picture for which for some reason I do
> not understand is not in a healthy state and might, in a few years, be in such a
> condition as to be unfair to your husband's memory.[4]

Damp and poor storage had evidently done its worst. Anne Mackie then took a
knife and slashed it. In her own words, 'I have always regretted that hasty decision.'
   We can, fortunately, imagine a little of the colour and movement he had
captured. *The Scotsman* saved the day again, by giving us the verbal building
blocks to recreate the image. In the fourth notice for the exhibition, it explained:

> Charles Hodge Mackie's *Ride to Nowhere* is a clever attempt to give an impres-
> sion of colour in movement. The subject is a merry-go-round with gorgeous
> canopy and hues of red and gold, spinning around with juvenile riders on the

wooden horses. It is set in the open air under vivid sunshine with brilliant blue sky, and gazing at it in wonder is a line of village children. Broadly brushed in, the picture shows originality of treatment.

Such an evocative description makes one long for a glimpse of that destroyed original.

The commercial success of his French pastorals, coupled with Torrey's purchase of his Spanish watercolours must have helped fund the longed-for visit to La Serenissima. Possibly he had also acquired Scottish patronage — two names have been mentioned in this regard: Auldjo Jamieson and James Cowan. The latter lived in Murrayfield and often visited Mackie in his studio at Roseburn, nearby. It was within easy walking distance and in his autobiography the patron described a relationship built on friendship as well as artistic respect. Cowan built up an impressive art collection, which included a Manet, many by the Glasgow Boys, Crawhall, Hornel, Henry, Lavery and Walton, as well as East Coast landscapists, such as Wingate. His walls also displayed the rising Colourists such as Cadell, J.D. Fergusson and Peploe. Such were his comfortable circumstances that Cowan could afford to have his portrait painted by Whistler, with whom he was in regular correspondence. Since he sat for over sixty sessions in London, there must have been much to discuss. On Whistler's death in 1903, the portrait was still unfinished but he can be seen, clad in his knickerbocker suit, in the NGS. At the special retrospective exhibition held for Whistler at the RSA, Cowan lent more than fourteen examples of his work. Cowan appreciated Mackie's sense of humour and their correspondence seemingly contained many examples. Unfortunately, the letters testifying to this friendship have disappeared. On the painter's death Cowan took care to return them to his widow who did not preserve them to aid future biographers. However, there is an undated reference in Cowan's autobiography which hints at the painter's excitement on encountering Venetian art *in situ*. He recounts:

> I had the privilege of hearing Charles Mackie expound, in the Venice National Gallery, how his scheme of colour was exemplified in the works of Carpaccio, and I have happy memories of him...[5]

A similar conclusion on the importance of Venice for the painter was reached by the Walls family. Acknowledging the wilderness years when Mackie was perfecting his theory and practice of colour, Hamish Walls thought that:

> the effort certainly paid off when he got to Venice, and he painted some marvellously glowing pictures of that colourful city and its life by day and night.

Venice is still a city that exists to be painted, with its interplay of grandeur and decay, set against the sound of the lapping Adriatic. The colours and shades of light are an ever-shifting backdrop to the public spaces and the ongoing daily life of the citizens. Though tourist-infested in the twenty-first century, Mackie's eyes would have largely seen the Venice we can admire today. The Campanile of San Marco had collapsed (gracefully, it was reported) in 1902, but had been rebuilt by 1912. The only casualty was the caretaker's cat, so Venice carried on as before. The Mistress of the Mediterranean was no longer her own mistress due to decline, war and occupation during the nineteenth century. The Austrians had finally ended its insular isolation in 1846 by building the railway link across the lagoon from Mestre. This is still the easier option, though arriving by sea might have appealed more to the Mackies' romantic instincts. His memories of Turner's portrayals of the city, bathed in golden light, would have fired his imagination many years before. One can only begin to guess what the impact of gazing at the reality must have done for such an ardent colourist. Faced with so many choices for his canvas, whether in the sparkling daytime sunlight or the romantic shadows cast by the gaslight on the piazzas, he worked furiously. Though Anne provides little detail on their time there, she does acknowledge his prodigious work rate:

> There he worked day after day, all through the summer in intense heat when even the Venetians groaned under the burning sun or fled to the mountains, grudging the time he took for a swim at the Lido.

For a man used to the chill north-easterly winds of Edinburgh, it took stamina and dedication. His passion for his art was undimmed and he was driven to paint like never before.

Venice still has a certain quality of light, whether by day or night, that carries a magical softness of its own. Mackie was not the first to be entranced by the intensity of colour and all the vantage points offered for his easel. Views of Venice had been reaching Britain for many years, helping to build the mindset that would allow artists to reach for a new vision. Ruskin's *Stones of Venice* (first published in 1853, in its third edition by 1874) must have been essential reading and whetted artistic appetites. Venice was now within the reach of more ordinary travellers, not just those who could comfortably afford a Grand Tour. Ruskin did go on to write a handbook to the city, as well as a guide to the pictures in the Accademia Gallery. Perhaps Mackie made use of these? With more than 170 canals, stretching for over sixty-two miles, there was peace and tranquillity abounding. The Grand Canal's two miles were studded with palaces, all appearing to date from the twelfth and thirteenth century, though some had only just been renovated to match the Gothic revival style. He would have been able to study the latest construction — a new fish market had been built on the Rialto in 1907.

Looking at his work from Venice there is passion, fire and glory in colour. There is also a numinous quality in the night scenes, where shadows cast by the lamps are captured with a delicate touch. These paintings integrate people with the backdrop of the city in a way that melds them with their piazzas, balconies and bridges. Whistler suggested that the city and its citizens existed solely to provide the artist with material for his art. Turner had also found limitless inspiration. Their admirer and disciple, Charles Mackie, would flourish here as never before. Any catalogue of his Venetian works would be frustrated by the number that are in inaccessible private hands as his output in the years 1908-12 was impressive. They comprise a wide variety of themes, with the usual grand vistas sitting side by side with more mundane realities, such as depicted in *Woman on a Bridge*, *Workshop in Venice*, *A Gondola Maker's Yard* and lastly *Band Night in Venice*. Set in one of the piazzas, the Campanile formed a striking backdrop to that lively night scene. Not surprisingly, *The Scotsman* deemed it 'a lovely work', noting 'its stately architecture and luminous blue night', in its 1912 review of the RSA exhibition.

Mackie's patron, James Cowan, certainly owned some of the choicest works but one of his former possessions has found its way, via the London art market, to the Mackie home in Melbourne. An impressive oil, it is entitled *Evening in Venice* (Pl. 31). First shown at the RSA in 1912, Cowan had lent it to their 1920 exhibition, so others could share in its pleasures. Its fine rendering, drawn from a shadowed background, highlighted what *The Edinburgh Evening News* praised as:

> a rich symphony of pulsing colour, from brilliant yellows to cool and reposeful blues deftly correlated.

Santa Maria del Salute was also in the Cowan collection and it, like his acclaimed *Bridge of Sighs*, were to be casualties of financial stringency when he was forced to sell in later years. Also set in the evening hour, the Venetian *passeggiata* is depicted against the background of the famous Bridge of Sighs. First shown in the 1911 RSA exhibition, alongside two other Venetian oils, it had one very distinguished viewer. Queen Mary visited Edinburgh on 18 July 1911, so she would have seen his Venetian pictures when she visited the recently opened new RSA Galleries. This painting achieved wider recognition, winning a Gold Medal in July 1912 in Amsterdam, proving that Mackie's talent had merited reward outside his own land. Held at the Stedelijk Museum, the show had focused on 'works by living masters', and contained two Mackie oils and two woodblock prints, all of Venice. This venture might well have been under the auspices of the SSA, as he was often in the top group selected to send their pictures. For the Munich exhibition of that same year, he came third in voting selection, with William Walls fifth, John Duncan ninth and Stanley Cursiter a lowly nineteenth. It must all have been some consolation since he had not yet been recognized as an Academician in Scotland. Cowan again lent the Gold Medal painting to the 1921 RSA exhibition, where its effect was deemed an 'immediate, spontaneous, snapshot'. Art sales have moved it on in private hands, so the original is not there for all to share. Only Munro's lithograph can provide a small 'snapshot' of what must have been an impressive painting.

By contrast, public collections, in Aberdeen, Perth, Glasgow and his home city of Edinburgh, contain a fine range of Venetian oils which underline Mackie's achievement and talent. Although the bulk of his output was executed in oil, also used for the production of sketches, he did produce a fair number of water-colours. Most of these cannot be traced but one fine example can be studied in Perth's basement store, *St. Mark's, Venice* (Pl. 29). The skill of the consummate watercolourist is clear in this fine work, which makes one long to see all the others which have been lost. In my researches, I was able to document at least ten exhibited Venetian watercolours. What one would give for a chance to see *Pranzo al Fresco, Venetian Supper Party* or *Night in Venice.*

Given his preferred technique of utilizing a watercolour for a woodblock print, *The Palace Gardens,* showing children playing at twilight on the Dogana would have surely been another (Pl. 25). The Dogana was the old customs building and the term was also used to describe the point of land at the junction of the Grand and Guidecca canals, close to the Mackie *pensione.* This was the print which Sickert had prized so highly. The other woodblock print from Venice, alternatively known as *The Ducal Palace* or *The Molo, Venice,* sets a brilliantly red–hued sail against the palace of the Doge in the background (Pl. 24). The Molo was the 'front door' to Venice, so to speak. It lay at the entrance to that very familiar Piazzetta and the broad stone quay had once provided a ceremonial landing-spot for officials, VIPs and other dignitaries. Distinctively flanked by the two huge granite columns that had been imported from the Byzantine East in the twelfth century, it would have been instantly recognizable. One column is surmounted by the winged lion of St Mark supporting a book, while the other has a representation of Venice's first patron saint, St Theodore. Both these prints were widely exhibited, and both elicited praise, notably from that doyen of print-making, Malcolm Salaman. *The Ducal Palace* was, he thought, 'perhaps Mr Mackie's most sumptuous print, rich in colour and design, and amply suggestive of the live character of Venice.'[6] Thankfully, copies of both are in public hands, in the NGS, the Hunterian, Perth Museum and Art Gallery, and further afield, in the Walker Art Gallery in Liverpool.

Some oil sketches have also survived. The Scottish Arts Club has a fine view of *Santa Maria del Salute* hanging in their dining room. A gift from the widowed Mrs Mackie, it looks down on a room which he would have frequented and known well. She might well have remembered joining their artist friends at the regular SAC Saturday evening 'At Home' where social conviviality was the order of the day.[7] Although it is unfinished and carries her initials as well (AMM), it might well have provided the basis for the Cowan picture mentioned previously. A trip to London and gaining access to the corridors of finance in a private bank was my necessary prelude to see the oil sketch in the Fleming Collection, *La Piazzetta*. Small in scale (it only measures 26 x 20 cm), it might well have been the preliminary study for the larger work, now in Edinburgh's City Art Centre. They also own a small oil study of the same theme, but it is the larger work which commands attention (Pl. 28). The latter had been presented to the Scottish Modern Artists' Association by their President Sir John Stirling-Maxwell in 1911 as a parting gift when he resigned after three years' service. Minuted as 'Mr Charles Mackie's noteworthy and characteristic Piazzetta', it had been exhibited at the RSA the previous year when the Baronet had purchased it for £250. When the SMAA became defunct, the painting was presented to the City Art Centre in 1964. It originally carried the date 1902 in their records but this cataloguing error has been amended, so it now has the correct 1909. The mistake was there for a number of years, emphasising yet again how Mackie errors abound. In 1902, he was enjoying the chill breezes of the North Yorkshire coast, not the sultry heat of a Venetian summer. What is indubitable is the praise it was accorded when it was first shown. *The Studio* magazine asserted that the picture 'in brilliance and subtlety, reaches a higher level than he had previously attained as a colourist'. While, closer to home, *The Scotsman* stated:

> praise may be freely accorded to Mr Charles Mackie for his accomplished and attractive rendering ... where the fading blue of the sky and the artificial light of the colonnade, with people seated at tables, have been skillfully contrasted.

The other gift from the SMAA in 1964 was *La Musica Veneziana* sometimes shortened to *La Musica* (Pl. 33). An earlier work, it had been first exhibited at the RSA in 1909. The SMAA had purchased it for their own collection in that year, no doubt partly influenced by the positive critical reception in the press. At over ten lines, the review in *The Scotsman* gave a detailed description in ecstatic language, such as:

> The hour is the twilight. The sunset glitter is of the city, which is seen in a soft serene grey light, to which colour is imparted by the lighted paper lanterns on the further gondolas ... The quiet tonal harmony is perfect.

Mackie had used the backdrop of the Doge's Palace, in all its Gothic grandeur, with the Campanile to its left. Fascinated by light and shadow, he captured this interplay of natural fading light and artificial illumination. It was a challenge he relished and turned to time and again in Venice.

The same scene was also executed for Ernest Auldjo Jamieson, the other putative patron. Named *La Serenata Veneziana*, it now hangs in the home of his granddaughter. She had fond memories of her grandfather although she was very young when he died; but she thought that he had been a support to Mackie. Though there is no documentary proof, it would explain the superb collection of Mackies that the family own. *La Serenata* is an exquisite work. One could imagine the present-day *Scotsman* waxing equally lyrical about its qualities and the skill of the painter as a colourist and impressionist. Another large, fine Venetian work in the same collection shows a very different subject. Entitled *Venice: Arch on the Rialto Bridge*, it depicts a scene under the central main arch on the south side. People and place are brought together, as a man leans on the balustrade to watch the canal below, while a busy scene of street life on the bridge itself is shown under that distinctive flash of Mackie red (Pl. 32). The final Venetian oil, *St Mark's from the Piazzetta*, carries an inscription 'To my friend E.A.J.' and underneath it is dated 'Xmas 09'. The relationship between patron and artist was a warm one, just as it was with James Cowan.

Night scenes were a Mackie speciality and his own very distinctive 'nocturnes' show his particular skill in capturing the effect of both artificial and natural illumination. Artistic nocturnes could capture nostalgia, atmosphere and the poetry of an urban landscape transformed by gaslight and electricity. *St Mark's by Moonlight* (Pl. 30), housed in Aberdeen Art Gallery's storage facility, deserves to see the light of day and entrance more eyes than mine. John Warrack, a well-known ship owner in Leith, lent it to the RSA exhibition in 1911. His daughter Mary Milne bequeathed it to Aberdeen in 1915 in memory of her first husband George Cooper, stockbroker in the granite city. He had died in March 1898 at the young age of thirty-seven. Did they go there on their honeymoon? The picture is a romantic scene, with the colours of the arch of St Mark's clearly visible. Yet, in the ordinariness of the cool evening life in the piazza the signature Mackie flash of red can again be spotted.

The other vantage point for a good painting could be found on one of Venice's many balconies. An integral part of the city's architecture, they allowed Venetians and visitors to watch all that passed below. Café life was also part of this ongoing bustle, observed and unobserved. Mackie painted both, again opting for the added challenge of lamplight. The NGS houses *Belvedere*, painted in 1910. This is a study of the colour effect produced by the juxtaposition of artificial light and the blue left by fading daylight. The awning over an open-air café, the group of figures below and the outlook to the Grand Canal are all offset by the twinkling lights and twilight glow. Beyond the balustrade of the café, the light is seen reflected in the waters of the canal. This sumptuous painting was bequeathed to the NGS in 1929 by Mr A.F. Roberts of Fairnilee, Dunfermline. An avid collector of Scottish art, he had bought paintings by William Walls as well as Charles Mackie. Described in his obituary as a man who delighted in the society of his friends, it was noted that many of these were members of the

Academy. It is not improbable that he knew the painter of *The Belvedere*. It has been deservedly much exhibited, with the British Council in the USA and Canada, at the RA in London and in Edinburgh, in the Law Courts and Parliament House. First seen by the public in the new RSA Galleries in March 1911, *The Scotsman* said that in Room IV they would find 'a delightful Venetian picture ... by Mr Charles Mackie, whose accomplished hand is seen at its best in this work'.

The other Venetian work owned by the NGS, though also languishing in its Granton store, is *Entrance to the Grand Canal, Venice*, where the painter has positioned himself and the viewer on a terrace with an open balustrade. (His signature is on the said balustrade, in duplicate.) The light of sunset illuminates the Grand Canal, the Doge's Palace, Santa Maria del Salute and the Customs House, with the usual traffic of gondolas and sailing boats passing by. Bill Mackie's researches have shown this balcony to be the Casa Frollo, in the Guidecca.

The Mackie pensione's interior also furnished the theme for a small painting in the Hunterian (Pl. 37). The painter has positioned a small vase of purple flowers on a table in the foreground, while the open window to the balcony frames a view looking towards Santa Maria del Salute. Small in size it may be, but the lively colour and very fluid brushwork show Mackie to be every inch the colourist. Its size could be accounted for by its use — it was presented as an award to D.M. Sutherland, an appreciative student of Mackie. Such a prize would surely have been much valued and perhaps passed from the hands of his widow into the safe care of the Hunterian.

It is disappointing to say that Mackie's painting of one of the most magnificent buildings in Venice, shown at the RSA in 1915, has not been traced. The subject was the *Ca'd'Oro* or House of Gold. No wonder this building on the Grand Canal attracted his painter's eye. Over twenty-two thousand sheets of gold leaf had been fixed on its surface. In addition, the ultramarine used on the façade had been made from powdered lapis luzuli all the way from Badakhasan. Originally constructed between 1421 and 1437, it was the most famous house in Venice, and the sunshine ensured that its embossed and gilded wall appeared as a brilliant sheet of coruscating light. He exhibited the painting again at the RGI in 1916, asking a mere £63, but there is no record of sale. It was also shown at the Royal Academy in London the next year. It must have found an appreciative buyer since it was loaned to the 1921 Memorial Exhibition by 'Sir P. Jeffrey Mackie Bart', as noted in Anne Mackie's handwriting. Perhaps it will surface again. His wife might have been by his side when he painted this, since she and their son had travelled with him to Venice. Donald received the bulk of his education from his mother and from his experience of life as they visited France and Italy.

One personal anecdote from the family's time in the Venetian sun was recounted by Hamish Walls. Asked about his time in the city, Donald's strongest reminiscence was of seeing a female nude in the flesh. Though the experience was over fifty years distant, he was able to recall a lot of detail. Apparently, the Mackies had become friends with a young English nurse, whom they deemed suitable company for their teenage son. Little did they know that she liked to swim naked and had found a deserted beach where she could do this without observation. She evidently thought that Donald was too young to notice or appreciate her charms. The reverse was the case but he did not enlighten her or his parents. Perhaps it was a relief that one of Mackie's friends, Robert Lorimer, gave Donald an architectural apprenticeship in 1912, curtailing his travels and exposure to life in the raw.

In her journal, Anne singled out the importance of Venice in Mackie's voyage as an artist: 'the crowning moment of this aesthetic life came when Venice was revealed to him.' Many of his contemporaries agreed with her and the praise garnered in the reviews was the most fulsome to date. In many ways, Venice had always been waiting for him. Perhaps he had not been ready up to that point to paint her as she deserved. His art had matured, as had the man. The earlier years had seen rejection, isolation and criticism before his own ideas could settle. The colour theorist became the colourist practitioner. The teacher showed he could apply his own lessons and respond with verve to La Serenissima. Piazzas, canals, humble Venetians and grand palaces all flowed from his brush. But the love affair with Italy was not over.

NOTES

1 Vittore Carpaccio (1465-1526) painted scenes of fifteenth-century Venetian life and religious themes; his best-known painting, *St Ursula's Dream*, best illustrates his use of colour and appeal to Mackie's imagination.
2 Peploe, Guy, *S.J. Peploe 1871-1935* (Edinburgh: Mainstream, 2000), p. 27.
3 Salaman, op. cit., p. 296.
4 Mackie family correspondence, courtesy of Bill Mackie.
5 Cowan, op. cit., p. 158.
6 Salaman, op. cit., p. 296.
7 *The Scots Pictorial's* social commentary noted the attendance in 1904 of 'Mrs Charles Mackie' and her dress 'black, with a fichu of white and gold embroidery'. It was the only reference to her, in contrast to many of her social circle.

Eleven
An Immoral Display

What had Charles Mackie done to occasion the wrath of the Reverend Jacob Primmer? Hard at work at his easel, earning his living between his continental journeys, his paintings usually elicited praise and found a ready market. Indeed, following the success of his depiction of his parents in the SSA exhibition of 1900, he found himself executing a number of portraits. Some of the sitters were located in nearby North Berwick and such family commissions must have helped to pay pressing bills. *Miss Frances Esson* figured in the 1902 SSA Exhibition, alongside *Ronald & Frances Patten.*[1] While *Mrs Esson* herself appeared at the SSA in 1904, followed by an unknown *Gavin* in 1908. Perhaps they are still somewhere in East Lothian, gracing a wall of some fine residence or gathering dust, unloved and unrecognized, in an attic?

A more than competent figure-painter, portraits were not his usual or favoured genre but Mackie did accept the invitation to paint a full-length study of the worthy Ella Carmichael Watson (1870-1928). This was a commission which would have attracted Mackie, since she was a woman of note and known to him. A Gaelic speaker, she had commenced her studies in 1892 and helped found the Celtic Union in 1894. She had combined the fight to advance Gaelic studies with the academic inclusion of women, founding the Women Students' Celtic Society, in robust response to her gendered exclusion from the Edinburgh University Celtic Society. Immersed in all things Celtic from an early age, she had acted as an amanuensis to her father Alexander Carmichael, whose portrait shares the same room.[2] *Carmina Gadelica* (published 1900) was the result of their joint efforts. One of the prime instigators in the launch of the *Celtic Review*, she had acted as editor for twelve years, 1904-16. They both gaze down at us from a room in the Department of Celtic and Scottish Studies in George Square. There is no date but careful observation can detect the presence of a wedding ring, so it must have been painted after 1906, the date of her marriage to William J. Watson, later appointed Professor of Celtic at Edinburgh in 1914.[3] The couple had moved initially to Inverness and she did not return to Edinburgh until 1909, so it might be surmised that the painting was commissioned after that date. It cannot be considered Mackie's finest work but the family would have been pleased with the sensitivity of the rendering and the attention to telling detail. The scroll was not accidental, as Watson had earned her academic laurels in her chosen field. Clock and candle were possible artistic allusions to the passage of time? Her long evening gown was secondary to her seat at a desk – she was no decorative ornament. The painter has emphasized her strong personality, uncompromising gaze and femininity in that single pose. Those who knew her testified to a serene idealism, coupled with kindness – qualities that Mackie has tried hard to capture. Given his own contribution to the Celtic Revival and strong friendship with Patrick Geddes, they would have moved in the same circles. She and Mackie had shared a common ambition – the love and promotion of all things Celtic. Gifted to the University in 1974 by her nephew, Michael Carmichael, the portrait is easily accessible today.

It is not such an easy matter to view his *Musical Moments*, since this fine oil had followed earlier works on the long journey to the National Gallery of Victoria in Australia (Pl. 34). The alternative title of *Les Moments Musicaux* refers to a composition by Schubert but I could not make out the composer's name on any of the sheet music present in the picture. The model remains unidentified but the busy musical setting has allowed the painter to make this much more than a portrait. The provenance of the painting echoes how far Mackie had travelled in his own journey as a practitioner. In stark contrast to the earlier Melbourne consignment, this work had been exhibited at Agnew's in London, in an exhibition entitled 'Independent British Art' in 1906. *The Studio* judged it to contain: 'some of the finest examples of modern painting as exemplified by the more advanced forms of artistic thought.' Referring specifically to the work from the 'Scottish Schools', the critic praised the 'absolute sincerity of the work', assuring the public that these were 'men who take their art very seriously, men who have something to say, and who say it each in his own individual way'.[4] Mackie was in good company, as other exhibitors included John Lavery, James Paterson and William McTaggart. One foreign visitor in London at the time had not only visited Agnew's but took the time to write to Mackie. The San Francisco art dealer and Mackie admirer, Frederick Torrey commended him on this fine work. The painter's openness and sincerity were evident in his reply. In a letter dated as 14 May 1906, he writes:

> My dear Torrey, I am awfully glad and not awfully surprised to find that you liked my 'Musical Moments'.... Everything in that picture was meant and the feeling of music in saturated light is a very recurrent one with me'.

What follows next in the letter is the clearest statement of his *raison d'être* as a painter:

> Now I cannot say what I am going to do – nor whether I will attain much but I
> do know that whatever I do shall not be for any other reason that it shall express
> honestly the me that happens to be behind it at the time.

He then explains the constraint he now feels:

> I cannot now do what other people want me to do. You put it well when you say
> an artist shows his interests and so only is interesting.[5]

Critics, unaware of this *cri de coeur*, also lined up to add their positive endorsements. *The Studio* judged that the artist 'has successfully mastered the difficulties of lighting and composition which the subject presents'. *The Art Journal*, in the context of an article detailing the purchases being made for the permanent collection of the Melbourne Gallery noted that it was 'by a talented ARSA' and 'the largest picture at the Agnew exhibition in the spring'. It also reproduced the painting for their readers to admire.[6] Using the funds of the generous Felton Bequest, it had been bought for £105. The Felton adviser in London was George Clausen, himself a skilled landscape painter. An early member of the New English Art Club, he had undertaken some of his artistic training in France and been influenced, like Mackie, by French Impressionism. Many of his works had graced the walls of SSA exhibitions in Edinburgh. As the agent for Melbourne, his selection in June 1906 was understandably influenced by an artist's rather than a collector's perspective. Seeking out living painters of distinction to broaden the gallery's collection, his acquisitions were judged as being in sound taste. Corot's *Sketch of Scheveningen* was purchased at the same sale for £35, so the Gallery had paid a lot more for their magnificent Mackie. Unlike many of the Mackies in British collections, it has seen the light of day and is much admired on the other side of the world.

Encouraged by this public success, Mackie persevered with completing several other large-scale easel paintings. His earlier letter to Torrey, dated 22 April 05, had referred to 'large, unfinished oils on hand', so more than one composition was on the blocks. Once again, we find the destructive hand of history has robbed us of seeing the whole Mackie original. Within the City Art Centre collection, there is a small head study of *Margaret Cumming*, given by the good lady herself in 1973. This part had been excised from the larger original, *For Harvest Festival*. First shown at the RSA in 1907, *The Scotsman* had enthused over its 'rich colour and light', reflecting that the 'eye rests on it with pleasure and delight.' The following year it was selected (cat. 568) to appear in the Fine Art Section of the Scottish National Exhibition held in Edinburgh, so it must have indeed delighted the eye.

Unfortunately, as with many Mackie paintings, it was a large painting. Given to Margaret Cumming, one of the original models, she had stored this gift from

Mrs Mackie in her hallway. Living in a small Roseburn flat, close to the site of the former Coltbridge Studio, there was insufficient space to hang such a large work. She was advised to cut out the section that contained her head and that of her friend, a fellow model. The rest of this fine painting was destroyed. Our only glimpse of the complete original is in a small, faded and scratched photograph, given to Bill Mackie by Margaret Cumming. There is one other image, a professional photograph showing Charles Mackie in front of the painting (Fig. 9). The latter is a better guide to its size and the former to its content. Unfortunately, they are both in black-and-white though the adult figure standing by the doorway is thought to be Anne Mackie.

Andrew Carnegie, purchaser of *The Return of the Flock to the Fold*, was also to buy the work that had occasioned Reverend Primmer's wrath and indignation at its immoral display.

Two versions of *Artis Ancilla* exist.[7] Exhibited at the RSA in 1912, in its English translation as *The Handmaid of Art*, it had been described in *The Studio* as 'an ensemble of richly harmonic beauty'.[8] The earlier version (Pl. 35) was indeed bought by Carnegie (possibly direct from the artist in his studio) but was sold by the Carnegie Trust in 2012. Purchased on the advice of his friend William Walls, Carnegie hung it in his Scottish home at Skibo Castle and it was never exhibited. Mackie's father-in-law knew the magnate well and had been his guest in the USA in the 1880s. In a letter to the Walls family in 1901, Carnegie said he regarded his beloved pictures as his friends, making it hard for him to part with them. Unlike money, which he felt he could give away readily.[9]

Fortunately, the City Art Centre owns the later version of the painting so we are still able to judge it for ourselves. A group of enthusiastic subscribers, encouraged by William Walls, had purchased it in 1913 and presented it to the SMAA. The Edinburgh City Art Collection then inherited it in 1964, on the demise of the latter organization. When it was shown in 2015 as part of the Curator's Choice Exhibition, the label explained the reason for its inclusion:

> Stunning! Stunning! The wow factor from the twentieth century. If this building was on fire I would save this stunner.

This was a view that the Reverend did not share, although he did view it as stunning in another sense. *The Glasgow Herald* carried a report from a righteously indignant Mr Primmer on 22 August 1912. Having ventured east to the fleshpots of the capital, he had viewed the RSA Exhibition and was shocked that it had contained at least half a dozen grossly nude paintings and sculpture. His fire and brimstone fairly bubbled over, condemning it all as 'An Immoral Display', he judged it an outrage on the morality of Edinburgh. Indeed, it was so awfully corrupt that he thought that *Artis Ancilla* should have been denounced from the pulpit. There is no record of his Edinburgh brothers of the cloth rising to the

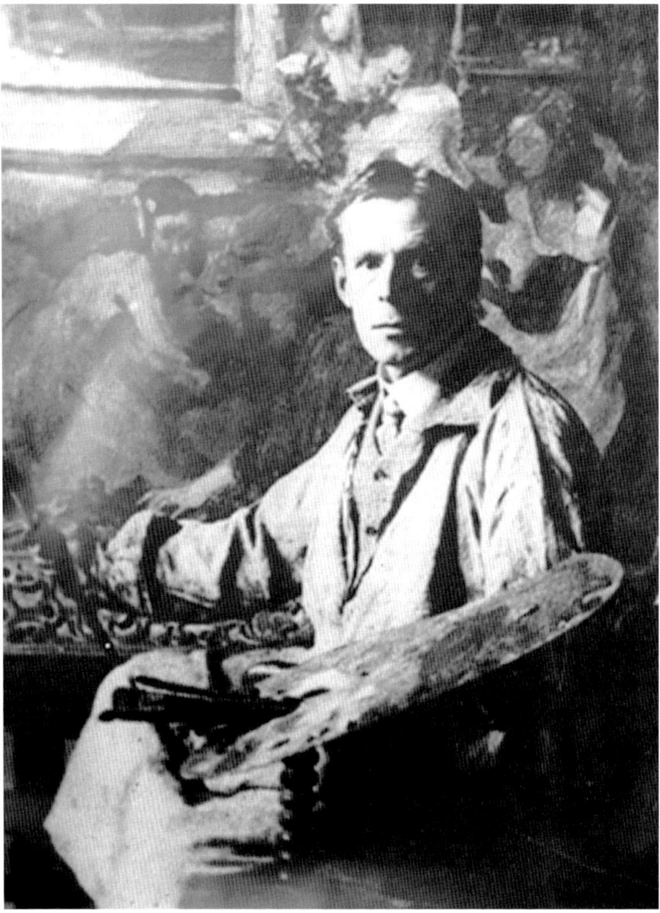

9 Photographic portrait of Charles Mackie, sitting in front of his oil painting *For Harvest Festival*, shown at the RSA Annual Exhibition in 1907. There is a small, faded black-and-white snapshot print of the whole painting which was given to Bill Mackie in 1982 by one of the models. This might be the only record of its true scale, since Margaret Cumming excised her head from the whole and the rest was destroyed. She can be seen in the studio photograph to the right behind the painter's head and her portrait *Margaret Cumming* was given to the City Art Centre in 1973. Oil on canvas, it measures 38.5 x 30.2cm and is the only part of the original which remains. It can be seen at the website www.artuk.org
Courtesy of Bill Mackie who was given this print by the Walls family

challenge and perhaps the painter would have been wryly amused at such vitriolic condemnation. In contrast to the Glasgow denunciation, the press in Edinburgh was fulsome in its praise for the composition, colour and charm of the picture. The *Edinburgh Evening News* carried a long review on Friday, 10 May 1912, where its initial commendation asserted that 'Charles Hodge Mackie is primarily a colourist'. It then went on to provide a detailed description of the composition itself, lauding the use of colour while expressing some reservations regarding the reclining nude. The review continued:

> in his *Handmaid of Art* he shows how skilfully he can compose. The foreground is the retiring room or rest chamber of an atelier, with a nude model enjoying in sleep a respite from the arduous work of posing. A curtain, just withdrawn by a student, shows the strongly lit studio behind, filled with workers. It is in the clever manner in which the colour composition is carried from the brilliant yellows of the distance to the red curtain line, and then on to the cool greens, blues and purples of the foreground textures that the great charm of the picture lies.

It evidently had not charmed the Reverend Jacob Primmer.

In fact, Mackie's own encounter with the nude female form had been late in emerging. Indeed, in his student days, he seems to have had difficulty in dealing with what was on offer at the RSA. A letter dated 17 November 1884 merely states: 'I regret having to inform you that I am unable any longer to attend the poses of the female model at the Life Class.' He did not explain why and it has left his biographer puzzling over his motivation or reservations. His attendance by then had plummeted, so he had possibly just moved on to fresher and more enticing pastures.

However, by 1911, his mental and physical horizons had widened considerably and many nude studies as well as actual paintings flowed from his pencil and brush. Contained in the print room at the NGS is a large collection from his sketch books. Bequeathed by his widow, they offer a fascinating insight into his preparatory work and determination to wrestle with the female body. Exquisite head studies are present too, often executed in red chalk. These all provide valuable evidence linked to later commissions and his final works. As for *Artis Ancilla,* the last word should be left to Anne Mackie. After her husband's death, she judged this handmaid to be 'the purest and one of the most lovely of nudes'. Fortunate indeed that the SMAA had been given this fine painting in 1913 when that committee of subscribers had presented it to the collection, in recognition of its importance in the history of modern Scottish art.

Mackie had been a member of the SMAA from the outset and remained so until his death. The worthy J.J. Cowan had also lent his support and served on the first executive committee. Present at that first meeting where the organization was conceived, on 21 May 1906, Mackie found himself flanked by many of his friends and artistic associates. They had convened at the Edinburgh home of James Cadenhead in Inverleith Terrace and the number included Robert Lorimer, Duddingston Herdman, D.Y. Cameron and other like-minded spirits. The detail of their discussions, aims and strategy can all be found in the minute book of the SMAA, secreted deep in the bowels of Edinburgh City Chambers. The handwriting proves difficult to decipher on occasion but their intent rings out loud and clear from the pages.

The main aim was markedly patriotic, since they felt that the British National Collections did not do justice to modern Scottish art. They considered that it was a good time to act, to achieve the 'removal of this blemish upon our national patriotism'. The old rebuke was made again – English did not equate with British. They went on to lament 'the indifference and ignorance which prevails regarding the Scottish School of painting', a complaint that had been voiced by their predecessor the SSA. However, the aim of this new sister organization was markedly different and they aimed to enlist the great and good, and their funds, to achieve their objective. Two of Mackie's erstwhile patrons figured on that list – Henry Beveridge in Dunfermline and J.J. Cowan in Murrayfield. The appeal for money was essential to realise their ambition – nothing less than the creation of a Scottish Luxembourg. In a later printed appeal for funds, unfortunately timed in 1914, the succinct but proud summary stated:

> the ideal has been a National Collection of Modern Art, something in the shape of a Scottish Luxembourg in which modern art in all its most significant phases should be represented. The Scottish Modern Arts Association was the first organization started in English-speaking countries for the purpose of acquiring, through voluntary subscription, works of modern craftsmen to serve as a national collection.[10]

They were keen to stress that they were not there as 'a Society of mutual admirationists', despite the initials. Herein lay the genesis of the impressive collection housed in the Modern Art Galleries in Edinburgh today.

The final realization of their dream was far distant in pre-1914 Scotland but Mackie was at the forefront in his support for this new, ambitious venture. His presence is recorded at the follow-up meetings held in 1906 and 1907, but he declined to join the executive committee, given the amount of extra work that would entail. He was ever mindful of the need to make a living but did agree in July 1914 to join a small sub-committee to discuss how to increase their available funds. There were many comments in the minutes regarding their main problem – lack of money to purchase art and increase the collection.

The available funds had already been put to good use, to purchase the works that would provide the core of this national collection of modern art. It can be no surprise that several of Mackie's works were among those presented to the association. In addition to works by John Duncan, Cadell, Peploe, Lavery and

Hornel, the purchasing committee decided early on to buy one of Mackie's Venetian studies. The 1910 Report notes that *La Musica Veneziana*, exhibited at the RSA the previous year, was bought for £70. Mackie's letter of acknowledgement and thanks can still be read in the file. As a contemporary Scottish artist he was deemed well worthy of inclusion.[11] Connections were strengthened between the art establishment and the SMAA, which aided their cause. James Caw resigned from the executive committee in June 1907 to take up his appointment as director at the NGS, possibly always aware of the SMAA dictum 'to secure for Scotland a collection of modern art suited to its distinguished position among the art centres of the world'. The association also tried to spread the word through securing Scottish representation at other galleries and exhibitions, as well as providing free lectures on topics of artistic interest, such as Japanese colour printing. Free tickets were provided for the students at the art college, to further the education of the next generation of young, modern Scottish artists. The 1913 report noted that over 750 young people had been brought to see the collections; the SMAA must have felt pleased with its progress to date.

After his own acknowledged success and the acclaim accorded his Venetian studies, Mackie left Edinburgh for further travel. He returned to the entrancements of Italy, venturing further afield. Rome was a major challenge and attraction, resulting in some substantial oils as well as watercolours. Many have disappeared, only being glimpsed when they occasionally come back on to the art market. His subject matter covered the expected tourist sites such as the River Tiber, the Castel Sant'Angelo, St Peter's, the Pincio and the Borghese Gardens. Roman bridges, porticoes and gardens all attracted this painter's eye and he also sought to bring his usual magic to the night scenes. A particular (lost?) watercolour, *Moonrise on the Tiber at Rome*, was shown at the RSW in Glasgow in both 1913 and 1914; £25 would have secured it for a Glaswegian of good taste. His Roman *oeuvre* attracted the usual paeans of praise, since his reputation was by now well established. All of the press comments emphasize his artistry with colour: 'radiant colours ... crisp and clear'; 'fluently painted'; and, for *Rome*, 'a work of singular beauty.' This had been shown at the RSA in 1913 and Mackie had followed it up in 1914 with a *Borghese autumnal*. Again, an unkind fate has robbed us (literally) of his vision of the *Borghese Gardens*. Anne Mackie presented this to the SMAA in 1946 and it was then presented in turn to the City Art Centre in 1964. Sometime after that date, it was lent out to be hung in the City Chambers. Some enterprising thieves made off with computers from that building and decided to take the Mackie as well. It has not been seen since and 'STOLEN' is written on the record. Truly, some events have not treated him or his work kindly (Pl. 36).

Mackie's travels further afield in northern Italy also date from this brief interlude before the outbreak of the World War I. *Asolo* and the *Red Bridge at Bassano* had been completed when he extended his horizon into the Veneto, beyond Venice itself. These paintings and the *Nomentano Bridge* (just outside Rome) provide some much-needed clues to his Italian peregrinations since he did not always identify his location. An instance of this vagary can be found in Perth Museum and Art Gallery, whose basement houses a delightful small oil study *The Pomegranate Tree*. A 1916 SSA exhibit, *The Nut Gatherers*, which 'takes rank with the finest of his larger work in respect of the sumptuous quality of its colour' is also from his Italian palette. This critic was so impressed that *The Studio* included a colour reproduction to allow readers to concur with his view.[12] Seeking out new subjects on which to try out his brush was made more challenging by the Italy of that time. There was limited transport available to the tourist, given the poor roads, inaccessibility and difficult terrain. This led Mackie to embrace modern horse-power, in the form of a motorbike, a mode of transport with which he was familiar. His son related that he and his father had a whole series of them for 'buzzing around' in Scotland as well. No doubt the warmth of the Italian climate made a welcome change. Easel, brushes, paints, parasol and all necessary artistic accoutrements would have taken precedence in his baggage. Anne tells us that in his quest, he took to 'scouring the almost impassable roads of the Campagna on his motorcycle and living in lovely villages where he met with not a few amusing adventures'. Frustratingly, she does not relate what these were but she makes a brave stab at the unfamiliar names – Marta, Valentano, Soriano, Viterbo, Toscanello. Apart from Toscanello, these small towns can all be located in the province of Lazio, accessible from Rome. With the provincial capital Viterbo fifty miles north of Rome, the other sites were also within this painter's range. Valentano was twenty-one miles from Viterbo; Marta was twelve miles to its north west; and Soriano is also located within motorbike distance, overlooked by Monte Cimino. Anne's memory must have let her down with regards to Toscanello, since I could find no trace of any commune or township with that name, though it is a famous brand of Italian cigar. The nearest candidates for the missing destination are Tuscania or Tessennano, but we will never know for sure what she meant. After 1914, he would never again return to that warm Italian sunshine and historic hill-towns which had provided so much inspiration.

Mackie's final visit to northern France also took place at this time before those fields would be engulfed by the horror of the war. *La danse du village* shown at the RSA in 1914 was described briefly by *The Studio* as 'a village dance by moonlight, in which the effect of motion is happily realized'. He would later repeat this theme for his diploma painting for the RSA, when he was elected an academician in 1917. We can glimpse a little of the passion of the original in this later rendition (Pl. 38). Harold Cowan (son of his patron) purchased the original, a loss that Anne Mackie regretted in later years. She felt that it had been one of his finest works and in a later letter to her relatives she described the circumstances in which it was painted.

The original title was *La Ducasse*, referring to the village feast and dance in honour of its patron saint. Mackie had watched it all evening and was evidently haunted by the spectacle he had observed. Anne explains:

> Next day he locked himself into a ramshackle studio he had made at the top of an old granary and worked ferociously for two hours and produced at white heat. I wish that I had it ... so much finer than the one he painted from it for his diploma picture...

She goes on to lament having had to sell it. Despite the RSA picture being the second-best, produced when he was already ill, it is still evocative of that heady scene and fierce artistic passion. Mackie was no conventional academic dullard, painting from preset techniques. He painted from his heart as well as his head, with inspiration guiding his brush and passion infusing his colours. For him, that fusion of people and place had to be at the core of his art.

Forced now to return to his native Scotland by the engulfing politics and consequent outbreak of war, he must have looked back wistfully on these travels. He must have missed the sunshine and vibrant colours of the continent. New horizons had opened up to him and his output proved he could rise to their challenge. The works from these years were some of his finest, since the synthesis of vision and technique had finally come to fruition.

NOTES

1 The Mackie file in the National Portrait Gallery in London contains a copy of a painting entitled *The Young Anglers*, painted 1902, which shows two young boys. This might be another missing portrait; it was unsold at the 2003 Christie's sale.
2 Painted by William Skeoch Cumming (1864-1929).
3 Her younger son, James, succeeded his father but died on active service in 1942.
4 *The Studio*, 1906, Vol. 37, p. 30.
5 The two letters to Torrey are held by the Victoria and Albert Museum, MSL/1959/3600A/1, MSL/1959/3600A/2; permission to quote therefrom courtesy of Bill Mackie.
6 *The Art Journal*, 1906, pp. 334, 336.
7 The term was used by Lucretius in *De Rerum Natura*.
8 *The Studio* 1912 Vol. 56 p.153.
9 Letter in the Walls Family papers, NLS ACC10448, courtesy of the National Library of Scotland.
10 Scottish Modern Arts Association yearbooks and minutes, ED3, courtesy of City of Edinburgh Archives.
11 SMAA's collection contained three Mackies: *La Musica Veneziana*; *La Piazzetta*; *Artis Ancilla*. All were presented to the City Art Centre in 1964 when the SMAA became defunct. By 1918 it had 84 paintings in its collection, including works by Cadell and Peploe.
12 *The Studio*, 1916, vol. 68, p. 63.

Twelve
Vistas of enjoyment?

The final chapter of Mackie's life would be spent largely on native soil and it would include a novel challenge, the creation of sculpture. Nothing would have been known about this achievement had it not been for the sterling work of Dr Louise Boreham and Dr Belinda Thomson, both members of the Society for Scottish Art History. What they found was the only extant sculpture executed by Mackie. A forgotten art treasure, it is unique and was very nearly lost to the world. Described as one of the most important lead sculptures and garden statues in the whole of Scotland, it had been abandoned in the grounds of Westerlea, in Ellersley Road in Edinburgh, left to its fate amid the garden weeds and vagaries of harsh weather. Formerly the grand home of Mackie's Murrayfield patron J.J. Cowan, by 2002 it was in the ownership of Capability Scotland. The SSAH's members' advocacy secured the support of Dr Godfrey Evans, Principal Curator of European Applied Art at the National Museums of Scotland. Had they not mounted this rescue mission and argued the case for its preservation, Mackie's only surviving sculpture would have disappeared forever.

Capability Scotland indicated their willingness to donate the sculpture to the National Museum of Scotland, asking only for due acknowledgement on the resultant display. After protracted negotiations, the much-needed funding was secured and with the appropriate conservation expertise, it was restored to life. The pond which it had dominated had long been filled in, no doubt for reasons of health and safety. The sculpture group itself had been deposited on garden paving and forgotten. Thoughtless neglect meant that it long had been in a sorry state but can now be viewed in all its splendour in the National Museum of Scotland. *Nymph and Faun* is to be seen when one exits the lift on Level 5, *en route* to the Tower Restaurant. Sited here, it surely provides an intellectual *hors d'oeuvre* and Mackie would have been delighted to think his work would be viewed by a much wider public (Pl. 40). Originally produced as a garden fountain, it would have delighted the eye of its owner and any of his visitors. Cowan also envisaged it would be a magnet for his grandchildren, querying the architect's pursuit of Galashiels cobblestones. In a P.S. he expresses his worry:

'They don't sound comfortable for the grandchildren's wading.' As it turned out, this was not a deterrent to youthful frolics. When viewing a private collection in Edinburgh, I did meet someone who remembered the fountain well. As a child she had observed the naughty prank of a friend, who had tipped her own sister Mary into the water. She did not mention if the sculptor was aware of the unintended use to which his ornamental fountain had been put by these school-girls. Mackie would probably have laughed, as his own 'vistas of enjoyment' had possibly not encompassed such pursuits.

Fortunately, it is possible to trace the genesis of the idea and the commission itself in the archives held in the University of Edinburgh. The Lorimer Papers reside in the Special Collections Department and they contain the correspon-dence between all those involved in the project. The letters are indicative of a strong, warm working relationship and an easy honesty.[1] Two of Mackie's friends considered him for the project — Sir Robert Lorimer, the architect and James Cowan, the stalwart patron. Lorimer had been asked to oversee some alterations to Westerlea and its garden. Cowan suggested that Mackie be approached to provide the design for the garden centerpiece, the ornamental fountain. This pond would have contained waterlilies and would have drawn the eye from every direction. At this time, Mackie's son Donald was already apprenticed to Lorimer and these Edinburgh circles were close-knit. Mackie's reputation and reliability were well-established. An early SSA exhibition catalogue also showed that he had tried his hand at small-scale sculpture in 1898. Exhibit 276 was entitled *The Budding Time* and was priced at £10. Nestled amid reliefs and statuettes, it was definitely not a painting but no other information has surfaced on its theme or material.

However, it showed he was not a complete novice in the field of applied art, albeit not on the scale now being envisaged. His studio was almost on site, so to speak, since it was situated round the corner from Henshaw's foundry and within walking distance of Westerlea itself. Having spent several summers in the Veneto and Lazio areas of Italy, Mackie brought with him his knowledge and observation of their piazzas, baroque fountains and garden statuary. Nymphs had long been deemed to be appropriate figures for a fountain, given their association with water. He would provide the idea and create the work of art. Henshaw's firm, still located at 29 Murieston Crescent, had the skill to cast the lead group which Mackie would design.

Cowan's taste accorded with the artist's ideas. Cowan is known to have collected contemporary sculpture and had been prevailed upon to lend his two Rodins to the SSA exhibitions, *Mother and Child* in 1899 and *La Défense* in 1905. He had bought several Mackie paintings, particularly on Venetian themes and often visited the artist in his studio, so he was well familiar with his output. The subject finally chosen was that of *Nymph and Faun*, where this mythical maiden holds a large, flat waterlily leaf over her head; she is teasing the faun below by spraying the water over his head. In action, surrounded by waterlilies, it must have been a truly lovely and restful sight (Fig. 10). In the NGS Print Room, there are a number of preliminary sketches which show possible ideas for the final design as Mackie toyed with ways of addressing this new challenge. When the project was first mooted in May 1913, Mackie costed his 'time' price as fifty guineas but stressed that the main attraction was that the project offered 'vistas of enjoyment to do a bit of applied art'. Lorimer visited Mackie in person in his Coltbridge Studio to look at his proposed design. He was sufficiently impressed to write to Cowan that 'the idea was good ... it might work out into a fine thing'. The other consideration was aesthetic since Lorimer stressed that he felt 'strongly the desirability of having a thing that can be ranked as a work of art, rather than a stock or trade production'. Lorimer's discussions with Henshaw about the amount of work involved in the creation and casting of the sculpture alerted him to the inadequacy of Mackie's estimate.

Lorimer felt sufficiently concerned to caution Cowan that fifty guineas was a very low estimate and that seventy or eighty guineas would be nearer the mark. In his own words: 'Regarding Mackie's price, I do not think he quite realises what he is letting himself in for offering to do the work for Fifty Guineas.' Mackie had not embarked on such a demanding work before and the cost of paying models, the creation of the figures and the time necessary to complete the work would all be ventures into new artistic territory. What can be gauged from the correspondence is his keenness to take it on. Lorimer, in asking Cowan to agree to some flexibility on the final costing, stressed that: 'Mackie, is, of course, tremendously keen to do the work.'

The increase in the fee was agreed and Lorimer kept Mackie informed. His response was not mercenary: 'All this makes me the more anxious to rise to the occasion.' In fact, he had been worried that the original financial estimates, including the cost of Henshaw's work, seemed to be 'staggering' though he knew that the foundry had to be responsible for the final casting. Henshaw originally estimated £105 for the casting but amended this to £135 as the size of the group was increased. Mackie had been anxious to reassure Henshaw that this was all in order:

> I am sure that neither Sir Robert Lorimer nor Mr Cowan would expect you to stick to the original estimate when the group had been made so much larger than was at first intended. Indeed Mr Cowan is one of those who like to pay well for a good job and I consider yours is very good indeed.

Mackie agreed that the foundryman's work would entail 'any amount of the finest craftsmanship to cast such a thing'. Mackie's emphasis was on the artistic adventure not the financial bottom line. Work apparently progressed satisfactorily — Lorimer had drawn out the plan for the exact siting of the fountain group

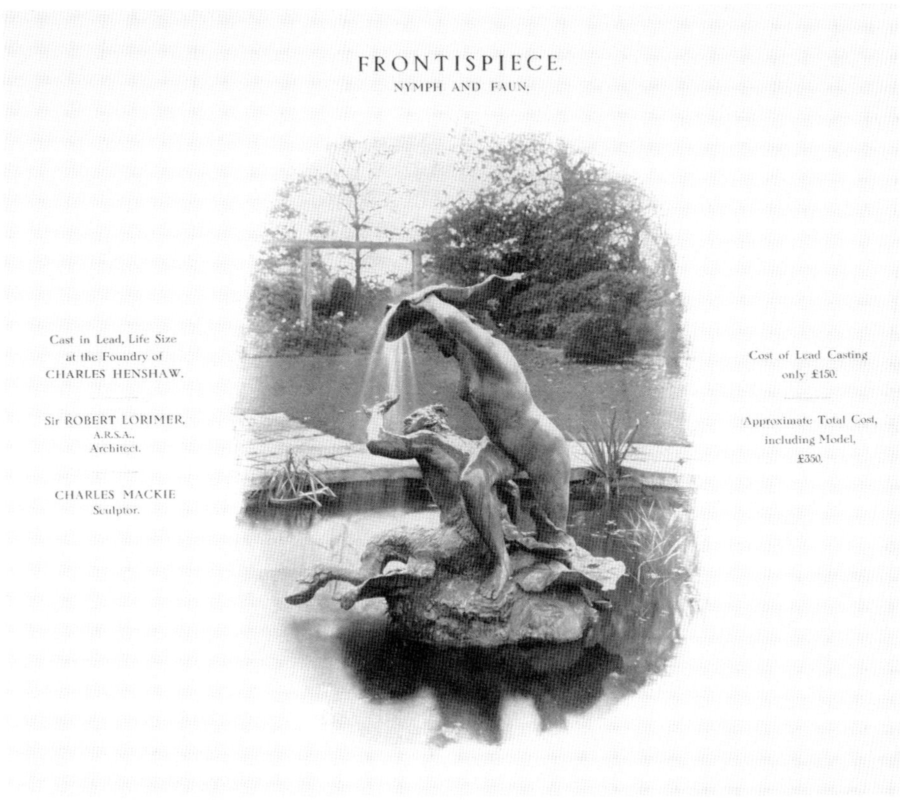

10 Henshaw Trade Catalogue photograph of fountain sculpture 1914, which shows Mackie's *Nymph and Faun in situ* in the garden of Westerlea, Murrayfield, home to his patron J.J. Cowan.
© Courtesy of Historic Environment Scotland, Licensor canmore.org.uk

and it was put in place by 1914. It featured prominently as the illustrated frontispiece for the Henshaw trade catalogue of 1914. The final cost of the lead casting was given as 'only £150' but the overall approximate 'Total Cost, including Model' was £350. This photograph shows the lead group *in situ*, as an impressive, functioning water-feature in a beautiful garden. It was stressed that this had been cast in lead, life-size at the Foundry of CHARLES HENSHAW. (Fig. 10)

The conservation report, drawn up by Janet and Andrew Naylor for the National Museum provides a detailed analysis of Mackie's work and the extent of the wear and tear of the intervening years. This led to the decision not to restore it as a working fountain, but as a sculptural group. The conservators judged it to be a complex work, both in terms of composition and technique. In their judgement this 'jolly moment in time' revealed a 'technically and compositionally complex work' with 'impressive grasp of form and technique'. The metal of choice had been lead, which had made it vulnerable to the damage it had sustained, despite its usually stable nature and corrosion resistance. The lead patina would have been an important and deliberate colour choice for the artist/sculptor. This colour would complement both the water and the surrounding waterlilies. Its grey tone would add to the overall effect. It was not an unusual choice for a fountain and was appropriate to its aquatic surroundings.

Unfortunately, as we now know all too well, it also had detrimental effects on those who came into contact with it. Lead was and is a highly toxic material, absorbed easily through the skin. If any part of the hand is contaminated through contact, particles can then be ingested. The process of creating his first garden sculpture was not only time-consuming but might have held hidden dangers for Mackie, particularly when he was attending to the finishing. From the original sketches, he would have composed a detailed drawing, from which he would have created a maquette. Nothing has survived, but he might well have used the traditional wax model approach. Henshaw then made his own plaster cast of the group from the artist's model and the foundryman's costs included removing it to the workshop round the corner at Murieston Crescent. The inscription records that it was 'MODELLED BY C.M. MACKIE AND CAST BY C. HENSHAW EDIN. 1914'.

For his part, Mackie had sent acknowledgement of receipt of £25 in his letter in the June of 1914, although there is no documentary definitive last word on his final fee. This major essay into sculpture so impressed the architect that he asked him to consider a similar venture for another Murrayfield residence, Kinellan. At this point we are made aware that not all was well with Mackie's health — a worrying sign of the long illness that was to be his constant affliction in the years ahead. In the same letter, he tells Lorimer 'I am home again but a perfect wreck, able to see no one and with orders not to touch work for another month'. With this in mind, he reluctantly declined the sculpture commission for 'the Herdman project' and yet he remained optimistic, 'One takes badly with illness when it is the first shot of it, and yet I suppose I shall be the better of it in the end'. Unfortunately, that was not to be the case.

However, Lorimer's initial concern had been justified. The final extant letter from Mackie, dated 4 November 1914, confirmed that he had not emerged the richer from the enterprise. To his regret, he tells Lorimer 'that after paying all my expenses on the Cowan fountain, I had little left but the fun of doing it'. A wiser man, he felt able to give an upwardly revised estimate for the statue at Kinellan House: £120. The war had been underway since August and travel abroad was now out of the question, so he had revisited that earlier request. There is no evidence that it progressed beyond the paper estimate and he was not a well man in the years that followed. Undertaking another large-scale sculpture might well have been beyond his physical and mental capacities. His handwriting in these letters showed a marked deterioration as a result of his illness.

Nevertheless, success had greeted his first and only completed major sculpture and his patron must have been well pleased with the outcome. Once again, Mackie had accepted the gauntlet of artistic challenge. He had mastered new techniques and shown impressive skill in a different medium. As an artist, he still felt a compelling need to wield his paint brush and engage with the landscape. The Continent was not open to him and the east coast of Yorkshire, scene of earlier successful compositions, was also denied. Britain itself had come under attack on that side of the country by German naval bombardment in December 1914. Bridlington, Scarborough, West Hartlepool and Whitby had all suffered. The civilian fatalities amounted to 137 killed, with 592 wounded – numbers that would appear puny compared to the onslaught of the Blitz in the next war. Nevertheless, this unexpected attack had resulted in the deaths of innocent women and children, a fact which fed well into the propaganda riposte – 'Remember Scarborough! Enlist Now' appeared on posters throughout the country. Given this confirmed vulnerability of the east coast of the UK, defence against the enemy and national security took precedence over the needs of the artist. Mackie was forced to look to the west and beyond the Scottish border. New pastures beckoned – in Wales.

Mackie's movements are always hard to track down but in this instance he did lend a hand to the biographer. The RSA files contain a letter dated 23 October 1917 and headed 'Abersoch, Carnarvonshire'. Addressed to the secretary, Mr Hastings, it was primarily a polite apology for his inability to attend a meeting of the academicians. As a newly elected member of the RSA in that year, his invitation would have meant a lot to him and his old teacher, Lawton Wingate. The latter had delayed the meeting to secure his attendance but Mackie felt compelled to stay in Wales.

I have had no address until now, having been forced to knock about a lot in Wales to get a place where one might work. Weather and windstress have played havoc with the foliage I wanted and I am now forced to content myself with waves.

> I hope to remain here for a few weeks indeed until the snow sends me away.
> I haven't done a scrap of work yet.

Frustration with his circumstances was coupled with determination to paint, whatever might be happening in the wider world. The results of these final journeys were exhibited at the wartime exhibitions, as Mackie still had to make a living. In fact, his presence in Wales must have pre-dated this letter since *Where the River Conway meets the sea* was shown at the RSA in 1916 (cat. 215), though there is no record of it being bought. Other possible candidates for this Welsh period could be *Autumn ploughing at Conway* (RSA 1917, Cat. 230) and *Pastures by the sea* (RSA 1918, Cat. 371). There are a number of unidentified landscape studies in the Perth collection which might also belong to this final flourish of landscape endeavour.

No one was immune from the impact of World War I but the Mackies suffered less than most Scots families. Their son Donald was commissioned in the Royal Engineers on 28 July 1915 and found himself serving King and country on the other side of the world, as part of the Egyptian Expeditionary Force, acting in the responsible position of works officer under the Works Directorate in Egypt. He was also in the field with the 52nd Lowland Division in Sinai and Palestine and did eventually return home, safe and sound, in June 1919. If he had served with any other Scottish regiment in the mud of Flanders, there might have been a very different outcome.

Mackie himself was too old for active service but tried to make his own contribution. The Gold Medal which had been awarded to him at Amsterdam in 1912 was donated to the government, to be melted down and help towards paying for the insatiable demand for munitions. In common with many of his fellows, he purchased war bonds. As a patriotic gesture, it was to be applauded but it was not to prove a wise financial investment. His will lists a number of these, inherited by his widow and son. Two issues of national war bonds amounted to £110 and two war savings certificates had been purchased for approximately £154. While not an impoverished artist by any means, this was a major amount of money, as these were all purchased in 1918/19. Mackie's financial contributions to the war effort were the best that he could do at that time. However, he did also attempt to contribute in the way that he knew best, through his art.

In the catalogue for the 1916 RSA exhibition, the picture numbered as Cat. 374 is Mackie's only painting directly linked to the war itself. It was controversial in terms of title, subject choice and composition. It did not receive good reviews and remained unsold, priced at £150. Nevertheless, it was his response to actual events and provides a glimpse into his reaction to the issue of conscientious objectors. Entitled *He that taketh not the sword to save the righteous, his soul shall perish*, it has vanished without trace and it might well have been destroyed. It was linked to two events: the atrocity carried out by the German army at

Aerschot in Belgium in 1914 and the passage of the first Military Service Act of January 1916. In response to the ever-mounting casualties, the latter had ended voluntary recruitment and brought in compulsory military service for all unmarried males between the ages of eighteen and forty-one. This had resulted in approximately 16,000 conscientious objectors registering their refusal to fight and engage in the mass slaughter being enacted on the Western Front.

The earlier Belgian atrocity was not the usual by-product of British propaganda and was documented in detail in the independent report produced by the US ambassador in September 1917. According to Brand Whitlock in his report to the Secretary of State, the Germans had entered Aerschot on 19 August 1914. A large number of the inhabitants who had not already fled were locked up in the church for several days, without receiving any food. They were then marched off to Louvain (the scene of another atrocity, the burning of the famous library). Those who had not been shot there were apparently marched back to Aerschot where men and women were separated. Many women and young girls were assaulted and raped. In total, 150 of the inhabitants of Aerschot were killed, many more brutalized and the dead numbered eight women and several children. Pillage and arson continued for a number of days, with furniture and art being sent to Germany, along with three hundred of the citizens, carted off in the same wagons. Burning, brutality, rape and pillage would all be scenes that would be associated with the name 'Aerschot'. The picture conjured up would remind all those at home why they were fighting to help plucky little Belgium against the brutish Hun. A famous propaganda poster of the time also conveyed this theme, as a small boy bravely faces a Goliath of a German soldier bearing down on him. The linking of these two events and the general revulsion at German barbarism, albeit later embellished by the deliberate exaggeration of the British government, produced one of Mackie's more unusual art works. Military tribunals had been set up to verify the claims of 'conchies' to exemption and many of these were rejected by these unsympathetic listeners. *The Scotsman* thought that their work would be reinforced by mounting a replica of this particular Mackie as a backcloth. Once again, we are indebted to its anonymous critic for a description that allows us to visualise the vanished painting, although the tone of the critique published on 16 March 1916 was less than enthusiastic. While paying tribute to 'the brilliant and diverse colour scheme' doubt was expressed as to its suitability to the subject matter. A colourful scene indeed was outlined in detail:

> the scene of rapine and murder of defenceless women and children ... With Huns to right and left engaged in their murderous work, women appeal to him in their hour of shame and misery, the 'Conscientious Objector' stalks through the blazing ruins of Aerschot, a self-righteous figure, waving aside calls for help.
>
> Seemingly proffered a sword by a half-naked woman struggling with a German

soldier, he passes by heedless to her plea and the warning of the artist, emphasised in his choice of title.

Mixed feelings greeted this war work by Mackie. The critics acknowledged his passion and the veracity of its noble intent but were ill at ease with the result. It was felt to be insufficiently stern, suffering from an 'uncomfortable combination of realism and symbolism'. The final judgement was that 'one feels its tragedy turgid rather than terrible'. The same reaction was voiced in *The Glasgow Herald* in its 3 June RSA review. While praising his Conway picture for its 'paeans of colour' and 'extraordinary skill', it damned the Aerschot image as 'artificial'. The evidence is not there to allow us to judge for ourselves but he never executed another work related to the war, which raged on till November 1918.

The exigencies of war also curtailed the activities of the organisations he had helped found in more peaceful times – the SSA and SMAA. The 1914 and 1915 SSA exhibitions still went ahead but it was not felt appropriate to hold a reception 'owing to the war'. Women were in greater evidence in committee and supportive duties, due to the gaps left by artists away on active service. In addition, novel methods were employed to advertise their activities – sandwich boards were paraded along George Street, Shandwick Place, George IV Bridge and the Mound, with additional advertising being placed in Edinburgh's tramcars. It was also agreed, in the light of slow sales, that war bonds and war saving certificates could be used in lieu of hard cash to purchase pictures. It was no wonder that the temporary secretary alluded to the 'troublesome times we are going through'. The SMAA faced an additional challenge, since it now had its own collection which had to be protected against risk of damage. Many members were also on active service, including the Secretary G.L.D. Hole (he of the illegible handwriting mentioned in the previous chapter). The NGS agreed to store the paintings, insured against the perils of war. Members were informed that the collection was in storage 'secure from deterioration by damp, and damage by fire, and untouched by any of the bombs dropped upon Edinburgh by the enemy'.

This referred to the Zeppelin raid which had occurred on 2 April 1916, when L14 and L20 had appeared in the skies over the capital. Given the nickname of 'baby-killers', Zeppelins had already carried out raids in the south of England. Thwarted by the heavy defences at Rosyth, they dropped their load on Leith and the city of Edinburgh itself. High explosive and incendiary bombs rained down and accounted for nine deaths, more than twenty injured citizens and much damage to the building fabric. A bonded warehouse in Leith went up in flames while the Grassmarket, Castle Rock and Lothian road suffered damage to tenements, hostelries and shops. Shards from the Castle Rock littered the streets and steps were taken to ensure the safety of the Scottish regalia. Even the one o'clock gun fired at the raiders in futile and indignant response. The machine-gun on Arthur's Seat did try to force them to leave but, thankfully, did not hit these highly combustible airships. If either had been brought down, the subsequent conflagration and loss of life would have been much greater. That reassurance from the SMAA held very real meaning for its members, since even the home front was now not immune to the impact of war. The one positive outcome was that the pupils at Mackie's old school, George Watson's, were allowed to start their Easter holidays ahead of schedule, due to the number of broken windows. In reality, Zeppelin raids made very little impact on the progress of the war but provided much-vaunted moral justification for the Allies. The surprised casualties were now regarded as innocent victims of German brutality and Hunnish barbarism. This might perhaps have also figured in Mackie's choice of subject for that controversial 1916 RSA submission, though no patriot had stepped forward to endorse it with purchase.

The post-war situation was to prove economically challenging, due to inflation, financial pressures and the reluctance to invest in art. Money was tight and the purchase of art was not a priority. Though J.J. Cowan was still a leading light and vice president of the SMAA, even he would also find himself a victim of these financial constraints, being forced to sell the bulk of his collection in 1926. The war would leave no-one unscathed, whether collector, entrepreneur or artist.

It seems ironic that it was during this period of difficulty and uncertainty that Mackie finally achieved the professional *imprimatur* of being elected an academician and full public acknowledgement of his status as an artist. His relationship with the awarding body had been troubled at times and his doughty espousal of the SSA had perhaps delayed this overdue recognition. For any Scots painter of his generation, living in Edinburgh in sight of its imposing building, this official endorsement by his fellow professionals was much valued. Pragmatically, it also helped with sales, since RSA could appear after his name and assure the buyer that he had invested in a sound product.[2]

Given the public acclaim which his work had received in the years after 1907, it was fully to be expected that he would be proposed as a full RSA. This had actually happened in 1911 but he lost out on that occasion, to a name familiar to him from the 1901 failure. *The Art Journal* records: 'voting was equally divided between Mr R. Gemmell Hutchison and Mr C.H. Mackie for membership of the RSA: by the casting vote of the President, Sir James Guthrie, Mr Hutchinson was chosen.'[3] That must have been another bitter blow but it had spurred him on to immerse himself deeper into his art and travel further afield. The years which followed saw him produce some of his finest works and venture into new territory, like sculpture. He must have known in his heart that he was worthy of the world's honours and would prove it through his art.

Earlier, the RSA had indeed recognised his ability and teaching skill in 1909, when he was appointed as Visitor to its Life School. He would be following in the footsteps of distinguished academicians such as William McTaggart whom the young Mackie had encountered when he was a student. The position was teaching and supervisory in the RSA Life Schools and would offer the young art students an opportunity to benefit from the knowledge of an experienced and successful artist. As usual with Mackie, his determination to do his best was apparent in his acceptance letter dated 11 March: 'I accept my appointment and shall do my best to do all that is required of me.' His skill was remembered and acknowledged by his students. The future Head of Gray's School of Art in Aberdeen, D.M. Sutherland, was said to have been 'much inspired by the teaching of Charles Mackie'.[4]

However, Mackie's integrity and self-imposed high standards resulted in his resignation the following year. He had found it impracticable and impossible to combine the teaching with the needs of a working artist. Indeed, he had erred on the side of over-involvement, to the detriment of the time vital to his own art. In the letter of 13 December 1910, he felt it important to outline this in detail. In theory, the role of Visitor was originally envisaged as a time-limited, weekly half-hour, to give advice and encouragement. Mackie seems to have been drawn in by the delights of teaching and exceeded this minimal amount:

> I find that I have devoted more time to the work of the Life School than I can well afford. This has demanded lately not less than 24 hours per week. I have not grudged this, but I am afraid I cannot continue it after the end of this month. Accordingly I wish to be allowed to resign then and to ask you to appoint someone in my place.

Ever the emollient gentleman artist, he concluded 'it has been a great pleasure to me to act as Visitor to the Life School'. Though this position had been short-lived, as a result of his own volition, it must have given him some career satisfaction. After all, he would possibly recall that the same Life School had refused him admission on his first attempt in October 1882. Now he felt sufficiently secure as a professional artist to reject the position and concentrate on his art. As ever, he had given it his best shot and decided that his priority was painting.

It was not until 14 February 1917 that he received the full recognition which was his long overdue reward: 'At a Statutory General Assembly Mr Charles Mackie was elected academician.' This final accolade was almost too tardy and he would not live long to enjoy it. He was already suffering from the illness that would prove terminal. It can be seen in the drawn face and sad look captured in the RSA official photograph, where he stands in painter's smock, holding the tools of his trade, palette and paintbrush (Fig. 12). The painting on the easel might well be his last major unfinished oil *The Bathing Pool*, which also carries the initials AMM, as his wife signed it on his behalf. It was still a work in progress when he died. In many ways the official 'encumbrance' of RSA had come too late to help him in his career or aid his financial security. Surrounded by the constraints of war and increasingly handicapped by illness, the distinction would be with him in life for only three more years. Perhaps Whistler's comment was all too apposite: 'Whom the gods wish to destroy, they make Academicians.'

People and place would have heightened meaning for Mackie at this time when he could no longer enjoy the sun of his beloved Italian piazzas. Family, confrères and friends would provide support and solace as he faced his final challenge. His home and heart would be in his Coltbridge Studio in his native Edinburgh and he would be surrounded by the memories of an artistic life well-lived. The Mackie family lived in the downstairs of the old Roseburn primary school, while the headmaster of the new school (opened in 1896) resided upstairs (Fig. 11). The building was numbered as 17 Corstorphine Road by Anne after her husband's death, when it ceased to be an artist's studio. It no longer exists since it was demolished in 1977 and in its place stands Murrayburgh House, a four-storey office block of ugly brutalism erected in 1978.

Mackie's studio can now only be seen in the old photograph overleaf. This was where he painted at his easel, worked on his woodblock prints and created his sculpture. It would have been possible to see the Pentland Hills in the near distance and they would be the subject for one of his final paintings. *Gathering Cloud – Pentland Side* was painted with help from one of his friends and fellow artists, William Miller Frazer.[5] With unrecorded provenance, it is acknowledged as a joint work and is in the permanent collection of the RSA. Both artists might have remembered the monogrammed Mackie painting *Girl and Calves crossing a Ford* inscribed 'From C.H. Mackie to W.M. Frazer 1897.' Their friendship was of long-standing and that final landscape is a sad work, redolent of dark days.

Many memories of the young students who had visited him during happier times must have remained with him. One member of this coterie was a young man called Joyce Cary, who would later achieve recognition as a celebrated author of fiction and poetry.[6] Apparently the attractions of Montmartre were proving too enticing for Cary, who was a seventeen-year old art student in Paris in 1906. They had met in a Parisian café and Mackie was worried that Cary might fritter away both his money and talent in a life of libertarian dissipation. It was at Mackie's suggestion that Cary came to Edinburgh in 1907 to undertake a more disciplined approach to his artistic training and joined the classes in the School of Art on the Mound. Though he ultimately decided that his true calling was not art and lay instead in the world of literature, he did recall time spent with his mentor in Murrayfield. In the company of his fellow students such as his friend Adam Bruce Thomson, they would gather in Mackie's Coltbridge Studio and talk 'art'. The new trends, merits and demerits, would be discussed. Fauvism and Impressionism would rouse their passions and these would be set against the Victorian academic art which still dominated the galleries. Cary, a committed Impressionist, and Mackie could bring their recent experiences of the Paris art scene to the discussion, and the older man surely had many

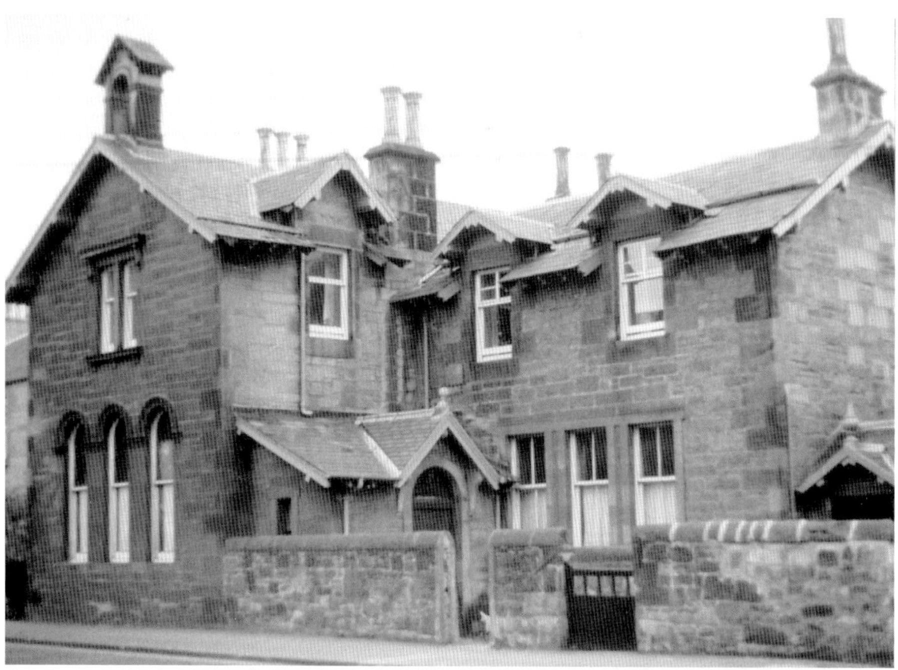

11 Photograph of the Old Roseburn Primary School 17-19 Corstorphine Road, Edinburgh.
Mackie's studio occupied the ground floor; the headmaster of the new Roseburn Primary School (opened 1896) lived upstairs. The whole building was demolished in 1977.
Photograph courtesy of Bill Mackie

anecdotes and observations to contribute. After all, he had met Gauguin in person and was an intimate of 'les symbolistes'.

Perhaps the young student was also invited to Mrs Mackie's 'at home' day, held on Fridays, when afternoon tea and talk was followed by an evening musical session with coffee, more tea, sandwiches and cakes. Donald remembered these popular occasions vividly:

> any number of invited and uninvited people up to twenty or more in number would turn up. Artists, musicians, authors, journalists, lawyers, doctors, professors, Scotch, English, Irish, French, German, Italian, Russian, Swedish, Danish and all points east turning up at one time or another. I was allowed to be present for a time at least as a small boy provided I kept quiet, staying longer and taking a greater part as I grew older, handing round food and drink and smokes, chatting to the least errudite [sic] of our guests, though by keeping one's ears open and one's mouth shut, one learned a lot from the babel [sic] of talk, argument and discussion.[7]

Cary would draw on similar memories for his book *The Horse's Mouth*, which describes the life of a reprobate artist, committed to his trade but living from hand to mouth, given to worldly indulgence despite his impoverished existence. He started writing the book on the wartime train home from Edinburgh, which he had revisited in November 1942 in order to accept the James Tait Black Memorial Prize and deliver a lecture at the university. Visiting his old haunts had awakened many memories of his youth as an art student all those years before. Their poignancy and his vivid recollection of the profession he had abandoned provided the inspiration for his fictional creation of the central character, an artist. The picture painted in words bore no relation to Mackie but many of the painter's utterances seem to echo some of his precepts. The main character, Gulley Jimson, is determined to paint no matter what, and will do anything – lie, steal, cheat, blackmail – in order to acquire colours and canvas. He talks with passion about the importance of the juxtaposition of certain colours and the shock of encountering a Manet. His beliefs and artistic vocation would have been endorsed by the Edinburgh artist, if not his dissolute lifestyle. Perhaps Cary was projecting what might have been his own fate if he had not come under the benign guidance of Mackie. Cary enjoyed his student days and recounted a social life in Edwardian Edinburgh which was bohemian, if not as dangerously seductive as Paris.

When these young art students visited Mackie's home for their sociable evening discussions, they walked into a building filled with the memorabilia of Mackie's life. Inside, they would have seen many reminders of his travels and links with the wider community of artistic brotherhood. In the final years, one hopes that all this would have given him some consolation, as his more immediate world contracted to his bed of pain and suffering. The description provided by Hamish Walls is a colourful guide to the building's interior, detailed in words of wonder by the writer, who had visited as a child: 'It wasn't so much a home as a museum. Within its walls ordinary domestic comfort had to compete with the cult of the Beautiful and lost decisively.' Since the building had been a school, the layout consisted of a number of interconnecting rooms, designed for use as classrooms, not living quarters. These appeared large, cold and full of empty space. According to the young observer, they were:

> sparsely occupied by breathtakingly beautiful but savagely uncomfortable pieces of furniture, a few magnificent rugs and mats lost in the great open spaces of the stained floors, Japanese screens, pictures and objets d'art of all sorts.

One object that stood out in his recollection was 'an extraordinary Islamic (?) fretted brass free-standing hollow pillar about five feet high'. It was of uncertain origin but must have loomed large to any small boy taken into such unusual surroundings. This unsettling atmosphere would have been further compounded by the party trick Mackie performed for his young nephew, which consisted of sticking his tongue out and drawing it in again by pulling his ear. Given his age at the time, Hamish Walls was apparently alarmed and mystified. He acknowledged that his extreme youth meant that he was 'too young to appreciate him as the original character he undoubtedly was'.[8]

As no photographs of the interior exist, Donald Mackie's description can supplement the memories of his cousin Hamish. His knowledge was first-hand, having lived there from 1897 to 1946 and seen his father at work *in situ*:

> Ours was an old rambling house with huge rooms, a converted school ideal for an artist, as almost every (room) was suitable for a studio, and at one time or another most of them had been used as until a final choice of one was arrived at. Our drawing room or lounge as it would now be called was a room some forty feet long by twenty wide with a polished floor covered by Persian carpets. Adjoining was my father's studio, a room of similar size, folding or rather sliding doors between, which when opened made the two a grand place for dances. My mother's full-size grand piano looked quite a small piece of furniture in a room of these dimensions.

Charles Hodge Mackie died here at noon on 12 July 1920. All who knew him alluded to the length of the illness and the common consensus is that it was some form of cancer, possibly of the bowel or rectum. The exact cause of death recorded on his death certificate was graphic in its detail: 'ulceration of rectum; operation; chronic septicaemia; heart failure'. In the era before antibiotics, sepsis seemed to have followed a failed operation, with fatal consequences. His wife

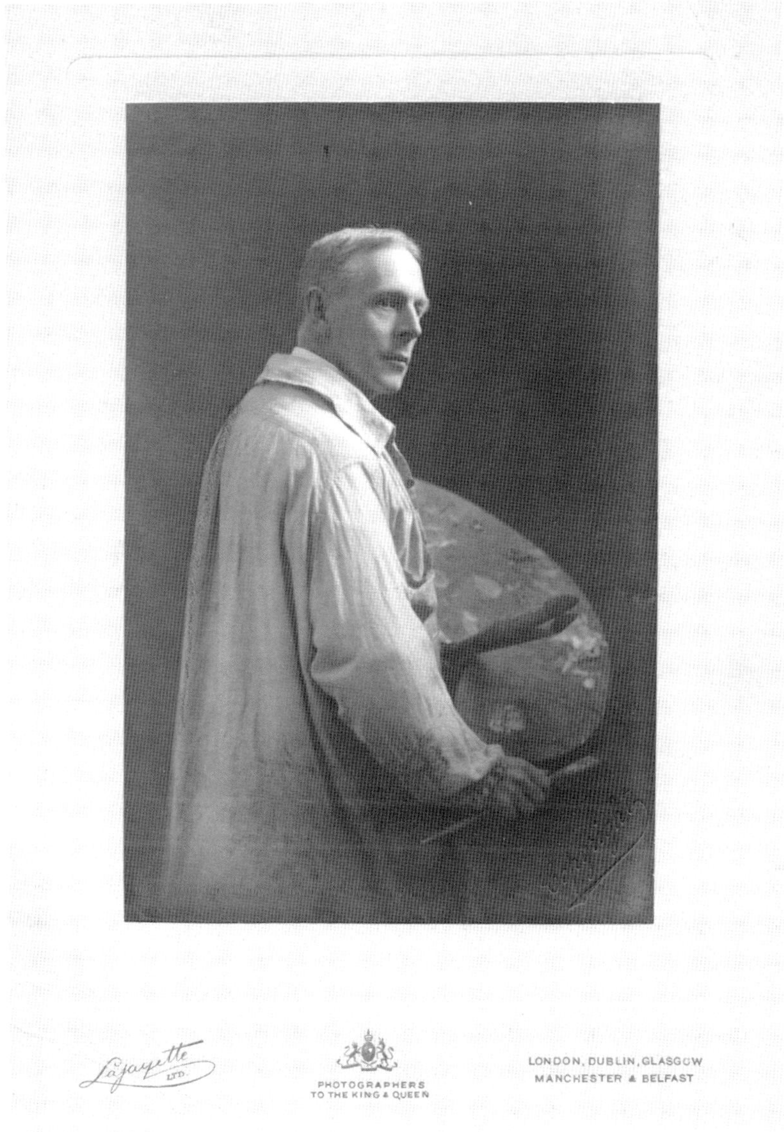

12 Studio photographic portrait of Charles Mackie by Lafayette Ltd, Glasgow.
This was probably taken in 1917 when he was elected an academician. The effect of his illness
can be clearly seen in his drawn face. He would not live long to enjoy his status as RSA.
Courtesy of Bill Mackie

and son had been by his side and it was Donald who had registered the death. There had been much pain and suffering but he never lost his humanity. His friend and patron James Cowan had been so moved by a letter he received from the dying artist that he referred to it in his autobiography:

> I have happy memories of him and admiration for his bravery in his latter days. In 1919 when our Golden Wedding took place, Charles Mackie, from a bed of suffering, wrote us a most kindly greeting, and also during his illness several other letters full of quaint humour.[9]

Such was the measure of the man. The death notice requested 'no flowers' and Mackie was interred at Warriston Cemetery on the 15 July 1920. His gravestone is still upright, held in place by the shade of the tree that overlooks his final resting place. The simple inscription is surmounted by a delicately carved cross and records:

> CHARLES H. MACKIE R.S.A. R.S.W. son of Captain Wm Mackie (2nd Queens Royal now West Surrey) died at Edinburgh 12th July 1920 in his 58th year.

It reads as a simple epitaph for a man who was well-esteemed at his passing. What were his last thoughts and words? His widow ascribed religious hopes of salvation but he had never been noted for religiosity. It was his art that had always been at the heart of his life. Possibly other words were nearer the mark. Despite suffering intense pain, he told one of his nurses that he longed to be back at his beloved easel: 'Give me two more years to live, I ask no more.' His journey had ended before he had reached his ultimate goal as a painter, artist and creative craftsman. His epitaph would reside in the obituaries, memorial exhibition and plaudits of the years immediately following his death. Then he would be largely forgotten, subsumed within a Scottish pantheon dominated by the Glasgow Boys and the Colourists.

NOTES

1 All Lorimer and Mackie quotations on the sculpture are taken from the Lorimer archive, courtesy of the University of Edinburgh Library, GEN.1963/15/9;1963/18/51/54/62/63, quoted by kind permission of Robin Lorimer and Bill Mackie.
2 Perhaps that explains the superscription 'Charles Mackie RSA' on the Stewartry painting of *John Copland*, executed in 1883, well before the event.
3 *The Art Journal*, 1911, p. 323.
4 Quoted in 'D.M. Sutherland MC, LLD, RSA (1883-1973)' catalogue of an exhibition held at Aberdeen Art Gallery, 5-26 October 1974, AAG, 1974.
5 William Miller Frazer RSA (1864-1961) Born in Scone, outside Perth, attended Perth Academy and died in Edinburgh. Mainly a landscape artist, he holds the record for exhibiting the most years at the annual RSA exhibition (78 in total). He was also a founder member of the SSA and served as its President in 1908. Perth Museum and Art Gallery holds a large number of his works. Elected RSA 1924 and subsequently president of the Scottish Arts Club.
6 Foster, Malcom, *Joyce Cary: A Biography*. (London: Michael Joseph, 1969) pp. 38-43 cover this period in Paris and Edinburgh. My grateful thanks to Dr Elizabeth Cumming for drawing my attention to the Mackie reference in the biography of Cary.
7 Mackie family correspondence, courtesy of Bill Mackie.
8 Walls–Mackie family correspondence, courtesy of Bill Mackie.
9 Cowan, op. cit., p. 158.

Epilogue

In Melbourne, Mackie's elder brother Copland did not long survive him, dying of cancer on 1 December 1921. Charles's widow and son continued to reside at 17-19 Corstorphine Road, now stripped of its title 'Coltbridge Studio', except when Donald chose to make use of it. Mackie's will shows that he had tried to make adequate provision for them both, since he had insured his own life for £200 on 14 April 1891, prior to marrying Anne. The estate in total was valued at £1,703. 18. 8. Savings, household effects, pictures, war bonds and certificates and a mysterious item of furniture at 45 Queen Street made up the total. Anne was not left impoverished, but her inheritance would equate to approximately £60,000 in today's money. In the years ahead, she would sell pictures and even resort to producing prints using Charles's woodblocks. Her main support would have to be her only son and other family members, such as her brother William Walls who lived nearby in Kaimes Road, Corstorphine. Donald Mackie pursued a fairly undistinguished career as an architect and quantity surveyor, marrying Irmgard Holzapfel in 1932. His artistic output was equally lacking in distinction, with a handful of exhibits at the RSA in 1929, 1932 and 1933. The designation was architect and each was a house design — in Davidson's Mains, Balerno and North Berwick respectively. In the field of applied art he had earlier exhibited a memorial case for a roll of honour at the SSA exhibition in 1920 (cat. 415). Indicative of the mood of the time, it was priced at £20. He had parted company with Robert Lorimer shortly before his father's death and having tried various options, set up in business as an architect at the former Coltbridge studio. As a footnote, one of his proposers for admission to the LRIBA[1] in October 1930 was Sir Frank Mears, the husband of an old childhood acquaintance, Norah Geddes. Having reached the rank of captain in World War I, Donald served out World War II as a reserve officer, apparently assessing compensation claims for any damage to property inflicted by the army. His architectural practice failed to flourish in the difficult post-war years and he instigated a move to Blairgowrie in 1946.

At that point, their home had to be cleared and while some bequests were made to the NGS, there must have been difficult choices to make with regard to sale, destruction or preservation. Given their weight, the original woodblocks for his prints must have met their end in flames. After the hustle and bustle of the capital, the move to a quiet rural Perthshire town must have been a form of social death for the lively Anne who also survived major surgery and a car crash. She died aged ninety-six in December 1960 and left all her remaining wordly goods to her much-cherished only son. He wrote to his Australian relatives that her last months had been very trying, 'as she was very deaf, almost blind and confined to bed, not able to read, knit or write and found life a dreary affair ... she often said she was tired of life.'

She was laid to rest in Blairgowrie cemetery, many miles distant from her beloved Charles. This was not a good year for Donald, since he also lost his wife Irmgard, known to all as Irmie. She had died before her mother-in-law, on 29 January 1960. Donald's dotage seems to have been somewhat sad and lonely, dependent on the comfort and companionship of his dog, Lindy. He referred to himself as 'the last of the Mohicans', as there were no other Mackies in Scotland, in contrast to the flourishing Mackie clan in Australia. His letters lament the dire Scottish weather, in both summer and winter, as well as his isolation, commenting that he found life: 'a pretty dull affair'. Recalling happier times on his motorbike, when he was scared stiff or frozen, he said that he had 'loved the life'. His words painted a melancholy picture of his last years at Balmoral Road in Blairgowrie. This last direct witness of Mackie's work and home life died on 17 February 1970 of cancer of the liver and was buried beside his wife. Although he left no memoir, he did have the good sense to bequeath the remaining Mackie paintings to Perth Museum and Art Gallery. In his will, he also left a third of his estate to Hamish Walls, who duly acknowledged his generosity alongside the unhappiness of the latter years. Donald Mackie did not die a rich man but his gift to Perth ensured that Charles Mackie's legacy was not lost for future generations.

Returning to Edinburgh, the writers of the glowing tributes in 1920 could not foresee how Charles Mackie would be all too easily pushed to the footnotes of Scottish art history. His stature as an RSA and RSW, achievement in a range of media and distinctive contribution to Scottish art in the twentieth century were all noted. The other marked feature of these eulogies was their emphasis on his fine qualities as a humane and well-liked brother artist. Several key points were highlighted, tracing the uneven trajectory of his career. Early recognition in the RSA exhibition of 1888, the pursuit of his colour theories and eventual public re-emergence with his more mature works by 1907 were seen as the distinguishing features. It was noted that he had exhibited on the European stage, citing Munich, Buda Pesth (sic), Dresden and Amsterdam, the occasion of his gold medal triumph. His travels in France and Italy were also cited as inspiration for some of his finest works, particularly his Venetian studies. The external 'encumbrances' were also duly acknowledged – ARSA and RSW in 1902, RSA in 1917 and his chairmanship of the SSA in 1900.

Personal and heartfelt tributes were paid by his friends at the Scottish Arts Club, where he was held in high regard by all who had known him. Seen as an artists' painter, he was placed in the first rank by his fellow practitioners who admired his determination to work out his colour theory, even at the cost of material advancement. His love affair with colour was deemed to have been vindicated by the sensuous and masterly works which achieved public renown after 1907. In his day it was said that he was acknowledged as one of Scotland's finest colourists — a label that has been unjustly removed. The SAC pronounced him 'a painter of considerable gifts as a colourist'. *The Studio* in 1916 had earlier endorsed that delineation:

> Charles H. Mackie occupies an outstanding position as a colourist. Fertile in ideas, he is attached to no school of painting, but has worked out the problems of colour and composition for himself ... the expression of an original mind.[2]

Banality and the commonplace were not his métier. He achieved his own ideal through undaunted dedication, unwavering commitment and hard work, bearing the criticism that came his way as a result. The rewards were finally being reaped in those twilight years. In his tribute in *The Scotsman*, one friend of long-standing, W.M. Frazer, lamented that Mackie had died too soon:

> His early work betokened great promise, based on close observation of nature. A worker of indomitable perseverance, he has been known to be out in the fields from dawn to sunset of a mid-summer day ... No artist ever set before himself a higher ideal; few have worked harder to attain it; and, just as he was nearing the goal — when his trained hand and receptive brain would have given us of his maturest — the veil is drawn across the canvas.

The SMAA concurred, deploring the loss to Scottish art: 'His power for good was great ... The value of such an example ... cannot be measured ... [and they hoped that] his influence may endure as an active force.' Given the number of artists whose life Mackie had touched, that was a wish which would be fulfilled. Throughout his career, Mackie had always found time to help, teach and inspire students and fellow artists. Laura Knight was one among many who testified to his fine qualities as a teacher. She judged that his methodology was both deliberate and yet inspired, since every brush stroke was a careful application of theory and imagination. She judged him both a painter of great distinction and a great teacher, whose lessons stayed with her for life. Her verdict was that Scotland should be proud of him. Her comments echoed many others who had learned so much from the example set by Mackie.

In Dunfermline, Anne Mackie's home town, the public tribute singled out his work amongst the poor. Acknowledging the praise for his art, the heading given was 'A FRIEND OF THE OUTCAST AND FALLEN'. *The Dunfermline Journal* cited a friend who had known of Mackie's unsung work among the poor of the

Edinburgh slums. As a young man, he had spent time trying to help them towards a better life. He had not sought money for this work but had stressed it was time and emotional empathy that mattered most. Mackie's own gentle words were quoted:

> It is not your money I want, but your personal service, as I have experienced that by visiting these unfortunate people, and by encouraging conversation, I gain their confidence and trust, and have thereby succeeded in leading them in many cases to useful lives.

This instinct to help those less fortunate than himself can be dated back to his youth. Anne's journal provided further confirmation:

> stronger than his aesthetic tastes was the urge to help the unhappy and the fallen. In spite of bitter opposition he and a young doctor took a house in the slums – West Port – to try and alleviate the misery round them, to bring some sweetness and light into their sordid lives, point the way to cleaner living and higher thinking, to feed, clothe, exhort, redeem from prison, plead their cause in courts of justice... But severe illness, which left a lifelong mark, ended for the moment that complete devotion.

Mackie's companion in the missionary enterprise was a Dr Arthur, who contracted pneumonia. The latter also did some work in London but had eventually to seek out the sun of Sydney, Australia to repair the damage to his health. The West Port had a notorious reputation as the worst district in Edinburgh. The Edinburgh Association for the Improvement of the Conditions of the Poor (known colloquially as 'The Help') said that 'the people were sunken, their habits infamous'. It relied on a huge army of volunteers like these two idealistic young men to address society's ills. Such social work would have endeared him further to Patrick Geddes and his University Settlement strivings on Castle Hill.

Mackie's own life had turned out more than useful, not just to his admirers but also to those to whom he had extended the hand of help and friendship along the way. Eddie Hornel, Hugh Munro, D.M. Sutherland, Joyce Cary and Laura Knight would surely all had reason to remember him with gratitude. His friends from the west would have read in *The Glasgow Herald* that he was also remembered for his work in applied arts. The account also referred to his notable success in 'the invention of a process for reproducing pictures in colour, which was applied to the boards of a publication on Greek pottery'. And, as has been shown, to much else besides. Those delicate colour prints were the legacy of his fifteen years of experimentation.

The fullest tribute was paid in the RSA Council Report which recorded his passing and his achievement. The eloquent summation confirmed the evolution of both artist and man, expanding the catalogue to include the mural work in the Infirmary, Ramsay Garden and Pitreavie Castle. His talent was justifiably deemed 'versatile' and J. Lawton Wingate lavished particular praise on his Venetian studies and *The Handmaid of Art*. Mackie's especial delight in discussion and analysis of his art was acknowledged as a major influence on his fellow-artists – a definite contrast to that scathing judgement of an RSA in earlier years. Wingate had known the Mackie family personally, had helped steer the young man in his youth and painted his portrait,[3] so this tribute reads as both genuine and sincere (Pl. 39).

The laurel wreath of RSA status was placed on his coffin and the pictures in the RSA exhibition following his death would have been graced with an eloquent bow of black ribbon, as was the custom. Among those who represented the RSA at the funeral at Warriston cemetery was his former teacher, past president of the SAC, current RSA president and obituarist, J. Lawton Wingate. Another notable presence was Robert Gibb, RSA, who had seen the young man in the life class all those years ago in the early 1880s, when he had been the Visitor. Although Geddes was not present, their old associate from the university, Professor Baldwin Brown was there. Other colleagues and friends read like a roll-call from the history of Scottish art – J.H. Lorimer, R.D. Herdman, W. MacGeorge, William Walls, Robert Nisbet, Robert Hope, W.M. Frazer and many more. They would all have lamented the loss of a good man and fine artist.

Walking on lyart leaves in rural Perthshire, I reflected on my years spent in the company of Charles Mackie and the journey we had taken together. Uncovering his life, the strongest impression was his essential decency as a human being. His constant striving to attain his own artistic vision could only be understood in the context of the integrity which was central to his character. Bridging the gap between the east and west of Scottish art, cultivating French comradeship, he had shown a facility for friendship and loyalty. Humour does not travel well across the decades but he was possessed of ready wit, inventive jest and self-mocking deprecation. Such self-awareness is not always commonplace in the art world but his was genuine. Passion for colour, an intimate sense of place and the impression of a singular moment can all be found in his paintings. Accessible to all, their power and charm can still bewitch us.

The judgement of posterity has not been so kind, possibly due to the double misfortune of his long illness coinciding with World War I. Not only the size of his canvases but the change in prevailing public taste meant that his art passed out of fashion and into that dark hinterland of obscurity. Charles Hodge Mackie was referenced in the art books and journals covering this period of Scottish art, but the vogue for the promotion of the Glasgow Boys and the Colourists meant that he was overlooked and all but forgotten. The flame of due recognition was kept burning by those who knew of him and the fine qualities of his art but his own modesty was paralleled by widespread ignorance of the man and his achievement. Whenever I mentioned his name, the most common response was 'Who?' I trust this book has at last answered that question.

NOTES

1 RIBA (Royal Institute of British Architects) had created a class of licentiate members as early as 1905. This was open to architects who could show evidence of competence without examinations. In 1925 the Society of Architects had amalgamated with the RIBA and most of the incoming members were accommodated within this category. Given Donald's inadequate formal schooling and the disruption of World War I, he would have been eligible.
2 *The Studio*, 1916, Vol. 67, pp. 58, 262.
3 The Wingate portrait was placed first in the catalogue for the 1921 memorial exhibition and had been lent by his sister, Annie Mackie. Although unsigned and undated, it would appear to have been painted c.1900.

Index

Page numbers in bold indicate illustrations

Aberdeen 113, 115, 138
Aerschot, Belgium 135, 136
Agnew's Gallery, London 119, 120
Aitken Dott 30
Aldershot 10, 58
Alma-Tadema, Lawrence 78
Antwerp 14, 17-21, 24, 47, 73
Armour, Margaret 31, 33, 34
Australia 9-11, 14, 56, 64, 103, 119, 147, 149

Bagshawe, Joseph 89
Baldwin Brown, Professor 36, 45, 150
Bassano del Grappa 99
Behrens, Reinhard 28
Beveridge, Henry 33, 34, 124
Blacklock, Tom 16, 18, 19, 75
Board of Manufactures 16, 78, 79
Bonnard, Pierre 51, 103
Boreland Wood 29
Boudin, Eugène 61
British Museum 49, 102
Brittany 29, 48, 50, 51, 53, 55
Broughton House 13, 15, 18, 24, 26, 27, 70
Burns, Robert 12, 41, **81**, 82, 84
Burton, Mary Rose Hill 33, 36

Cadell, Francis (Bunty) 76, 98, 110, 124, 127
Cadenhead, James 41, 73, 124
Caillebotte, Gustave 50
Cameron, D.Y. 124
Capper, Stewart Henbest 28, 35, 36
Carnegie, Andrew 108, 121
Carpaccio, Vittore 107, 110, 117
    St.Ursula's Dream 117
Cary, Joyce 139, 141, 149
Castle Cottage, Cardoness Castle 21, 29
Caw, James 69, 125
Cézanne, Paul 54, 56, 61, 71, 72
Chevreul, Michel-Eugène 72
City Art Centre, Edinburgh 6, 70, 114, 120, 121, 122,
    125, 127
Clark, Andrew 9
Clark, Evelyn 9
Clement, Gad Frederik 49, 56
Clausen, George 120
Cockburn Association 34
Coltbridge Studio 26, 66, 67, 69, 95, 110, 121,
    130, 139, **140**, 146
Constable, John 77
Copland, John 13
Corot, Jean-Baptiste-Camille 78, 120
    Sketch of Scheveningen 120
Cowan, John James 66, 69, 70, 73, 110, 112-115, 123,
    124, 128-130, 133, 137, 144
Crane, Walter 61, 64

Crawhall, Joseph 110
Crawshaw, Lionel Townsend 89, 91
Culross 20, 62
Cumming, Margaret 120, 121, **122**
Cumming, William Skeoch 127
Cursiter, Stanley 54, 109, 112

Dade, Ernest 89
Degas, Edgar 61
Denis, Maurice 49, 51, 56
    Homage to Cézanne 56
    Madame Ranson with Cat 56
Douglas, William Fettes 76, 77
Duncan, John 30, 37, 41, 42, **43**, 45, 69, 73, 112, 124
Dundrennan 13, 14, 18
Dunfermline 21, 33, 40, 67, 108, 115, 124, 148
The Dunfermline Journal 148
Dunragit, Wigtownshire 23
Durand-Ruel 41, 50, 61, 100, 108

Edinburgh 14, 17, 20, 22, 27, 30, 33, 35, 37, 39, 41,
    58, 60, 64, 67, 69, 73, 84, 99, 112, 121, 124, 128,
    136, 139, 141
Edinburgh Evening Dispatch 65, 82
Edinburgh Evening News 40, 41, 123
Edinburgh Social Union 33-36
Edinburgh Summer Schools 30, 41, 42, 45, 46
Étaples 92, 105, 107-109

Faeds 12
Fergusson, J.D. 110
Findlater, Lydia 75, 86
Findlay, Sir John 77
Fletcher, Frank Morley 106
Frazer, William Miller 139, 145, 148, 150
Frier, Harry and Robert 59

Gatehouse of Fleet 21, 22, 30, 31
Gauguin, Paul 10, 21, 29, 50, 51-54, 71, 100, 101, 141
    NOA, NOA 101
    Vision après le sermon 51
Geddes, Anna (formerly Anna Morton) 30, 42, **43**, **44**, 66
Geddes, Alastair 28, 44
Geddes, Norah 28, 29, 31, 33, 36, 41, 44, 146
Geddes, Patrick 12, 21, 23, 28, 30, 31, **32**, 33-42, **43**,
    44, 45-47, 50, 55, 64, 65, 75, 78, 119, 149, 150
George Watson's College (school attended by Copland
    and Charles Mackie) 27, 58-60, 137
Gibb, Robert 16, 150
Glasgow 9, 17, 22, 23, 35, 57, 73, 98, 100, 113, 123, 125
Glasgow Arts Club 73
The Glasgow Evening News 23
The Glasgow Herald 40, 104, 121, 136, 149
Gold Medal, Stedilijk Museum, Amsterdam 112, 134

Gordon, Esmé 26, 27, 56, 65, 75, 82
Goupil 105
Grafton Galleries 61, 108
Grosvenor Gallery 100
Guthrie, Sir James 50, 80, 137

Henry, George 21, 22, 29, 30, 110
Henshaw, Charles (Foundry) 129, 130, **131**, 132
Herdman, Robert Duddingston 16, 73, **81**, 124, 132, 150
Hill, Rowland Henry 89, 92, 93
Hope, Robert 73, 150
Hopwood, Henry Silkstone 89, 108
Hornel, Edward 10, 12-14, 16-24, 26, 27, 33, 64, 65, 70, 72, 95, 100, 101, 110, 125, 149
    Among the Wild Hyacinths 100
    Madame Chrysanthème 23
    Summer 23
    The Wounded Butterfly 26
Hornel, Margaret 12
Hornel, Tizzie 21, 27
Huelgoat 48-50, 54
Hunterian Gallery, Glasgow 29, 54, 70, 113, 116
Huntly, Marquis of 79
Hutchison, Robert Gemmell 24, 137

Jackson, Fred W. 89, 92, 93, 108
    The Last Load 108
Jamieson, Auldjo 110, 114-115
Jobling, Robert and Isa 89
Johnson, Laura (also see Knight, Dame Laura) 10, 70, 88-90

Keppie, John 23, 27
Kirkcudbright 12-14, 18, 20, 22, 23, 27, 45, 62, 70, 73, 95
Kirkcudbrightshire Advertiser 22
Kirkcudbrightshire Fine Art Association 12
Knight, Harold 89
Knight, Dame Laura 67, 68, 89, 93-95, 148, 149

Lavery, John 50, 110, 119, 124
Leeds Art Gallery 87, 96
The Liverpool Echo 23
London 16, 17, 47, 49, 61, 67, 82, 100, 106, 108, 110, 112, 114, 116, 119, 120, 149
Lorimer, Robert 117, 124, 129, 130, 132, 133, 146, 150

MacGeorge, William Stuart 19, 24, 27, 72, 73, 75, 76, 104, 150
Macgillivray, James Pittendrigh 76
Mackie, Anne (formerly Anne MacDonald Walls), married to Charles Mackie 10, 11, 21, 27, 33, 42, **43**, **44**, 47-49, 52 - 54, 56, 58, 59, 62, **68**, 91, 100, 102, 103, 105, 107, 109, 111, 113, 116, 117, 121, 123, 125, 126, 127, 134, 138, 139, 141, 146, 147, 148, 149
Mackie, Anne (formerly Young) wife of Captain Mackie 57, 60, **81**
Mackie, Annie, younger sister of Charles Mackie

27, 41, 56, 57, 58, 60, 75, 86, 98, 103, 151, **pl.13**, **pl.15**
Mackie, Bill, grandson of Copland Mackie 9, 10, 27, 57, 60, 64, 65, 75, 116, 121, 122
Mackie, Charles Hodge: works by
Drawings and Paintings:
    Annie Mackie 60, 61 **pl.13**, **pl. 15**
    Asolo 125
    Artis Ancilla (The Handmaid of Art) 121, 123, 127, **pl.35**
    Autumn Ploughing at Conway 134
    Bait-Gatherers 92
    Band Night in Venice 112
    Barges on the Thames 61
    The Bathing Pool 138
    Belvedere 115, 116
    Benderloch 62
    Borghese Autumnal 125
    Borghese Gardens 125, **pl.36**
    Boy, with a Strayed Lamb 62
    Breton Girl Crocheting 50, **pl.10**
    Bridge of Sighs 112, 113
    Busking the Cross at Daybreak 20, 62
    Ca d'Oro 11
    Captain and Mrs Mackie 60, 80, 81, **(7)**, **pl.11**
    Cattle grazing beside a Farm Pond 66
    A Colonsay Cowherd 62
    Crofterland 65
    La Danse du Village/ La Ducasse 126, 127, **pl.38**
    An Early Frost at Sunrise 65, **pl.17**
    Ella Carmichael Watson 118, 119
    Entrance to the Grand Canal, Venice 116
    Mrs Esson 118
    E'ening brings a' hame 62, 64
    Étaples 91, 107
    Evening in Venice 112, **pl.31**
    The Faggot Gatherers 29, **pl.6**
    A Field Worker 12
    Folding Sheep at Gloaming 108
    Miss Frances Esson 118
    Gathering Cloud – Pentland Side 139
    Gavin 118
    Girl and Calves crossing a Ford 139
    Girl weaning a Calf 62
    A Gondola Maker's Yard 112
    The Harbour Bridge, Whitby 88, 101
    Harrowing the Field 66
    For Harvest Festival 120, 121, **122**
    The Hay Cart 108
    He that taketh not the sword to save the righteous, his soul shall perish 134, 135, 136
    The Hill, Runswick 90
    The Hill-Farm Pond 80
    A Homely Old Body 18
    The Incoming Tide 98
    An Interior, Venice 116, **pl.37**
    A Japanese Album 56, **pl.13**
    John Copland 13, 145
    Kirkcudbright Town 18, 29, **pl.1**
    Landscape of a Lakeside View (The River Tay ?) 66

The Last Load 108
The Little Dancers, Madrid 26
Looking towards St. Paul's 61
Margaret Cumming 120, 121, **122**
Moonlight on the Bay 89, 90, **pl.20**
Moonrise on the Tiber at Rome 125
La Musica Veneziana 114, 125, 127, **pl.28**
Musical Moments/ Les Moments Musicaux 119, 120,
    pl.34
Night in Venice 113
Nomentano Bridge 126
A Nor'Easter 91
The Nut Gatherers 126
Oak in Autumn 71
Peeling Potatoes 18, 95
La Piazzetta 114, 127, **pl.28**
The Pomegranate Tree 126
The Pool below the Bridge 90
The Pool of Ness 12, 55, **pl.2**
Potato Gathering 66
La Poursuite 55
Pranzo al Fresco 113
Preparing for Dinner 12
Raking the Stubble 66
Reapers returning at Sundown 64
The Red Bridge at/of Bassano 97, 99, 102, 125
The Return of the Flock to the Fold 108, 109, 121, **pl.27**
Ride to Nowhere (Merry-Go-Round) 109, 110
A Roadside Study 91
Ronald and Frances Patten 118
Round the Old Ash Tree 66, 108
Runswick 92
Saint Mark's, Venice 113, **pl.29**
Saint Mark's by Moonlight 115, **pl.30**
Saint Mark's from the Piazzetta 115
Santa Maria del Salute 112, 113
Sauntering Home at Sundown 18, 26
La Senorita 26
La Serenata Veneziana 114, 115
Shepherd bearing a Wounded Ewe 62, **63**, 108
The Shepherdess 108
Six designs for panels in the Royal Infirmary,
    Edinburgh 35
Snipe 64, 65, **pl.12**
A Sower 12
Still Waters on the Black Devon 66
Stokesay Castle 92
Sundown at Runswick Bay 91
At Sundown on Peat Moss 12
On the Tagus at Toledo 91
The Thames at Dusk 61
There were three maidens pu'd a flower / By the bonnie
    banks o' Fordie / The Bonnie Banks o' Fordie 41,
    54, 70, 71, **pl. 9**, **pl. 16**
Venetian Supper Party 113
Venice: Arch on the Rialto Bridge 115, **pl.32**
Weaning Time 62, 64
Westminster from the Thames 61

Where the River Conway meets the sea 134, 136
Whitby Bridge 88
Whitby Market 92
The Windmill 87, 88, **pl.18**
Woman on a Bridge 112
Woodland in Autumn 92
Workshop in Venice 112
Ye Olde Palette 14, **15**, 19, 101
The Young Anglers 127
The Ypres Tower, Rye 98

Book Covers:
The Evergreen 12, 23, 33, 37-41, 55, 70, 73,
    75, 99, 100, **pl.5**
Greeks and Persians 24, 101, 105
John Knox 46
The Scottish Arts Club. Opening Ceremonies 1894 39

Murals:
Pitreavie Castle, Dunfermline:
    The Battle 34
    The Call to Arms 33
    Hardyknute series 34
    O Lang, Lang may the Ladies Sit 33
Ramsay Garden, Edinburgh:
    Age 30
    Daisy Chain 30
    The Drinking Pond 30
    Felling Trees in a Beech Wood 28, 29, **pl.3**
    Gathering Winter Leaves 29, **pl.4**
    Seasons 29
    The Storks 30
    Summer 30, 34
    The wind scattering leaves (autumn breeze?) 30
Royal Infirmary, Edinburgh:
    Six Designs for panels: ploughing, sowing, harrowing,
    reaping, harvesting and grinding 34-36

Prints:
The Source of the Tay 61
The Tay above Aberfeldy 61, 62
The Tay below Aberfeldy 62, 64
Themistocles and the Delphic Oracle 105
Xerxes and the Hellespont 105

Prints (Woodblock, black and white):
By the Bonnie Banks o' Fordie 41
Chucks 41
Felling Trees 41
Hide and Seek 40, 41, 55, **pl.7**
Lyart Leaves 40, 55, **pl. 8**
Robene and Makyn 40
When the Girls come out to play 40, 55

Prints (Woodblock, coloured):
The Combat 99, 103, **pl.22**
The Donkey 100
The Doge's Palace / The Ducal Palace / The Molo, Venice
    100, 104, 105, 113, **pl. 24**
The Incoming Tide 98, 100, 103, 105
The Palace Gardens 9, 100, 104, 105, 113, **pl.25**
Picardy Poplars 100, 102, 105, 107, **pl. 21**
The Red Bridge at/of Bassano / Bassano Bridge 97,

102, **pl. 23**
The Return of the Flock 100, 104, 105, 108
Wild Hyacinths 96, 100, 104, **pl.26**
Sculpture:
The Budding Time 129
Nymph and Faun **122**, 128-133, **pl. 40**
Mackie, Copland, elder brother of Charles Mackie 9, 10, 58, 59, 146
Mackie, Donald, only son of Charles Mackie 58, 67, **68**, 87, 88 93, 97, 104, 102, 103, 104, 108, 116, 117, 126, 129, 134, 141, 142, 144, 146, 147, 151
Mackie, Helen (Nellie), older sister of Charles Mackie 57
Mackie, William (Captain), father of Charles Mackie 10, 13, 57, 60, **81**, 144
Mackie, Willie, elder brother of Charles Mackie **25**, 26, 47, 57, 58, 61, 99
McManus Gallery, Dundee 98
McTaggart, William 16, 36, 76-78, 82, 92, 119, 137
The Manchester Guardian 38
Manet, Edouard 50, 54, 61, 82, 110, 141
   Jeune fille au fichu 82
Mayor, William Frederick 89, 93
Mears, Sir Frank 35, 146
Melbourne 9, 10, 57, 60, 61, 64, 75, 112, 119, 120, 146
Millais John Everett 78
Millet, Jean-Francois 47, 48, 78, 108
   The Sheepfold, Moonlight 108
Mitchell, J. Campbell **81**, 84
Modern Art Gallery, Edinburgh 54, 74, 124
Monet, Claude 41, 61, 71, 72
Monogram 33, 34, 36, 50, 70, 71, 139
Montreuil-sur-Mer 92, 108
Morisot, Berthe 54, 61
Morlaix 49
Morris, William 64
Mouncey, William 12, 45
Munro, Hugh 104, 113, 149
   The Bridge of Sighs 104
Murdoch, William Burn 19, 25, 26, 27, 41, 45, 73, 75

Nabis 10, 21, 51, 55, 71, 72 101
Naismith, Robert and Annie 28
National Galleries of Scotland (NGS) 16, 51, 109, 110, 113, 115, 116, 112, 123, 124, 125, 130, 136, 146
National Library of Scotland (NLS) 10, 28, 30, 56, 59, 69
National Museums of Scotland (NMS) 128, 132
National Portrait Gallery, London 127
New English Art Club 92, 120
Nisbet, Robert 16, 72, 73, 75, 150
Noble, Robert 16, 72, 73, 75, 78, 84
Normandy 48, 60, 92, 107

Oliphant, James 35

Pagan, Elizabeth 24, 101
Pannett Art Gallery, Whitby 92, 108

Paris 10, 21, 26, 29, 30, 35, 41, 46, 47, 49, 50, 52-55, 82, 94, 100, 139, 141
Paterson, James 119
Peploe, Samuel John 13, 100, 107, 110, 117, 124, 127
   Tolbooth 13
Perth, Scotland 21, 113
Perth Museum and Art Gallery 62, 97, 104, 105, 108, 109, 113, 126, 134, 147
Perthshire, Scotland 21, 147, 150
Picasso, Pablo 83
   Cubist Picture 83
   Femme tenante une coupe 83
Pissarro, Camille 54, 61, 71
Pissarro, Lucien 105
Pitreavie Castle 33, 69, 150
Pont-Aven 29, 48, 51
Portobello 58, 62, 64
Puvis de Chavannes, Pierre 30, 35, 54

Ramsay, Allan 37, 42
Ramsay Garden 21, 27, 28, 29, 30, 31, **32**, 33, 35, 36, 39-42, 66, 69, 150
Ranson, Paul and Marie-France 40, 51-53, 55
Redon, Odilon 51
Reid, Alexander 21, 100, 106
Reid, Sir George 39, 77
Renoir, Pierre-Auguste 41, 50, 54, 61, 71, 72
Reynolds, Joshua 77
Rhind, W. Birnie 84
Robson, William 16, **81,** 84
Roche, Alexander 17, 24, 64, 65
Rodin, Auguste 78, 129
   Victor Hugo 78
   Mother and Child 129
   La Défense 129
Rouen 35, 54
Roussel, Ker-Xavier 51
Roxby Estate 88
Royal Academy, London (RA) 12, 67, 108, 116
Royal Association 18, 27
Royal Glasgow Institute (RGI) 17, 18, 26, 67, 75, 76, 116
Royal Hibernian Academy, Dublin 67
Royal Hibernian School, Dublin 58
Royal Infirmary, Edinburgh 33-35, 59, 64, 150
Royal Institution building 16, 17
Royal Institution for the Encouragement of the Fine Arts 16
Royal Scottish Academy (RSA) 6, 12, 16-20, 24, 26, 29, 35, 39, 41, 60-63, 65-67, 69, 70, 71, 73-80, 82, 84, 86-88, 91, 108-110, 112-116, 120, 121, 123-127, 133, 134, 136-139, 146, 147, 149, 150
Royal Scottish Society of Painters in Watercolour (RSW) 88, 98-99, 108, 125
Royal Watercolour Society 98
Runswick 87, 89, 92, 93, 99
Ruskin, John 98, 111

Salaman, Malcolm 101, 108, 113

San Francisco 91, 119
Sargeant, John Singer 77, 82
The Scots Observer 64
The Scots Pictorial 24, 60, 70, 79, 80, 82, 84, **85**
The Scotsman 18, 35, 36, 62, 64, 71, 77, 78, 79,
    91, 99, 100, 108, 109, 112, 114-116, 120, 135, 148
Scott, Tom 16, 20
The Scottish Art Review 64
Scottish Arts Club (SAC) 11, 39, 67, 69, 72, 73, 113,
    147, 148, 150
Scottish Artists' Golf Club 72-73
Scottish Modern Artists' Association (SMAA) 114, 121,
    123-125, 127, 136, 137, 148
Senior, Mark 89
Sérusier, Paul 40, 45, 46, 49-55, 67, 72, 103
   Louise/La Servante bretonne 50
   Pastorale bretonne 40, 49, 50
   The Talisman 51, 52
   ABC de la Peinture (book) 52
Sickert, Walter 92, 97, 100, 105, 106, 113
Sisley, Alfred 54, 61, 71
   View of the Thames 61
Society for Scottish Art History (SSAH) 128
Society of Graver-Printers in Colour (SGPIC) 104
Society of Scottish Artists (SSA) 12, 26, 28, 40, 60, 74-80,
    82-84, 86, 88, 90, 91, 101, 106, 112, 118, 120, 124,
    126, 129, 136, 137, 146, 147
Spain 26, 91, 97
Staithes 26, 87, 89-96, 107
Staithes Art Club 89-92
Stewartry Museum, Kirkcudbright 13
Stuart Prize 20, 62
Sutherland, D.M. 116, 138, 145, 149
Symbolists 49

Tay, River 61, 62, 99
Thomson, Adam Bruce 139
Torrey, Frederick C. 91, 110, 119, 120, 127
Toulouse-Lautrec, Henri 50
Traquair, Phoebe 36
Trevelyan, Sir George Otto 79
Trustees' Academy 14, 17, 60
Turner, Joseph Mallord William 47, 49, 62, 71, 97, 111,
    112

Ugthorpe Mill 87

Van Gogh, Vincent 54
Velasquez 26
   Las Meninas (*The Maids of Honour*) **25**
   The Spinners 26
Venice 9, 11, 92, 99, 100, 105-108, 110-117, 126
Verlat, Charles 17, 18
Victoria & Albert Museum 91
Vuillard, Jean-Edouard 10, 21, 51, 54, 55, 103
   Ouvrières dans l'atelier de couture (Seamstresses in the
    workroom) 54
   (*La Poursuite*?) 55

Walker Art Gallery, Liverpool 23, 105, 113
Walls, Hamish 48, 99, 110, 116, 142, 147
Walls, Provost of Dunfermline 47, 101
Walls, William, brother-in-law of Charles Mackie
    17, 19, 21, 24, 27, 47, 72, 73, 75, 76, **81**, 99, 100,
    112, 115, 121, 146, 150
Walton, Edward Arthur 110
Watson, Ella Carmichael 118, 119
Whistler, Rex 26, 107, 110, 112, 139
Whitby 87, 88, 91, 99, 133
The Whitby Gazette 89-91, 93, 107
Wingate, Lawton 64, 65, 110, 133, 150, 151
   Portrait of Charles H. Mackie **pl.39**

The Yorkshire Evening News 92
Yorkshire Union of Artists (YUA) 26, 90, 91, 95

Bibliography

PRIMARY SOURCES

City of Edinburgh Central Library, Edinburgh and Scottish
Collection: Edinburgh Social Union Annual Reports and
Minute Books

City of Edinburgh Archives: Merchant Company Archives:
George Watson's Prospectuses

City of Edinburgh Archives: Scottish Modern Arts
Association Yearbooks and Minutes (ED3)

City of Glasgow, Mitchell Library archive: Royal Glasgow
Institute of the Fine Arts exhibition catalogues

National Library of Scotland
John Duncan: Notebooks NLS ACC6866
Geddes Archive: NLS MS 19997
Norah Geddes (Lady Mears): 'Reminiscences' NLS
MS19266
Anne Mackie's Journal: NLS ACC 9177
Walls Family Papers (incl. RSA Diploma, photographs and
letters): NLS ACC10448

National Galleries of Scotland
Gallery of Modern Art Library: Society of Scottish Artists
Catalogues and Scrapbook GMA A57/5/1
Society of Scottish Artists: Minute Books GMA A57/01;
A57/02
Royal Scottish Academy of Art and Architecture
Archives: Annual Reports; Nomination Books; Registers of
Life Class; Annual Exhibitions Catalogues; Annual Sales
Records; Artist's file.
Skits on the Exhibition of the Royal Scottish Academy:
Publ. Cruickshank, Elder Street, Edinburgh 1888

Royal Scottish Society of Painters in Watercolour
Archive catalogue of exhibitions

University of Edinburgh Centre for Research Collections
Lorimer Papers: GEN.1963/15/9; 1963/18/51/54/62/63

Lothian Health Services Archives: Infirmary Reports and
Minute Books 1885-1890

University of Strathclyde Special Collections
Patrick Geddes Archive T-GED
2/2173;8/1/1;8/1/5;8/1/8;9/2173;9/76;9/77;9/78;9/228;
10/1/48;12/2/48/2

JOURNALS and PERIODICALS

The Art Journal: NLS Q66
1891 p126;1893 p30;1894 p30;1895 p319; 1896
p222; 1897 p320 ; 1900 pp124; 287-8; 1903 p284;
1906 pp334, 336; 1907 pp93,156; 1911 p323

Art and Antiques Weekly June 1979 Vol.36, no.11, pp22-
24: 'Britain's Impressionists' by Dr Peter Phillips NLS NB30

Art and Antiques Weekly October 1977 Vol.29, no.7,
pp22-24: 'Early Days and Hard Times at Staithes' by Dr
Peter Phillips NLS NB30

Quiz February 1895

The Scots Pictorial: Microfilm Mf.N.285 (NEWSPLAN 2000
Project) July 1898; August 1899; August 1900; March
1901; May 1901; April 1902; October 1902; April 1904;
July 1904

The Scottish Art Review June 1888-March 89 Vol.1 pp225
(Baldwin Brown) and Geddes (RSA Review) NLS Q53

Scribner's Magazine Vol.LV Jan-June 1914 Pages 271-2:
'The Field of Art. Contemporary Engraving on Wood' by
William Walton. NLS Shelfmark M258-9

The Studio NLS Shelfmark Q116
1897 Vol.10 p100; 1900 Vol.19 pp269-70; 1901 Vol.23
pp 274,292; 1901 Extra Edition p.48 Illus. 'The Harbour
Bridge, Whitby' and referenced in 'British Pen Drawings'
by J.M. Bulloch; 1904 Vol.31 p259; 1905 Vol.33 p83;
1906 Vol.37 Page 30; 1907 Vol.40 RSA Supplement:
colour illustration of 'La Senorita'; 1907 Vol.42 pp 63-4;
1908 Vol 43 p137; Vol 44 p232; 1909 Vol.45 p14;
Vol.46 p138; Vol.47 pp222-223; 1909-10 Vol.48 pp
229, 234; Vol.49 p229; 1912 Vol.54 p148; 1912-13
Vol.56 pp150, 153; 1913 Vol.58 pp152, 295-6; Vol.59
p136; 1914 Vol.61 p65; Vol.62 pp 65,144;1915 Vol.64
p60; Vol.65 p102; 1916 Vol.67 pp58, 262; Vol.68 p60;
1917 Vol.71 p59 Special number: Graphic Arts of GB, ed.
Charles Holme, text by Malcolm C. Salaman, with plates.
(S.293.a); 1919 Vol.75 p128; 1920 Vol.78 p120; Vol.80
p159

NEWSPAPERS (various years cited in text)
Dunfermline Journal
Edinburgh Evening Dispatch
Edinburgh Evening News
Glasgow Evening News
Glasgow Herald
Kirkcudbrightshire Advertiser
The Scotsman
Whitby Gazette
Yorkshire Evening News

With thanks to:
The British Library Board
The British Newspaper Archive
(www.britishnewspaperarchive.co.uk)

SECONDARY SOURCES

Aberdeen Art Gallery: 'D.M.Sutherland MC, LLD, RSA
(1883-1973)' catalogue of an exhibition held at Aberdeen
Art Gallery 5-26 October 1974 Publ. AAG 1974

Ackroyd, Peter: *Venice* Publ. Vintage Books, London 2010

Arts Council of Great Britain: 'French Symbolist Painters'
Publ.1972, to accompany Exhibitions held that year in the
Hayward Gallery, London & Walker Art Gallery, Liverpool

Baile de Lapierre, Charles (ed): *The Royal Scottish Academy
Exhibitors 1826-1990* Publ. Hilmarton Press 1991

Baldwin-Brown, Gerald: *The Fine Arts* (University Extension
Manuals) Publ. John Murray, London 1891

Barfoot, Michael (Lothian Health Services Archivist): 'The
Royal Infirmary of Edinburgh 1729-1948' (An Exhibition
of Records from the Lothian Health Services Archive May
2003) Publ. Edinburgh University Library 2003

Bezzola, Tobia & Prelinger, Elizabeth: *Paul Gauguin: the Prints*
Publ. Prestel 2012

Bolling, G. Fredric: *Graphic Work of Laura Knight*
Publ. Scolar Press, Aldershot 1993 NLS Shelfmark H8.94.29

Bomford, David & Roy, Ashok: *A Closer Look at Colour*
Publ. National Gallery Company, London 2009

Bourne, Patrick (ed): *Kirkcudbright: One Hundred Years
of an Artists' Colony* Publ. Atelier Books Edinburgh 2000

Bourne Fine Art Gallery Exhibition Catalogue 1988

Bourne Fine Art Gallery Exhibition Catalogue 2008

Boyer, Patricia Eckart (ed): *The Nabis and the Parisian
Avant-Garde* Publ. Rutgers Univ. Press 1988

Boyle-Turner, Caroline: *Paul Serusier* Publ. UMI Research
Press ('Studies in the Fine Arts: The Avant-Garde No.37')
1980

Bromberg, Ruth and Joseph: *Collection of Sickert prints
and drawings* Publ. Fine Art Society PLC 2004 NLS
Shelfmark HP4.205.0428

Caw, James L.: *Scottish Painting Past and Present 1620-1908*
Publ. T.C. and E.C. Jack 1908

Campbell, Mungo: *The Line of Tradition: Watercolours,*

Drawing and Prints by Scottish Artists 1700-1990
Publ. National Galleries of Scotland 1993 (to accompany
exhibition 4 Aug-12 Sept)

Cary, Joyce: *The Horse's Mouth*
Publ. Michael Joseph London 1985

Checkland, Olive: *Philanthropy in Scotland*
Publ. John Donald, Edinburgh 1980

Child, Dennis: *The Yorkshire Union of Artists 1888-1922*
Publ. Leeds Philosophical & Literary Society Ltd. 2001
NLS Shelfmark HP2 .202.04149

Child, Dennis: 'Painters in the Northern Counties of
England and Wales' Publ. Prof. Dennis Child, Univ. of
Leeds 2002 NLS Shelfmark: H8.202.0600

Cowan, John James: *From 1846-1932: Autobiography*
Publ. Edinburgh 1933 NLS Shelfmark R171a

Crane, Walter: *An Artist's Reminiscences*
Publ. Methuen (London) 1907 NLS Shelfmark S.156.c2

Cullen, Anthea: *The Work of Art: Plein-air Painting and
Artistic Identity in Nineteenth Century France*
Publ. Reaktion Books 2015

Cumming, Elizabeth: *Hand, Heart and Soul: the Arts and
Crafts Movement in Scotland* Publ. Birlinn Ltd. 2006

Cunningham, A.S.: *Romantic Culross, Carnock,
Cairneyhill, Saline and Pitfirrane* Publ. W. Clark & Sons
Dunfermline 1902 NLS Shelfmark R.245.h

Cursiter, Stanley: *Looking Back: A Book of Reminiscences
1887-1976* Privately publ. 1974 NLS Shelfmark H3.75.946

Devereux, David: *Kirkcudbright to Pont-Aven: artists in
search of inspiration*
Publ. The Stewartry Museum, Kirkcudbright 2005

Dunbar, Janet: *Laura Knight*
Publ. Collins 1975 NLS Shelfmark H2.76.64

Durand-Ruel, Paul: *Memoirs of the First Impressionist Art
Dealer*, revised, corrected and annotated by P. Durand-
Ruel & F. Durand-Ruel. Publ. Flammarion 2014

Edinburgh Council of Social Service: records of
Association for Improving the Condition of the Poor;
Publ. Edinburgh 1905/6 NLS Shelfmark QP.la.2561

Edinburgh Philanthropic Red Book; Publ. 1901 under the
auspices of the Edinburgh Association for Improving the
Condition of the Poor

Eldon, Kerry and Roberts, Rose (eds): *The Art Researchers'
Guide to Edinburgh* Publ. Art Libraries Society UK and

Ireland 2012

Ellridge, Arthur: *Gauguin and the Nabis: Prophets of Modernism* Publ. Terrail 1995

Errington, Lindsay: *Robert Herdman 1829-1888* Publ. NGS & Scottish Post Office Board 1988

Exhibition Catalogue: 'Painting the Century - Adam Bruce Thomson 1881-1976' Scottish Gallery 6-30 Nov. 2013

Ferguson, Lesley: *Wanderings with a camera in Scotland: the photography of Erskine Beveridge* Publ. RCAHMS 2014 NLS Shelfmark PB6.214.356/2

Findlay, William: *Ian Robertson: Art in Scotland* Publ. O.U.P. 1948 NLS Shelfmark X.39.d

Fletcher, Frank Morley: *Woodblock Printing. A Description of the Craft of Woodcutting and Colour Printing based on the Japanese practice* Publ. 1916 Edinburgh College of Art. Republished as an ebook by Gutenberg 2006

Foster, Malcolm: *Joyce Cary: A Biography* Publ. Michael Joseph London 1969 NLS Shelfmark NC.263.g.9

Fowle, Frances: *Van Gogh's Twin: the Scottish Art Dealer Alexander Reid 1854-1928* Publ. National Galleries of Scotland 2010

Fowle, Frances: *Impressionism and Scotland* Publ. National Galleries of Scotland 2008

Fowle, Frances and Thomson, Belinda (eds): *Patrick Geddes and the French Connection* Publ. White Cockade 2004

Furst, Herbert: *The Modern Woodcut* Publ. John Lane The Bodley Head Ltd London 1924

Garton, Robin: *British Printmakers 1855-1955* Publ. Garton & Co., in assoc. with Scolar Press 1992

Garton & Cooke: Fine Art Dealers and Publishers Catalogue 35

Geddes, Patrick & colleagues: *The Evergreen* 1895-1897 Publ. in Edinburgh at the Lawnmarket and also in London by T. Fisher Unwin. Paternoster Square, and in America by J. B. Lippincott & Co. NLS Shelfmark Ca.6/1

Gordon, Esmé: *The Royal Scottish Academy of Painting, Sculpture and Architecture 1826-1976* Publ. Charles Skilton Edinburgh 1976 NLS Shelfmark H4.98.1039

Gordon, Haig: *From Capri to Kirkcudbright: the life and work of William Robson (1863-1950)* Publ. St. Cuthbert Publications 2005 NLS Shelfmark PB6.208.771/7

Gordon, Haig: *Tales of the Kirkcudbright Artists*

Publ. Galloway Publishing Kirkcudbright 2008

Greutzner-Robins, Anna (editor): *Walter Sickert: Complete Writings on Art* Publ. Oxford University Press 2000 NLS Shelfmark H4.201.0423

Halsby, Julian: *Scottish Watercolours 1740-1940* Publ. Batsford 1986

Hannan, Thomas: *Famous Scottish Houses: the Lowlands* Publ. James Thin, The Mercat Press Edinburgh 1984 edition. NLS Shelfmark N3 205 2506L

Hardie, William: *Scottish Painting 1837 - Present* Publ. Waverley Books 2010

Harper, Malcom M'Lachlan: *Bards of Galloway: a collection of poems, songs, ballads etc. by natives of Galloway/edited, with an introduction and notes, by Malcolm McL. Harper* Publ. Dalbeattie Thomas Fraser 94 High Street 1889 NLS Shelfmark Hall.250.c

Hart, James: *The Secret Staithes Diary of Enid Lucy Pease Robinson* Publ. Historical Publishing 2010

Hartley, Keith S.: *Scottish Art since 1900* Publ. Lund Humphries in association with NGS 1989 Shelfmark GMN.2/1.(6)

Hartrick, Archibald Standish: *A Painter's Pilgrimage through Fifty Years* Publ. Cambridge University Press 1939 NLS Shelfmark R.190.1

Haycock, David Boyd: *A Crisis of Brilliance* Publ. Old Street Publishing Ltd 2009

Haswell, Jock: *The Queen's Royal Regiment (West Surrey): the 2nd Regiment of Foot* Publ. Hamish Hamilton 1967

Haworth, Peter: *Paintings by members of the Staithes Group* Publ. by Peter Haworth to accompany the 2002 Exhibitions at the Fine Art Society, Whitby Museum & Bourne Fine Art. NLS Shelfmark HP3.203.0680

Henley, William Ernest (1849-1903): *Century of Artists. A Memorial of the Glasgow International Exhibition of 1888* Publ. James MacLehose & Sons Glasgow 1889 NLS Shelfmark Co.1/2

Holloway, James & Lindsay Errington: *Discovery of Scotland: the appreciation of Scottish scenery through two centuries of painting* Publ. NGS 1978 NLS Shelfmark GMO.2.(28)

Holroyd, Michael: *Works on Paper* Publ. Little, Brown & Co. 2002

Holmes, Richard: *Footsteps: Adventures of a Romantic Biographer* Publ. Harper Perennial 2005

Howard, John: *Chapters from the History of a Seafaring Town* Publ. John Howard (Staithes) 2000

Howie, Les et al: George *Watson's College: an Illustrated History* Publ. Karen Tumblety 2006

Huntly, Charles Gordon, Marquis of, 1847-1937: *Auld Acquaintance/the Marquis of Huntly* Publ. Hutchinson & Co. London 1929 NLS Shelfmark N3.205.3474L

Irwin, David and Francina: *Scottish Painters at Home and Abroad 1700-1900* Publ. Faber and Faber 1975

Jordan, Rosamund (ed): 'Staithes Group Centenary Exhibition Catalogue' printed in York 2003

Kemplay, John: *Paintings of John Duncan: a Scottish Symbolist* Publ. Pomegranate Art Books, San Francisco 1st Edition 1994 NLS Shelfmark H8.95.576

Kirkcudbrightshire Fine Arts Association Catalogues: 1886, 1887 & 1888 NLS shelfmark APS.2.93.24

Knight, Laura: *Oil Paint and Grease Paint* Publ. London 1936 NLS Shelfmark R183c

Knight, Laura: *The Magic of a Line: the autobiography of Laura Knight* Publ. William Kimber London 1965 NLS Shelfmark NF. 1354.e.19

McConkey, Kenneth: *New English: a history of the New English Art Club* Publ. Royal Academy 2006 NLS Shelfmark HB3.207.10.62

McConkey, Kenneth: *British Impressionism* Publ. Phaidon Press Ltd. 1989 NLS Shelfmark H8.89.646

McEwan, Peter J.M.: *Scottish Art and Architecture* Publ. Glengarden Press 2004

McKay, W.D. & Rinder, Frank: *The Royal Scottish Academy 1826-1916* Publ. James Maclehose & Sons, Glasgow 1917 NLS Shelfmark H4.98.1126

Mackie, Bill: 'Colour Printing by Charles H. Mackie RSA' Unpublished manuscript which was generously shared with the author.

MacMillan, Duncan: *Scottish Art in the 20th Century 1890-2001* Publ. Mainstream 2001 edition

MacMillan, Duncan: *Scottish Art 1460-2000* Publ. Mainstream 2000

Maine, George F. (compiler): *Wind in the Pines. A Celtic Miscellany* Publ. T.N. Foulis Ltd. Edinburgh & London 1922 NLS Shelfmark NG.1168.h.16

Manguel, Alberto: *Reading Pictures* Publ. Random House trade paperbacks New York 2002

Meller, Helen: *Patrick Geddes: Social Evolutionist and City Planner* Publ. London Routledge 1990

Messum, David: *British Impressionism: a collection of British impressionist paintings 1880-1940: narrated by Laura Wortley* Publ. Studion Fine Art Publications 1988

Morden, Barbara C.: *Laura Knight. A Life* Publ. McNidder & Grace 2014

Morrison, Rhona: 'The Help, an Account of the Edinburgh Association for the Improvement of the Poor 1868-1906' Publ. Edinburgh Council of Social Service, 1968 NLS Shelfmark HP2.86.4123

Munro, Neil: *The Brave Days* Publ. Edinburgh The Porpoise Press 1931

Murray, D.P.: 'The History of Pitreavie Castle': bound typescript in Dunfermline Library, 1985

Myrone, Martin (editor) *Watercolour in Britain* Publ. Tate Publishing 2010 (accompanying the exhibition)

National Gallery of Scotland: 'Catalogue of Paintings and Sculpture' Published by the Trustees 1957 (NGS Art S4N)

Newsletter: The Friends of the Royal Scottish Academy: no. 53 Winter/spring 2001

Newton, Laura (ed.) *Painting at the Edge. British Coastal Art Colonies 1880-1930* Publ. Sansom & Co.2005 NLS Shelfmark HB5.207.11.121

Nunn, Pamela Gerish: *From Victorian to Modern: innovation and tradition in the work of Vanessa Bell, Gwen John and Laura Knight* Publ. Philip Wilson, London 2006 NLS Shelfmark HB5.208.2.142

Oliver, Cordelia: *Society of Scottish Artists: the first 100 years* Publ. SSA 1991 NLS Shelfmark H8.92

Oliver, Cordelia: *The Royal Scottish Society of Painters in Watercolours* Publ. RSW 2000

O'Reilly, G.H.: *History of the Royal Hibernian Military School, Dublin* Publ. Genealogical Society of Ireland 2001

O'Riordan, Ian & Patterson, David: *Scotland's Art* Publ. Edinburgh City Council 1999

Pagan, Elizabeth H.C.: *Greeks and Persians* Publ. Univ. Press of Liverpool 1900

Perth Museum and Art Gallery: 'William Miller Frazer, RSA 1864-1964', paintings and sketches of the Scottish landscape and beyond, 5 Aug.-3 Sep. 1978 Perth Museum and Art Gallery Publ. 1978

Peploe, Guy: *S.J. Peploe 1871-1935*
Publ. Mainstream 2000

Phillips, Peter: *The Staithes Group*
Publ. Phillips & Sons 1993; reprinted 1994

Roberts, Alasdair: *Ties that Bind: Boys' Schools of Edinburgh*
Publ. Steve Savage Publishers 2009

Rochdale Art Gallery: 'F.W. Jackson 1859-1918:
Exhibition Catalogue 1978-79' Publ. RAG 1978

Roxburgh, John R. (Compiler): 'The Edinburgh Philanthropic
Red Book: a handbook to the various institutions and
trusts available for the benefit and relief of persons in
Edinburgh and Leith who are suffering from distress'
Publ. under the auspices of the Edinburgh Association for
Improving the Condition of the Poor. McNiven & Wallace
1901 NLS Shelfmark R.251.h

Royal Academy Exhibitors (1769-1904; 1905-1970) Vol.5:
Publ. London 1906; 1981

Royal Association for Promotion of Fine Arts in Scotland:
The River Tay - illustrations of the Scenery of the River Tay
Publ. T & A Constable, Edinburgh 1891 NLS Shelfmark
M95b

Royal Glasgow Institute of the Fine Arts: *Dictionary of
Exhibitors at the Annual Exhibitions Vol.3*
Publ. Woodend Press 1992.

Royal Hibernian Academy of Arts: *Index of exhibitors and
their works, 1826-1979*, compiled by Ann M. Stewart;
with a summary history by C. de Courcy Publ. Dublin:
Manton 1986-87

Salomé, Laurent: ed. *A City for Impressionism: Monet,
Pissarro and Gauguin in Rouen*
Publ. SKIRA 2010 NLS Shelfmark HBS 210 12.5

Scottish Arts Club: *Scottish Arts Club, Edinburgh, 1874-1974*
Publ. SAC 1974 NLS Shelfmark: NE.11.a.39

Shone, Richard: *Walter Sickert* Publ. Phaidon Oxford
1988 NLS Shelfmark H8.88.645

Sitwell, Osbert (editor): *Free House! or, The artist as
craftsman being the writings of Walter Sickert*
Publ. Macmillan & Co. 1947 NLS Shelfmark X.167.d

Smith, Bill: *Hornel: the life and work of Edward Atkinson
Hornel* Publ. Atelier Books, Edinburgh 1997

Soden, Joanna: 'La Danse du Village' The Friends of the
Royal Scottish Academy Newsletter no. 53 Winter/Spring
2001

Stubbs, Peter: 'Edinburgh Photographic Society:
transactions recording Edinburgh's Photographic
Societies in the 19th c.' Edinburgh and Scottish
Library TR1

The Scottish Gallery: Exhibition Catalogue 1987:
'Charles Mackie 1862-1920'

Sweeney, Jan: *From Studio to Foundry. Preparation
for Casting* Publ. Bloomsbury 2014

Thomson, Belinda: 'Vainly Seeking Impressionism:
A Scottish Artist's Response to the Musée du
Luxembourg, c.1894' publ. in *Journal of the Scottish
Society for Art History* Vol.14 2009-2010

Wilkie, James: *Bygone Fife, from Culross to St.
Andrews. Traditions, legends, folklore and local history
of the kingdom* Publ. William Blackwood & Sons
1931 NLS Shelfmark R.245.e

Withington, Donald J. & Grant, Ian R., editors: *New
Statistical Account of Scotland* (originally edited by
Sir John Sinclair) Publ. E.P. Publishing Ltd. 1983

Wortley, Laura: *British Impressionism: a garden of
bright images* Publ. Studio Fine Art Publications
1988 NLS Shelfmark H8.89.173

Acknowledgements

It has been one of the joys of researching this book to encounter such a diverse, delightful and helpful range of individuals. They have all aided the cause of Charles Mackie and contributed to the book which resulted.

Pride of place must go to Bill Mackie in Melbourne, Australia. He has been more than generous of his time and shown a ready willingness to share his own research, family correspondence and images of the art in his own collection. A kind and thoughtful host during my visit to Australia, he helped clear the way through the thicket of copyright by granting me permission to quote from all the unpublished letters in public collections in the UK. This book would not have been possible without his cooperation, generosity of spirit and technological assistance. That debt can never be repaid in full but I hope that seeing his Uncle Charlie's story in print might provide some small recompense.

Also in Australia, Ted Gott, Senior Curator of International Art at the National Gallery of Victoria in Melbourne facilitated access to their Mackie. Sydney Art Gallery was similarly helpful.

In the UK, a long list of galleries and individuals opened up their basements, archives and storage centres as well as giving of their time and expertise: Liz Louis and Griff Coe at Aberdeen Art Gallery; David Patterson, Helen Scott and Maeve Toal at the City Art Centre in Edinburgh; Anne Dulau at the Hunterian Art Gallery in Glasgow; Dr Joanna Meacock at Kelvingrove Gallery in Glasgow; Nigel Walsh at Leeds Art Gallery; Kirsty MacNab at the McManus Art Gallery in Dundee; Hannah Brocklehurst, Alice Strang and Kerry Watson at the National Galleries of Scotland in Edinburgh; Rosie Broadley at the National Portrait Gallery in London; Paul Adair, Maria Devaney and Rhona Rodger at Perth Museum and Art Gallery; Helen Berry at the Pannett Art Gallery in Whitby; David Devereux at the Stewartry Museum in Kirkcudbright.

In addition, some private galleries and auction houses also offered information and assistance: Zoe Blamire, the McGill Duncan Gallery, Castle Douglas; Bonhams; Nick Curnow at Lyon and Turnbull; the Fleming Collection; the Staithes Gallery; and Emily Walsh and her excellent team at The Fine Art Society are all deserving of thanks.

The Print Room at the British Museum provided first-hand evidence of Mackie's print technique. The staff at the RCAHMS supplied the only extant picture of Mackie's sculpture in situ; Godfrey Evans, Principal Curator of European Art at the National Museums of Scotland and his colleague Maggie Wilson provided the records and image of Mackie's surviving sculpture, pre- and post-restoration. Similarly helpful, the National Trust for Scotland allowed access to the murals at Ramsay Garden and to the records at Broughton House in Kirkcudbright – thanks to Ian Riches and Sally Eastgate. In Glasgow, the custodian of the RSW archives was Lesley Nicholl, who tried to locate what could not be found. Dr John Croft and the Dame Laura Knight Society rendered timely assistance when it was needed.

Libraries were essential to this enterprise and the knowledge of their librarians proved a lifeline on more than one occasion. In Edinburgh, these were: the National Library of Scotland; the Fine Art, Edinburgh and Scottish Collections in the Central Library; the Centre for Research Collections at the University of Edinburgh; and the library at the Scottish Gallery of Modern Art. The Edinburgh City Archives and the Scottish Arts Club willingly opened up their archives and Joanna Soden and Sandy Wood allowed me easy access to the records of the Royal Scottish Academy of Art and Architecture. Local libraries in Dunfermline, Kirkcaldy and Perth confirmed their valuable role in adding to human understanding. In Glasgow, the staff at the Mitchell Library were equally helpful. The Geddes Archive housed in the University of Strathclyde Andersonian Library was a treasure-trove and special thanks are due to Rachel Pike and Dr Anne Cameron.

A long alphabetical list of individuals does not do justice to their cooperation, guidance and enthusiasm. Each one helped me on my journey to uncover more about Charles Mackie. Dr Barbara Morden willingly shared her understanding of Dame Laura Knight's art while Dr Belinda Thomson helped pin down the wayward chronology of the French visits. Thanks are due to Mo Bittker, Cordelia and Patrick Bourne, Dr Louise Boreham, Dr Elizabeth Cumming, Ian Devlin, Thelma Good, Christopher Gordon, Peter Haworth, Les Howie, Bob Isaat, Dave Jeffery, Ann Lanzl, Robin Lorimer, Conor McCutcheon, Nola Meikle, Christine Pybus, Jean and David Roberts, Robert Robertson, Alison and Ros Shirreff, Nigel Malcolm Smith, David Steel, Anne Wiseman and Simon Wood.

Finally, the patient and cheerful guidance of Clara Hudson and Paul Deaton at Sansom & Co. steered this novice in the right direction. The stalwart support of my good friends, Susan and Malcolm Chamberlain and Brian and Esther Henderson sustained me throughout. Thank you for listening and supplying much-appreciated photographic, editorial, technological and moral support over these past years.